MONTANA BIRDS

Caleb Putnam
Gregory Kennedy

Lone Pine Publishing International

Distributed by Lone Pine Publishing
1808 B Street NW, Suite 140
Auburn, WA, USA 98001

Website: www.lonepinepublishing.com

Library and Archives Canada Cataloguing in Publication

Putnam, Caleb, 1977–
        Montana birds / Caleb Putnam, Gregory Kennedy.

Includes bibliographical references and index.

ISBN-13: 978-1-55105-463-6
ISBN-10: 1-55105-463-9

        1. Birds—Montana—Identification. I. Kennedy, Gregory,
1956–   II. Title.

QL684.M9P88 2005   598'.09786   C2005-901749-X

Cover Illustration: Western Meadowlark, by Gary Ross
Illustrations: Gary Ross, Ted Nordhagen, Ewa Pluciennik
Scanning & Digital Film: Elite Lithographers Co.

Map, p. 13: based on the Montana State Library's Natural Resource Information System map of climax vegetation

PC: P1

CONTENTS

NONPASSERINES

PASSERINES

ACKNOWLEDGMENTS

Our knowledge and understanding of the birds of Montana are greatly increased by the legions of binocular-toting people who go afield to study them, and then take the time and effort to report their observations. We are particularly indebted to the contributors, authors and editors of *P.D. Skarr's Montana Bird Distribution,* which has for years been the primary source on the subject, and which provided the basis for all the range maps herein. We are also indebted to the birders who take part in Christmas bird counts, breeding bird surveys and other citizen science studies, as well as those who individually report their sightings to regional compilers of birding journals such as *North American Birds.* An important debt is owed the organizers and compilers of these efforts. We thank all the members of Montana Partners in Flight and the Montana Bird Conservation Initiative, who are working diligently to conserve Montana's imperiled species.

Thanks also go to John Acorn, Chris Fisher, Andy Bezener and Eloise Pulos for their contributions to previous books in this series. In addition, we gratefully acknowledge Gary Ross, Ted Nordhagen and Ewa Pluciennik, whose skilled illustrations have brought each page to life.

My own growth as an ornithologist and birder has been encouraged and supported by many, but I am especially grateful for the constant support of my wife Sara, and my parents Jeff & Pam Putnam, and for the mentorship of Jeff Marks and Mike Supernault, who have provided a lifetime of inspiration and friendship.
—*Caleb Putnam*

House Wren

WATERFOWL

Snow Goose
size 30 in • p. 20

Canada Goose
size 35 in • p. 21

Trumpeter Swan
size 5 ft • p. 22

Mallard
size 24 in • p. 23

Blue-winged Teal
size 15 in • p. 24

Cinnamon Teal
size 16 in • p. 25

Northern Shoveler
size 19 in • p. 26

Northern Pintail
size 24 in • p. 27

Green-winged Teal
size 14 in • p. 28

Redhead
size 20 in • p. 29

Lesser Scaup
size 17 in • p. 30

Harlequin Duck
size 17 in • p. 31

Bufflehead
size 14 in • p. 32

Common Goldeneye
size 18 in • p. 33

Common Merganser
size 25 in • p. 34

Ruddy Duck
size 15 in • p. 35

GROUSE & ALLIES

Ruffed Grouse
size 17 in • p. 36

Greater Sage-Grouse
size 26 in • p. 37

Blue Grouse
size 20 in • p. 38

Sharp-tailed Grouse
size 17 in • p. 39

DIVING BIRDS & PELICANS

Wild Turkey
size 3 ft • p. 40

Common Loon
size 32 in • p. 41

Red-necked Grebe
size 20 in • p. 42

DIVING BIRDS & PELICANS

Eared Grebe
size 13 in • p. 43

Western Grebe
size 25 in • p. 44

American White Pelican
size 5 ft • p. 45

Double-crested Cormorant
size 29 in • p. 46

HERONS & VULTURES

Great Blue Heron
size 4 ft • p. 47

Turkey Vulture
size 28 in • p. 48

Osprey
size 23 in • p. 49

BIRDS OF PREY

Bald Eagle
size 3 ft • p. 50

Northern Harrier
size 20 in • p. 51

Sharp-shinned Hawk
size 11 in • p. 52

Swainson's Hawk
size 21 in • p. 53

Red-tailed Hawk
size 22 in • p. 54

Rough-legged Hawk
size 21 in • p. 55

Golden Eagle
size 35 in • p. 56

American Kestrel
size 8 in • p. 57

Prairie Falcon
size 17 in • p. 58

RAILS, COOTS & CRANES

Sora
size 9 in • p. 59

American Coot
size 15 in • p. 60

Sandhill Crane
size 4 ft • p. 61

SHOREBIRDS

Killdeer
size 10 in • p. 62

American Avocet
size 18 in • p. 63

Willet
size 15 in • p. 64

Spotted Sandpiper
size 7 in • p. 65

SHOREBIRDS

Long-billed Curlew
size 23 in • p. 66

Marbled Godwit
size 18 in • p. 67

Wilson's Phalarope
size 9 in • p. 68

GULLS & TERNS

Franklin's Gull
size 14 in • p. 69

Ring-billed Gull
size 19 in • p. 70

California Gull
size 19 in • p. 71

DOVES

Black Tern
size 10 in • p. 72

Rock Pigeon
size 13 in • p. 73

Mourning Dove
size 12 in • p. 74

OWLS

Great Horned Owl
size 22 in • p. 75

Burrowing Owl
size 9 in • p. 76

Great Gray Owl
size 29 in • p. 77

Short-eared Owl
size 15 in • p. 78

NIGHTJARS, KINGFISHERS & HUMMINGBIRDS

Common Nighthawk
size 9 in • p. 79

Vaux's Swift
size 5 in • p. 80

Calliope Hummingbird
size 3 in • p. 81

Rufous Hummingbird
size 3 in • p. 82

WOODPECKERS

Belted Kingfisher
size 13 in • p. 83

Lewis's Woodpecker
size 11 in • p. 84

Red-headed Woodpecker
size 9 in • p. 85

Red-naped Sapsucker
size 9 in • p. 86

Downy Woodpecker
size 7 in • p. 87

Hairy Woodpecker
size 9 in • p. 88

Northern Flicker
size 13 in • p. 89

Pileated Woodpecker
size 17 in • p. 90

REFERENCE GUIDE

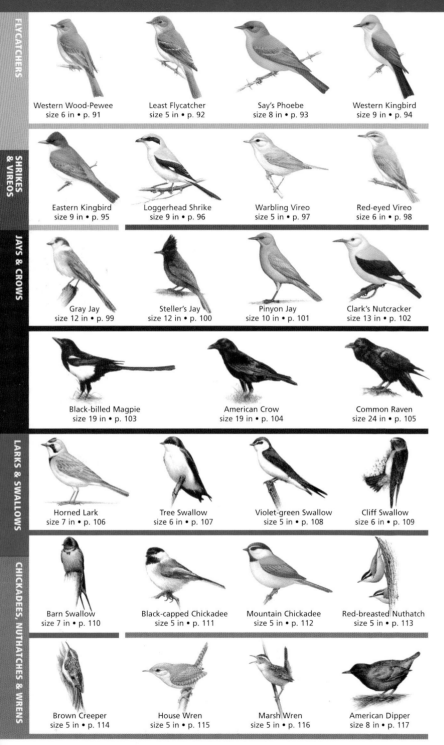

FLYCATCHERS

Western Wood-Pewee
size 6 in • p. 91

Least Flycatcher
size 5 in • p. 92

Say's Phoebe
size 8 in • p. 93

Western Kingbird
size 9 in • p. 94

SHRIKES & VIREOS

Eastern Kingbird
size 9 in • p. 95

Loggerhead Shrike
size 9 in • p. 96

Warbling Vireo
size 5 in • p. 97

Red-eyed Vireo
size 6 in • p. 98

JAYS & CROWS

Gray Jay
size 12 in • p. 99

Steller's Jay
size 12 in • p. 100

Pinyon Jay
size 10 in • p. 101

Clark's Nutcracker
size 13 in • p. 102

Black-billed Magpie
size 19 in • p. 103

American Crow
size 19 in • p. 104

Common Raven
size 24 in • p. 105

LARKS & SWALLOWS

Horned Lark
size 7 in • p. 106

Tree Swallow
size 6 in • p. 107

Violet-green Swallow
size 5 in • p. 108

Cliff Swallow
size 6 in • p. 109

CHICKADEES, NUTHATCHES & WRENS

Barn Swallow
size 7 in • p. 110

Black-capped Chickadee
size 5 in • p. 111

Mountain Chickadee
size 5 in • p. 112

Red-breasted Nuthatch
size 5 in • p. 113

Brown Creeper
size 5 in • p. 114

House Wren
size 5 in • p. 115

Marsh Wren
size 5 in • p. 116

American Dipper
size 8 in • p. 117

REFERENCE GUIDE

Ruby-crowned Kinglet
size 4 in • p. 118

Mountain Bluebird
size 7 in • p. 119

Townsend's Solitaire
size 9 in • p. 120

Swainson's Thrush
size 7 in • p. 121

American Robin
size 10 in • p. 122

Gray Catbird
size 9 in • p. 123

Brown Thrasher
size 12 in • p. 124

European Starling
size 9 in • p. 125

Cedar Waxwing
size 7 in • p. 126

Yellow Warbler
size 5 in • p. 127

Yellow-rumped Warbler
size 6 in • p. 128

Townsend's Warbler
size 5 in • p. 129

American Redstart
size 5 in • p. 130

Ovenbird
size 6 in • p. 131

Northern Waterthrush
size 6 in • p. 132

Common Yellowthroat
size 5 in • p. 133

Wilson's Warbler
size 5 in • p. 134

Western Tanager
size 7 in • p. 135

Green-tailed Towhee
size 7 in • p. 136

Spotted Towhee
size 8 in • p. 137

Chipping Sparrow
size 6 in • p. 138

Clay-colored Sparrow
size 6 in • p. 139

Vesper Sparrow
size 6 in • p. 140

Lark Bunting
size 7 in • p. 141

Savannah Sparrow
size 6 in • p. 142

SPARROWS & BUNTINGS

Song Sparrow
size 6 in • p. 143

White-crowned Sparrow
size 7 in • p. 144

Dark-eyed Junco
size 6 in • p. 145

Chestnut-collared Longspur
size 6 in • p. 146

Snow Bunting
size 7 in • p. 147

Lazuli Bunting
size 6 in • p. 148

BLACKBIRDS & ORIOLES

Red-winged Blackbird
size 8 in • p. 149

Western Meadowlark
size 9 in • p. 150

Yellow-headed Blackbird
size 10 in • p. 151

Brewer's Blackbird
size 9 in • p. 152

Common Grackle
size 12 in • p. 153

Brown-headed Cowbird
size 7 in • p. 154

Bullock's Oriole
size 8 in • p. 155

FINCHLIKE BIRDS

Gray-crowned Rosy-Finch
size 6 in • p. 156

Pine Grosbeak
size 9 in • p. 157

House Finch
size 6 in • p. 158

Red Crossbill
size 6 in • p. 159

Common Redpoll
size 5 in • p. 160

Pine Siskin
size 5 in • p. 161

American Goldfinch
size 5 in • p. 162

Evening Grosbeak
size 8 in • p. 163

House Sparrow
size 6 in • p. 164

INTRODUCTION

In recent decades, birding has evolved from an eccentric hobby of a few dedicated individuals to a continent-wide phenomenon boasting millions of professional and amateur participants. There are many good reasons birding has become so popular. Many people find it a relaxing pastime that can offer outdoor exercise and an opportunity to socialize with other bird enthusiasts. Others see it as a rewarding learning experience. Still others watch birds to reconnect with nature and monitor the health of the local environment.

Whether you are just beginning to take an interest in birds or have already learned to identify many species, this field guide has something for you. We've selected 145 of the state's most common and noteworthy birds. Some live in specialized habitats, but most are common species that you have a good chance of encountering.

BIRDING IN MONTANA

Whether you are looking out your back window or taking a walk on a secluded trail, you will find birds always close by. Some birds, such as chickadees and finches, are our neighbors year-round (although we often notice them more in winter, when they frequently visit our backyard feeders). Other birds visit Montana only in spring and summer to take advantage of the abundant food available and to raise their young. Included in this category are many waterbirds and songbirds. Still other birds pass through Montana only briefly each spring and fall on their way to more northern and southern locales. It is difficult to believe that Montana's sometimes harsh winters would be inviting to any bird, but a few species, such as the Northern Shrike, Common Redpoll and Rough-legged Hawk, are only winter visitors to our state.

Some of the birds featured in this book are so common and familiar that you will probably encounter them on a regular basis. Others are more shy and secretive or are restricted to certain habitats, so seeing them may be a noteworthy event. Likewise, some species are easily identified; if you see a Black-billed Magpie, you are not likely to confuse it with any other bird. Gulls, on the other hand, and many songbirds and raptors, can be more challenging to properly identify.

Montana has a long tradition of friendly birding. Birders are usually happy to help beginners, share their knowledge and involve novices in their projects. Christmas bird counts, breeding bird surveys, nest box programs, migration monitoring studies, feeder watch programs and birding lectures and workshops provide a chance for birders of all levels to interact and share their appreciation for birds. So, whatever your level of knowledge, you'll have ample opportunity to learn more and get involved. For further information on Montana bird outings and projects, contact your local naturalists' club or Montana Audubon: PO Box 595, Helena, MT 59624; (406) 443-3949; http://mtaudubon.org/.

Black-billed Magpie

TOP MONTANA BIRDING SITES

Montana is as diverse as it is large. From the alpine meadows of Glacier National Park to the alkali lakes of Westby; from the sage-brush seas of Bannack to the prolific marshes of Bowdoin National Wildlife Refuge, our state supports a rich flora and fauna.

Montana's western third is dominated by the Rocky Mountains. The mountain region includes montane coniferous forest, inter-mountain valleys with grassland, sagebrush, wetlands and riparian forest, and, above about 9000 feet, alpine meadows and snowfields with relatively few species.

East of the Continental Divide is the great open area that gave rise to one of our state's monikers: Big Sky Country. But the "plains" are far from uniform grassland. Hot, dry canyons border lush cotton-wood gallery forest. Prairie potholes complement nearby short-grass prairie and cattail marsh. Aspen parkland forests abut long-dry coulees. The variety of habitats in the Treasure State is remarkable. Hundreds of good birding areas can be found throughout Montana. The following 50 represent a diverse range of accessible bird communities.

1. Troy
2. Kootenai Falls
3. Eureka
4. Glacier NP
5. Blackfeet Indian Reservation
6. Kalispell
7. Flathead Lake
8. Swan Lake & Swan River NWR
9. Polson
10. Ninepipe NWR
11. National Bison Range
12. Lolo Pass
13. Lee Metcalf NWR
14. Rattlesnake NRA
15. Seeley Lake
16. East Front of Rockies
17. Pine Butte Swamp Preserve
18. Freezout Lake WMA
19. Benton Lake NWR
20. Giant Springs SP
21. Rogers Pass
22. Lake Helena & Helena Valley Regulating Reservoir
23. Canyon Ferry Lake
24. Warm Springs Settling Ponds
25. Georgetown Lake
26. Bitterroot Mountains
27. Lost Trail Pass
28. Bannack
29. Clark Canyon Reservoir
30. Dillon
31. Ennis Lake
32. Red Rock Lakes NWR
33. Bridger Range
34. Yellowstone NP
35. Havre
36. Lewistown
37. Molt & Big Lake
38. Red Lodge & Beartooth Mountains
39. Pryor Mountains
40. Bighorn Canyon NRA
41. Youngs Creek
42. Tongue River Reservoir, Decker
43. Bowdoin NWR & Nelson Reservoir
44. Charles M. Russell NWR
45. Fort Peck
46. Miles City
47. Ekalaka
48. Makoshika SP
49. Medicine Lake NWR
50. Westby

NP = National Park
NRA = National Recreation Area
NWR = National Wildlife Refuge
SP = State Park
WMA = Wildlife Management Area

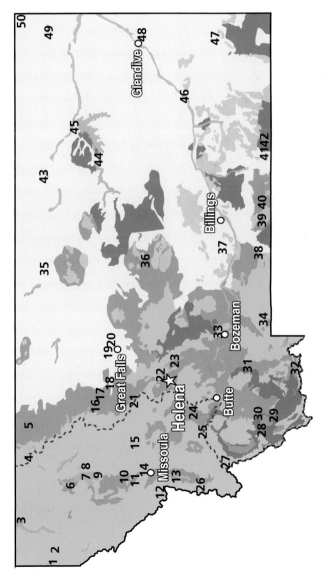

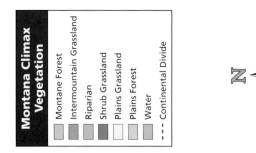

Montana Climax Vegetation

Montane Forest
Intermountain Grassland
Riparian
Shrub Grassland
Plains Grassland
Plains Forest
Water
- - - Continental Divide

13

MONTANA'S TOP 10

Bowdoin National Wildlife Refuge & Nelson Reservoir

Bowdoin NWR, just east of Malta, is one of Montana's premier birding locations. Particularly from June to August, the alkaline waters of Lake Bowdoin teem with waterbirds: American White Pelican, American Avocet, Black-necked Stilt, Wilson's Phalarope, Willet, Franklin's Gull, Eared Grebe, White-faced Ibis and the rare Piping Plover, along with various waterfowl and other species. Bowdoin is recognized as a stopover of global importance to migratory shorebirds, and in spring and late summer it is one of the top places in the state to observe them. The refuge also contains almost 9000 acres of upland prairie that supports Sharp-tailed Grouse, Baird's Sparrow, Sprague's Pipit, Grasshopper Sparrow, Chestnut-collared Longspur, Swainson's Hawk and a variety of breeding ducks.

Any trip to Bowdoin merits a side stop at Nelson Reservoir, six miles northeast, which hosts a similar assortment of waterbirds and songbirds.

Freezout Lake Wildlife Management Area

Lying on the mountain–prairie interface, Freezout Lake WMA has become a birder's mecca for its great variety of species. Its 12,000 acres of wetlands and short-grass prairie, as well as large nearby grainfields, make it attractive to an assortment of waterfowl, gulls, raptors and songbirds. Its most stunning spectacle is the annual stopover of hundreds of thousands of Snow Geese in late March and early April: up to 400,000 at once. Other prominent migrants include Ross's Goose, Northern Pintail and Tundra Swan.

Freezout Lake supports a large colony of breeding Franklin's Gulls, as well as many species of nesting ducks. It is also the best place in the state to view the uncommon Clark's Grebe among the numerous Western Grebes. Common grassland species include Short-eared Owl, Northern Harrier, Chestnut-collared Longspur, Western Meadowlark, Vesper Sparrow, Clay-colored Sparrow and Savannah Sparrow. The extensive marshes support Great Blue Heron, Marsh Wren, Black Tern, Red-winged Blackbird, Yellow-headed Blackbird, Common Tern and American Avocet.

Snow Goose

Red Crossbill

Glacier National Park

Ranging from 3000 feet to over 10,000 feet, this beautiful, diverse park features aspen parkland, wet redcedar–hemlock forest, montane forest and alpine tundra. Glacier NP is the best place in Montana to observe Harlequin Ducks, as well as alpine species such as the White-tailed Ptarmigan and Gray-crowned Rosy-Finch. Common forest species on the wetter west side of the park include Townsend's Warbler, MacGillivray's Warbler, Winter Wren, Chestnut-backed Chickadee, Golden-crowned Kinglet, Calliope Hummingbird, Swainson's Thrush, Steller's Jay and Red-breasted Nuthatch. The east side, in the drier rain shadow, can be good for Ruby-crowned Kinglet, Western Tanager, White-crowned Sparrow, Red-naped Sapsucker, Western Wood-Pewee, Wilson's Warbler and Yellow Warbler. Other species to watch for include Blue Grouse, Red Crossbill, Varied Thrush, Townsend's Solitaire, Vaux's Swift and Pine Siskin.

Benton Lake National Wildlife Refuge

Over 12,000 acres of prairie and wetlands make up Benton Lake NWR, 10 miles north of Great Falls. Birding access is easy via a small system of roads and dikes. The refuge's extensive marshes support large numbers of breeding and migrant water-birds, including California Gull, Franklin's Gull, American White Pelican, Western Grebe, Wilson's Phalarope, White-faced Ibis and many species of waterfowl.

The adjacent short-grass prairie supports Chestnut-collared Longspur, Marbled Godwit, Sharp-tailed Grouse, Horned Lark, Upland Sandpiper, Western Meadowlark, Grasshopper Sparrow, Savannah Sparrow, Vesper Sparrow, American Kestrel and occasionally Burrowing Owl.

Medicine Lake National Wildlife Refuge

Medicine Lake NWR is another of Montana's many great prairie wetlands. Nestled in the northeastern corner of the state, this park has relatively few visitors and can often be enjoyed in near solitude. Birding is great, especially during migration, when Medicine Lake swarms with waterbirds. It hosts a large breeding colony of American White Pelican, along with many other species including Western Grebe, Eared Grebe, American Bittern, American Coot, Tundra Swan, Black Tern, Common Tern,

Forster's Tern, Great Blue Heron and various waterfowl. The dense bulrush marshes support Marsh Wren, Black-crowned Night-Heron, Common Yellowthroat and the rare Nelson's Sharp-tailed Sparrow.

The extensive mixed-grass prairie surrounding the lake supports several Sharp-tailed Grouse leks, which become active in April. Other grassland species commonly observed here include Baird's Sparrow, Lark Bunting, Chestnut-collared Longspur, Upland Sandpiper, Long-billed Curlew, Short-eared Owl and Clay-colored Sparrow.

Red Rock Lakes National Wildlife Refuge

Red Rock Lakes NWR is located in the scenic Centennial Valley about 30 miles west of Yellowstone NP. The 42,000 acres of the refuge encompass a variety of habitats between 6600 feet and 10,000 feet. Two lakes, Upper Red Rock and Lower Red Rock, connect via Red Rock Creek, which widens into a large marsh. Surrounding the lakes is a great deal of open grassland and some impressive sagebrush flats. Farther uphill, montane conifer forest carpets the slopes of the Centennial Mountains.

Of special interest is the large population of Trumpeter Swans, discovered here in the 1930s when the species was thought nearly extinct. The refuge was created to protect this population, but swans are by no means the only birds present. Waterfowl and shorebirds abound during breeding and migration. Raptors and songbirds are prevalent in upland areas. Species of note include Red-naped Sapsucker, Mountain Bluebird, several swallows, Franklin's Gull, American Coot, Sandhill Crane, Eared Grebe and Western Grebe.

Charles M. Russell National Wildlife Refuge

Centered on Fort Peck Lake and the surrounding uplands, Charles M. Russell NWR comprises an impressive 1,100,000 acres. Not surprisingly, a wide range of habitats are represented, including open water, cottonwood gallery forest, short-grass prairie and dry canyons, coulees and buttes. The avifauna is correspondingly diverse.

Riparian forests support Ovenbird, Red-headed Woodpecker, Western Wood-Pewee, Gray Catbird, Warbling Vireo, House Wren and Yellow Warbler. Upland birds include Pinyon Jay, Say's Phoebe, Sharp-tailed Grouse, Greater Sage-Grouse, Common Nighthawk, Common Poorwill, Short-eared Owl, Burrowing Owl, Horned Lark, Lark Bunting, Mountain Bluebird, Western Meadowlark, Brewer's Blackbird and the rare Mountain Plover. Birders need to be aware of wet conditions and the resulting "gumbo" roads that will stop any vehicle in its tracks.

Lee Metcalf National Wildlife Refuge

In the shadow of the Bitterroot Mountains lies the 2800-acre Lee Metcalf NWR. Consisting mainly of marsh wetlands, riparian cottonwood forest, dry ponderosa pine forest and adjacent fields, this refuge is best known for its waterbirds and raptors. Osprey are particularly numerous in summer, and a Bald Eagle pair usually nests in the northern part of the refuge. The marshes support Great Blue Heron (often including a breeding rookery), Common Yellowthroat, Song Sparrow, Yellow-headed Blackbird, Red-winged Blackbird, Marsh Wren and a large number of waterfowl including Cinnamon Teal, Redhead, Ring-necked Duck and Common Goldeneye. Sora and Virginia Rail can sometimes be observed at the marsh's edge.

A walk on the kiosk trail will typically yield Great Horned Owl, Pileated Woodpecker, Tree Swallow and Hooded Merganser. Along the Bitterroot River you may find Lewis's Woodpecker, Bank Swallow, Belted Kingfisher and Spotted Sandpiper. The open fields along Wildfowl Lane often host Red-tailed Hawk and American Kestrel, and in winter Rough-legged Hawk and occasionally Prairie Falcon and Peregrine Falcon.

East Front of the Rockies

The East Front is an informal term for the area west of Great Falls near Highway 200. Here the Continental Divide cuts along the eastern edge of the Rocky Mountains close to the prairies, creating a beautiful "wall" of snow-capped peaks overlooking the flat grasslands. In addition to the incredible scenery, the East Front boasts a number of large reservoirs that attract migrating birds by the thousands. Some of the best examples are the Eureka, Bynum, Pishkun and Willow Creek reservoirs. Pine Butte Swamp, west of Choteau, is another excellent birding location where you may find Sandhill Crane, Mountain Bluebird, White-crowned Sparrow, Northern Waterthrush, Yellow Warbler, Song Sparrow, Savannah Sparrow, Vesper Sparrow and the rare Alder Flycatcher, among many others. Birders here should be on the lookout for grizzly bears.

Other birds that may be spotted on the East Front include Golden Eagle, Ferruginous Hawk, Swainson's Hawk, Long-billed Curlew, Horned Lark, Common Raven and Black-billed Magpie.

Flathead Lake & Polson

Flathead Lake, the largest natural freshwater lake west of the Mississippi, lies at the north end of the Mission Valley. Birdwise, the lake is at its best in spring and fall, when it serves as a magnet for migrating waterbirds. Winter is also good if the lake has open water (most years). Common Loon, Red-necked Grebe, Redhead, Lesser Scaup, Bufflehead, Common Goldeneye, Barrow's Goldeneye and Canada Goose are a few of the many species of waterfowl to be found here.

The Flathead River empties into the lake at the north end, and birding here is also productive. At the lake's outlet at the south end lies the town of Polson. Here the Flathead River is wide and often attracts Common Merganser, diving ducks such as goldeneye and scaup, and Ring-billed and California gulls. The Polson Sewage Lagoons, perched on the east bank of the river, often attract good numbers of Northern Shoveler, Ruddy Duck and gulls. Pablo Reservoir, a managed pool about four miles south of Polson, is worth checking during migration for songbirds, waterbirds and especially shorebirds.

Golden Eagle

ABOUT THE SPECIES ACCOUNTS

This book presents detailed, illustrated accounts of 145 common bird species of Montana. While this number may seem a bit overwhelming to the beginning birder, it is by no means a comprehensive list. Because you are likely to encounter other birds, many similar to those illustrated in this book, we have briefly described confusable species in each entry (see Similar Species, next page). The Checklist (p. 167) lists all the bird species that have been recorded in Montana. Common and scientific names and the order of the birds follow the American Ornithologists' Union's *Check-list of North American Birds*.

One of the challenges of birding is that many species look different in different seasons. Many birds have breeding and nonbreeding plumages, and immature birds often look different from their parents. This book does not describe or illustrate all the different plumages of a species; instead, it focuses on forms most likely to be seen in our area.

In addition to helping you identify the birds, the species accounts bring them to life by including points of interest about their behavior, physiology, ecology and the derivation of their names.

ID: This section describes the bird's features using as little jargon as possible (see the Glossary and its illustration, p. 165, for exceptions). Although birds may not technically have "eyebrows" or "chins," these and other terms are easily understood by all readers. Where appropriate, the description is subdivided to highlight differences between male and female birds, breeding and nonbreeding birds and immature and adult birds.

Size: The average length *(L)* of a bird's body from bill to tail, as well as its wingspan *(W)*, give the approximate size of the bird. Please note that birds with long tails often have large lengths that do not necessarily reflect "body" size. Unless otherwise mentioned, the sexes are about the same size. Where the difference in size is consistent and substantial, different sizes are given for each sex.

Status: A general comment, such as "common," "uncommon" or "rare," is usually sufficient to describe the relative abundance of a species. However, in a state the size of Montana, it can be difficult to make such sweeping generalizations. Some species are common in certain parts of the state but uncommon or rare in others. We have labeled many such species "locally common." "Fairly common" species may vary in abundance geographically or from year to year. Wherever possible, we have also indicated status at different times of the year. Situations are bound to vary as migratory pulses, seasonal changes and centers of activity concentrate or disperse birds.

Habitat: The habitats we list indicate where each species is most commonly found. In most cases, it is a generalized description, but if a bird is restricted to a specific habitat, the habitat is described accordingly.

Nesting: For each species that nests in Montana, nest location and structure, clutch size, egg color, incubation period and parental duties are noted. Remember that birding ethics discourage the disturbance of active bird nests, and laws prohibit the destruction or possession of nests, eggs or young.

Feeding: Birds spend a great deal of time foraging for food. If you know what a bird eats and where the food is found—information the accounts provide—you will have a good chance of finding that bird.

Voice: Many birds, particularly songbirds, tend to be heard and not seen. Easily remembered imitative phrases for their distinctive sounds will aid in identifying birds by ear. Please note that these phrases may only loosely resemble the call, song or sound. Should one of ours not work for you, feel free to make up your own.

Similar Species: Because bird species can differ in subtle ways, consult this section before finalizing your identification. The most relevant field marks of easily confused species are briefly described. Page references lead you to similar species that have their own illustrated accounts. If you think you're observing one of the other species (without a page reference), you may wish to consult a more comprehensive guide.

Concentrating on the most relevant field marks, and paying attention to habitat preferences and behavioral clues, make differences between species much clearer. Don't be discouraged when you're first learning. Even experienced birders make mistakes!

Best Sites: If you are looking for a particular bird, you will have more luck in some locations than others, even within the range shown on the range map. In this section, we list some easily accessible places where you stand a good chance of seeing the species. Abbreviations are defined on p. 12.

Range Map: The range map for each species shows the general Montana distribution of the species in an average year. Most birds confine their annual movements to this range, although each year some wander beyond their traditional boundaries. These small maps do not show differences in abundance within the range. They also cannot show pockets within the range where the species may actually be absent, or how the range may change from year to year.

Unlike many other field guides, we have attempted to show migratory pathways—areas of the region where birds may appear en route to nesting or winter habitats. The pathways as shown do not distinguish high-use migration corridors from areas that are seldom used.

RANGE MAP LEGEND

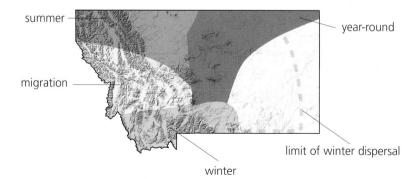

summer

migration

year-round

limit of winter dispersal

winter

SNOW GOOSE

Chen caerulescens

Among the greatest of Montana's avian spectacles is the annual spring gathering of more than 250,000 Snow Geese at Freezout Lake. These birds literally cloud the sky en route to their distant northern breeding grounds. Elsewhere in Montana, Snow Geese are found in much smaller numbers. • In recent years, Snow Goose populations have increased dramatically in North America, and there is concern that these birds may be degrading the sensitive tundra environment they use for nesting. • Snow Geese grub for their food, often targeting the belowground parts of plants. Their strong, serrated bills are well designed for pulling up the roots of marsh plants and gripping slippery grasses. • Unlike Canada Geese, which fly in "V" formations, migrating Snow Geese usually form oscillating, wavy lines. • Snow Goose plumage, like that of the Sandhill Crane, is often stained rusty red from iron in the water. • Until 1983, this species' two color morphs, a white and a blue, were considered different species.

blue morph

ID: white overall; black wing tips; pink feet and bill; dark "grinning patch" on bill; plumage is occasionally stained rusty red. *Blue morph:* white head and upper neck; dark blue gray body. *Immature:* brownish or dusky white plumage; dark bill and feet.
Size: *L* 28–33 in; *W* 4½–5 ft. Male on average larger than female.
Status: locally uncommon to abundant from March to April and September to November.
Habitat: shallow wetlands, lakes and fields.

Nesting: does not nest in Montana.
Feeding: grazes on waste grain and new sprouts; also eats aquatic vegetation, grasses, sedges and roots.
Voice: loud, nasal, constant *houk-houk* in flight.
Similar Species: *Ross's Goose:* smaller; petite bill with warty blue base; lacks black "grinning patch." *Tundra Swan* and *Trumpeter Swan* (p. 22): much larger; white wing tips. *American White Pelican* (p. 45): much larger bill and body.
Best Sites: Freezout Lake WMA; Benton Lake NWR; Medicine Lake NWR.

CANADA GOOSE

Branta canadensis

Canada Geese are among the most recognizable birds in our region, but they are also among the least valued. Few people realize that at one time these birds were hunted almost to extinction. Populations have since reestablished, and, in recent decades, these large, bold geese have inundated urban waterfronts, picnic sites, golf courses and city parks. Many geese overwinter in sheltered locations where food is available year-round. • Ornithologists recently divided this species into two, the diminutive Cackling Goose *(B. hutchinsii)* and the larger Canada Goose. Only the familiar Canada Goose is common in Montana. • Canada Goose pairs mate for life. Unlike most birds, the parents maintain a bond with their young until the beginning of the next year's nesting, almost a year after the young are born, thereby increasing the chance of survival for young birds. • Fuzzy goslings seem to compel people, especially children, to get closer. Goose parents, however, can be aggressive. Hissing sounds and low, outstretched necks are warning signs to give these birds some space.

ID: long, black neck; white "chin strap"; white undertail coverts; light brown underparts; dark brown upperparts; short, black tail.
Size: *L* 21–48 in; *W* 3½–5 ft. Male on average larger than female.
Status: very common from March to November; many overwinter.
Habitat: lakeshores, riverbanks, ponds, farmlands and city parks.
Nesting: on island or shoreline; usually on ground but often uses elevated platform such as broken-off tree or man-made structure; female builds nest of plant materials lined with down; female incubates 3–8 white eggs 25–28 days while male stands guard.
Feeding: grazes on new sprouts, aquatic vegetation, grass and roots; tips up for aquatic roots and tubers.
Voice: loud, familiar *ah-honk,* often answered by other Canada Geese.
Similar Species: *Snow Goose* (p. 20): blue morph has white head and upper neck; always lacks contrasting white "chin strap."
Best Sites: widespread around wetlands, lakes, reservoirs, suburban areas with water frontage and open fields; Freezout Lake WMA; Benton Lake NWR; Medicine Lake NWR.

TRUMPETER SWAN

Cygnus buccinator

The Trumpeter Swan was hunted nearly to extinction for its meat and feathers in the early 20th century. By the 1930s, one of the last known populations was found at Montana's Red Rock Lakes, prompting the formation of the Red Rock Lakes National Wildlife Refuge. Attempts to reintroduce the Trumpeter Swan to former parts of its breeding range are meeting with success in many areas, including Montana, and the bird's numbers continue to increase. • Both "trumpeter" and *buccinator* refer to this swan's loud, bugling voice, which is produced when air is forced through the long windpipe that runs through the keel of the bird's breastbone. The resulting low-pitched sound is the best means of separating this species from the extremely similar Tundra Swan, a common migrant in our state. • The Trumpeter Swan is the world's largest species of waterfowl and Montana's heaviest bird species; males routinely weigh more than 30 pounds.

ID: all-white plumage; large, solid black bill; black skin extends from bill to eyes; black feet; neck is kinked at base when bird stands or swims. *Immature:* gray brown plumage; gray and pink bill; light-colored feet.

Size: *L* 5–6 ft; *W* 6–7 ft. Male on average larger than female.

Status: uncommon year-round.

Habitat: lakes and large wetlands.

Nesting: always close to water, whether on shore, on small island or on muskrat or beaver lodge; male gathers marsh plants such as cattails, bulrushes, sedges and grasses; female constructs nest mound and lines it with down; mostly female incubates 4–6 creamy white to dull white eggs 32–37 days.

Feeding: tips up, surface gleans and occasionally grazes for vegetation; eats primarily pondweeds, duckweeds, aquatic tubers and roots.

Voice: loud, resonant, buglelike *koh-hoh.*

Similar Species: *Tundra Swan:* smaller; usually shows yellow spot in front of eye; higher-pitched voice; immatures often not separable. *Snow Goose* (p. 20): much smaller; black wing tips; pinkish bill.

Best Sites: *Breeding:* Red Rock Lakes NWR. *In migration:* Ennis Lake; Flathead Lake; Freezout Lake WMA; Canyon Ferry Lake.

MALLARD

Anas platyrhynchos

The male Mallard, with his iridescent green head and chestnut brown breast, is the classic wild duck. Mallards can be seen almost any day of the year, often in flocks and always near open water. These confident ducks have even taken up residence in local swimming pools. • Wild Mallards freely hybridize with domestic ducks, which were originally derived from Mallards in Europe. The offspring are a confusing blend of both parents. • Male ducks molt after breeding, losing much of their extravagant plumage. This "eclipse" plumage camouflages them during the flightless period when new flight feathers are growing in. The males usually molt again into breeding colors by early fall. • The body heat of a brooding hen is enough to increase the growth rate of nearby grasses, which she then manipulates to further conceal her precious nest.

ID: dark blue speculum bordered by white both fore and aft; orange feet; does not dive. *Male:* glossy, green head; yellow bill; chestnut brown breast; white "necklace"; gray body plumage; black central tail feathers curl upward. *Female:* mottled brown overall; orange bill spattered black.

Size: *L* 20–27½ in; *W* 35 in. Male on average larger than female.

Status: common to abundant from March to November; many overwinter on open water.

Habitat: lakes, prairie potholes, wetlands, rivers, city parks, agricultural areas and sewage lagoons.

Nesting: in tall vegetation or under bush, often near water; female builds nest of grass and other plant material lined with down; female incubates 7–10 light green to white eggs 26–30 days.

Feeding: tips up and dabbles in shallows for seeds of sedges, willows and pondweeds; also eats insects, aquatic invertebrates, larval amphibians and fish eggs.

Voice: *Male:* deep, quiet quacks. *Female:* loud quacks; very vocal.

Similar Species: *Northern Shoveler* (p. 26): much larger bill; male has white breast; female has blue forewing patch. *Common Merganser* (p. 34): thin, blood red bill and white underparts; male lacks chestnut breast. *American Wigeon:* blue bill; white crown; obvious white forewing patch in male and female. *Green-winged Teal* (p. 28): very small; white vertical bar on side of chest; speculum bordered by beige on leading edge in both sexes.

Best Sites: nearly any body of open water.

BLUE-WINGED TEAL

Anas discors

The small, speedy Blue-winged Teal is renowned for its aviation skills. These teals can be identified in flight by their small size, sky blue forewings and the sharp twists and turns that they execute with precision. • Despite the similarity of their names, the Green-winged Teal is not the Blue-winged Teal's closest relative. The Blue-winged Teal is more closely related to the Northern Shoveler and the Cinnamon Teal. These birds all share broad, flat bills, pale blue forewings and green speculums. Female Cinnamon Teals and Blue-winged Teals are so similar in appearance that even expert birders and ornithologists have difficulty distinguishing them in the field. • Blue-winged Teals migrate farther than most ducks, summering as far north as the Canadian tundra and wintering mainly in Central and South America. As a result they arrive later and depart earlier than Montana's other waterfowl species.

ID: does not dive. *Male:* blue gray head; white crescent on face; darker bill than female; black-spotted breast and sides. *Female:* mottled brown overall; white throat. *In flight:* blue forewing patch; green speculum.

Size: *L* 14–16 in; *W* 23 in. Male on average larger than female.

Status: fairly common from late April to August.

Habitat: shallow lake edges and wetlands; prefers areas of short but dense emergent vegetation.

Nesting: in grass along shoreline or in meadow; female builds nest with grass and considerable amounts of down; female incubates 8–13 white eggs, sometimes tinged with olive, for 23–27 days.

Feeding: gleans water's surface for sedge and grass seeds, pondweeds, duckweeds and aquatic invertebrates.

Voice: *Male:* soft *keck-keck-keck*. *Female:* soft quacks.

Similar Species: *Cinnamon Teal* (p. 25): female virtually identical to female Blue-winged Teal, but brown is richer, bill sturdier and eye line less distinct. *Green-winged Teal* (p. 28): female has smaller bill and black and green speculum; lacks blue forewing patch. *Northern Shoveler* (p. 26): much larger bill with paler base; male has green head and lacks spotting on body.

Best Sites: Freezout Lake WMA; Bowdoin NWR; Benton Lake NWR; Lee Metcalf NWR.

CINNAMON TEAL

Anas cyanoptera

If the Stetson is the "hat of the West," then the Cinnamon Teal is the "duck of the West." The principal distribution of both the headwear and the bird broadly define that great reach of arid country where water is dramatic and important. Cinnamon Teals push northward each spring from southwestern and middle-American wintering grounds to dot the reed-fringed pools of intermountain basins. Nesting is common in the valleys of western Montana, where marshes containing suitably dense cover for nesting are prevalent. • The intense reddish brown plumage of the male Cinnamon Teal, accented by its ruby red eyes, is worth an admiring gaze at any time of day, but can be a true showstopper in the low, slanting light of early morning and late afternoon. • Male ducks of most species abandon their mates early in incubation, but male Cinnamon Teals often accompany their partners throughout this period.

ID: small duck; big-billed; does not dive. *Male:* intense cinnamon red head, neck and underparts; red eyes. *Female:* mottled warm brown overall; dark eyes. *In flight:* conspicuous pale blue forewing patch; green speculum.
Size: *L* 15–17 in; *W* 22 in. Male on average larger than female.
Status: fairly common from late March to September.
Habitat: freshwater ponds, marshes, sloughs and flooded swales with surface-growing or submergent aquatic vegetation; usually prefers sites providing nearby marsh cover, and less apt than other dabbling ducks to feed in flocks far out in fields.

Nesting: in tall vegetation, occasionally far from water; female builds nest of grass and down placed in concealed hollow; female incubates 7–12 pinkish buff eggs 21–25 days; ducklings fly after 7 weeks.
Feeding: gleans water's surface for grass and sedge seeds, pondweeds, duckweeds and aquatic invertebrates.
Voice: not often heard; male utters whistled *peep*; female gives rough *karr, karr, karr*.
Similar Species: *Ruddy Duck* (p. 35): male has white "cheek," blue bill and stiff, upward-angled tail. *Green-winged Teal* (p. 28): small bill; no blue forewing patch. *Blue-winged Teal* (p. 24): male has white crescent in front of eye; female difficult to distinguish (see that species).
Best Sites: Lee Metcalf NWR; Freezout Lake WMA; Ninepipe NWR; Red Rock Lakes NWR.

NORTHERN SHOVELER

Anas clypeata

The initial reaction upon meeting this bird for the first time is often, "Wow, look at the big honker on that Mallard!" A closer look, however, reveals a completely different bird—the Northern Shoveler. The extra large, spoonlike bill allows this strangely handsome duck to strain small invertebrates and plankton from the water and from pond bottoms. The Northern Shoveler eats much smaller organisms than do most other waterfowl, and its intestines are elongated to prolong the digestion of hard-bodied invertebrates. The shoveler's specialized feeding strategy means that it is rarely seen tipping up—it is more often found in shallows where the mucky bottom is easiest to access. • The scientific descriptor *clypeata*, Latin for "furnished with a shield," possibly refers to the chestnut flanks of the male. This species was once placed in its own genus, *Spatula*, the meaning of which needs no explanation.

ID: distinctive, large, spatulate bill; blue fore-wing patch; green speculum; does not dive. *Male:* green head; yellow eyes; white breast; chestnut brown flanks. *Female:* mottled brown overall; orange-tinged bill.
Size: *L* 18–20 in; *W* 30 in. Male on average larger than female.
Status: common from March to November; rare in winter.
Habitat: shallow marshes, lakes, reservoirs, ditches and sewage ponds with muddy bottoms and emergent vegetation.
Nesting: in shallow hollow on dry ground, usually within 150 ft of water; female builds nest of dry grass and down and

incubates 10–12 pale greenish buff eggs 21–28 days.
Feeding: dabbles in shallow and often muddy water; strains out plant and animal matter, especially aquatic crustaceans, insect larvae and seeds; rarely tips up.
Voice: generally quiet; occasional raspy chuckle or quack, most often heard during spring courtship.
Similar Species: *Mallard* (p. 23): blue speculum bordered by white both fore and aft; lacks pale blue forewing patch; male has chestnut brown breast and white flanks. *Blue-winged Teal* (p. 24): smaller; much smaller bill; male has spotted breast and sides. *Northern Pintail* (p. 27): female has smaller, blue-sided bill; lacks blue forewing.
Best Sites: Lee Metcalf NWR; Ninepipe NWR; Freezout Lake WMA.

NORTHERN PINTAIL

Anas acuta

The trademark of the elegant male Northern Pintail is its long, tapering tail feathers, which are easily seen in flight and point skyward when the bird dabbles. This bird may represent the very definition of avian grace, with its slender build and delicate outline. • Migrating pintails are often seen in flocks of 20 to 40 birds, but some early spring flocks number in the thousands. Exceptional sites such as Freezout Lake sometimes host more than 200,000 Northern Pintails, with birds carpeting both pond and field. Although many pintails migrating through Montana are heading to and from breeding sites in northern Canada, Montana does support a healthy breeding population of its own. • Pintails breed earlier than most other waterfowl, and in the U.S. they begin nesting in mid-April.

ID: long, slender neck; dark, blue-sided bill; does not dive. *Male:* distinctive; chocolate brown head; long, tapering tail feathers; white of breast extends up sides of neck; dusty gray body plumage; black and white hindquarters. *Female:* mottled light brown overall; plain face. *In flight:* slender body; brownish speculum with white on trailing edge only.

Size: *Male: L* 25–30 in; *W* 34 in. *Female: L* 20–21 in; *W* 34 in.

Status: common from March to November; rare in winter.

Habitat: shallow wetlands, prairie potholes, fields and lake edges.

Nesting: in small depression in low vegetation; female builds nest of grass, leaves and moss, lined with down; female incubates 6–12 greenish buff eggs 22–25 days.

Feeding: tips up and dabbles in shallows for seeds of sedges, willows and pondweeds; also eats aquatic invertebrates and larval amphibians; eats waste grain in agricultural areas during migration; diet more varied than that of other dabbling ducks.

Voice: *Male:* soft, whistling call. *Female:* rough quack.

Similar Species: *Mallard* (p. 23) and *Gadwall:* females are chunkier; orange on bill; dark eye line; two white wing stripes (Mallard); rectangular white patch on inner upperwing (Gadwall). *Blue-winged Teal* (p. 24) and *Cinnamon Teal* (p. 25): females smaller; blue forewing; dark eye line. *Green-winged Teal* (p. 28): female much smaller; dark eye line.

Best Sites: Freezout Lake WMA; Bowdoin NWR; Medicine Lake NWR; Ninepipe NWR; Benton Lake NWR.

GREEN-WINGED TEAL

Anas crecca

The Green-winged Teal is one of the speediest and most dexterous fliers of all waterfowl. With its red head, green "mask" and amazing flying speed, it might bring to mind a comic book superhero. • When intruders cause these small ducks to rocket up from the wetland's surface, the birds circle quickly overhead in small, tight-flying flocks, returning to the water only when the threat has departed. Unlike many other ducks, Green-winged Teals often feed on mudflats, and are commonly seen alongside shorebirds at the marsh's edge. • Green-winged Teals often undertake a partial migration before molting into their postbreeding, "eclipse" plumage. During this time, like most waterfowl, they become temporarily flightless as their new flight feathers grow in. • The name "teal" possibly originated from the medieval English word *tele* or the old Dutch word *teling*, both of which mean "small" and which originally referred to the Green-winged Teal's Eurasian counterpart, the Common Teal *(A. crecca crecca).*

ID: small dark bill; green and black speculum; does not dive. *Male:* chestnut brown head; green swipe extending back from eye; white vertical shoulder slash; creamy breast spotted with black; pale gray sides. *Female:* mottled brown overall; dark eye line; light belly.
Size: *L* 12–16 in; *W* 23 in. Male on average larger than female.
Status: common from March to November; some overwinter.
Habitat: shallow lakes, wetlands, beaver ponds, ditches, sewage lagoons and meandering rivers.

Nesting: well concealed in tall vegetation within a few hundred feet of water; female builds nest of grass and leaves, lined with down; female incubates 6–14 cream to pale buff eggs 20–24 days.
Feeding: dabbles in shallows, particularly on mudflats, for aquatic invertebrates, larval amphibians, marsh plant seeds and pondweeds.
Voice: *Male:* crisp whistle. *Female:* soft quack.
Similar Species: *American Wigeon:* male lacks white shoulder slash and chestnut brown head; female has blue bill and white forewing patch. *Blue-winged Teal* (p. 24) and *Cinnamon Teal* (p. 25): female has blue forewing patch.
Best Sites: Freezout Lake WMA; Ninepipe NWR; Lee Metcalf NWR; Bowdoin NWR; Benton Lake NWR.

REDHEAD

Aythya americana

Redheads are diving ducks with very different summer and winter habitats. During the breeding season, pairs scatter across the wetlands of central and western North America, but in winter most are found in coastal bays of the southern U.S. and Mexico. • For a diving duck, the Redhead consumes a large amount of plant material, and it is often found in shallower waters than other divers, regularly feeding from the water's surface. • Redheads prefer large marshes for nesting. Female Redheads usually incubate their own eggs and brood their young as other ducks do. They do, however, regularly lay eggs in nests of neighboring Redheads or of other duck species, a strategy called brood parasitism.

ID: black-tipped, blue gray bill; single pale gray stripe on speculum; dives. *Male:* rounded, red head; black breast and hindquarters; gray back and sides. *Female:* dark brown overall with rusty tinge to head; uniform body plumage lacks mottling; lighter "chin" and "cheek" patches.
Size: *L* 18–22 in; *W* 29 in. Male on average larger than female.
Status: fairly common from March to November; small numbers may overwinter.
Habitat: *Breeding:* large prairie potholes, bulrush and cattail marshes. *In migration:* large wetlands, ponds, lakes, bays and rivers.
Nesting: usually in shallow water, sometimes on dry ground; female builds deep basket nest of reeds and grass suspended over water at base of emergent vegetation

and lines it with fine white down; female incubates 9–14 greenish eggs 23–29 days; female may lay eggs in other ducks' nests.
Feeding: dives to depths of 10 ft; eats primarily aquatic vegetation, especially pondweeds, duckweeds and plant leaves and stems; occasionally eats aquatic invertebrates.
Voice: generally quiet. *Male:* catlike meow in courtship. *Female:* rolling *kurr-kurr-kurr; squak* when alarmed.
Similar Species: *Canvasback:* clean white back; bill slopes onto forehead. *Ring-necked Duck:* female has more prominent white eye ring, white ring on bill and peaked head. *Lesser Scaup* (p. 30): male has dark head and whiter sides; female has more white feathering at base of bill.
Best Sites: *Breeding:* Freezout Lake WMA; Medicine Lake NWR; Bowdoin NWR. *In migration:* Flathead Lake; East Front Reservoirs.

LESSER SCAUP

Aythya affinis

The male Lesser Scaup mimics the colors of an Oreo cookie—black at both ends and light in the middle. Although the female is less distinguishable than her counterpart, both sexes are easily recognized in flight by the white stripe extending halfway to the wing tip. • The Lesser Scaup is more at home in lakes of forested areas than are many other ducks, but it also nests in marshes. • The scientific descriptor *affinis* is Latin for "adjacent" or "allied"—a reference to this scaup's close association to other diving ducks. "Scaup" might refer to a preferred winter food of this duck—shellfish beds are called "scalps" in Scotland—or it might be a phonetic imitation of one of its calls. • Scaups are known by the nickname "Bluebill."

ID: yellow eyes; dives. *Male:* purplish black head; black breast and hindquarters; dusty white sides; grayish back; black-tipped, blue gray bill. *Female:* dark brown overall; well-defined white patch at base of bill.
Size: *L* 15–18 in; *W* 25 in. Male on average larger than female.
Status: fairly common from March to November; some overwinter.
Habitat: *Breeding:* woodland ponds, margins of prairie potholes and lake edges with grassy margins. *In migration:* lakes, large marshes and rivers.
Nesting: in tall, concealing vegetation, generally close to water and occasionally on island; female builds nest hollow of grass and lines it with down; female incubates 8–14 olive buff eggs about 21–27 days.

Feeding: dives underwater for aquatic invertebrates, mostly mollusks, amphipods and insect larvae; occasionally eats aquatic vegetation.
Voice: alarm call is deep *scaup. Male:* soft *whee-oooh* in courtship. *Female:* purring *kwah*.
Similar Species: *Greater Scaup:* rare in Montana in winter and migration; nearly identical but with white wing stripe extending more than halfway to wing tip; more rounded head; slightly larger bill; male's head greenish black. *Ring-necked Duck:* male has white shoulder slash and black back; female has white-ringed bill. *Redhead* (p. 29): male has red head and white-ringed bill; female lacks white at base of bill, has rusty-tinged head, gray wing stripe.
Best Sites: Freezout Lake WMA; Medicine Lake NWR; Benton Lake NWR; Red Rock Lakes NWR.

HARLEQUIN DUCK

Histrionicus histrionicus

The showstopping Harlequin Duck is an ornithological oddity in more ways than one. Favoring rushing mountain streams over marshes, this gaudy fowl is perhaps the most uniquely patterned bird in Montana, and one of the rarest. Nonchalantly braving even the most turbulent whitewater currents in search of animal matter, these birds often pause to stand atop an exposed boulder. In June or early July, the males leave the nesting females and travel to the Pacific coast to molt on marine waters. The females keep to the rapids and torrents, raising their families in a pleasantly chaotic setting. • Harlequin Ducks are considered a Montana species of concern due to small population size and apparent region-wide declines. • The Harlequin Duck gets its name from the male's striking plumage—a harlequin is an actor who is colorfully made-up or wears a mask.

ID: small, rounded duck; blocky head; short bill; raises and lowers tail while swimming; dives. *Male:* gray blue body; chestnut sides; white spots and stripes on head, neck and flanks. *Female:* dusky brown overall; light underparts; 2–3 light patches on head.

Size: *L* 16½ in; *W* 26 in. Male on average larger than female.

Status: rare and local from May to September.

Habitat: *Breeding:* shallow, fast-flowing mountain streams; prefers undisturbed waters. *In migration:* occasionally uses larger rivers or lakes in valleys.

Nesting: under shrub or among rocks near stream; female builds shallow nest lined with grass, other plant material and down; female incubates 3–7 cream-colored eggs 28–30 days and rears young alone.

Feeding: dabbles and dives down to 5 ft for aquatic invertebrates, mainly caddisfly and stonefly larvae; searches river bottoms, probing rock crevices for invertebrates and fish eggs.

Voice: generally silent outside breeding season. *Male:* descending trill and squeaky whistles during courtship. *Female:* harsh *ek-ek-ek* or low croak during courtship.

Similar Species: *Bufflehead* (p. 32): smaller; never found on fast-flowing water; female lacks white between eye and bill. *Other diving ducks:* different habitats; longer necks; less rounded bodies.

Best Sites: McDonald Creek (Glacier NP); Yellowstone NP; Kootenai River; Yaak area.

BUFFLEHEAD

Bucephala albeola

With their bold, simple coloration and tiny size, Buffleheads are among the first diving ducks identified by beginning birders. These birds are noticeably abundant on park ponds and urban reservoirs. Males are strikingly dressed in black and white, with a characteristic large white patch on the rear of the head. Females are more subdued but appealing, their sooty heads ornamented with a pretty white "cheek" spot. • In migration and in winter, Buffleheads dive for mollusks, mostly snails. If you are lucky, you may see a whole flock dive at the same time for these tasty morsels. • The genus name *Bucephala*, meaning "ox-headed," refers to the shape of this bird's head; *albeola* means "white," referring to the male's plumage.

ID: very small, rounded diving duck; white patch on inner wing in flight; short gray bill; short neck. *Male:* white wedge on back of head; head otherwise iridescent dark green or purple, usually appearing black; dark back; white underparts. *Female:* dark brown head; oval white ear patch; light brown sides.

Size: *L* 13–15 in; *W* 21 in. Male on average larger than female.

Status: locally common from March to November; regularly overwinters on open water.

Habitat: open water of lakes, large ponds and rivers.

Nesting: in tree cavity or artificial nest box, usually near water; nest cavity lined with down; female incubates 6–12 ivory eggs 28–33 days.

Feeding: dives for aquatic invertebrates; takes water boatmen and mayfly and damselfly larvae in summer; favors mollusks (particularly snails) and crustaceans in winter; also eats some small fish and pondweeds.

Voice: *Male:* growling call. *Female:* harsh quack.

Similar Species: *Hooded Merganser:* male has white crest outlined in black; long, thin bill; female lacks white head patch. *Harlequin Duck* (p. 31): mountain stream habitat; female has 2–3 light spots on head. *Common Goldeneye* (p. 33) and *Barrow's Goldeneye:* males larger, have white patch between eye and bill; females lack white head patch. *Other diving ducks:* females much larger, none with single white patch behind eye.

Best Sites: *Breeding:* Seeley Lake; Glacier NP. *In migration* and *winter:* Flathead Lake.

COMMON GOLDENEYE

Bucephala clangula

The male Common Goldeneye performs an interesting winter courtship display, often in front of apparently uninterested females. He arches his puffy, iridescent head backward until his forehead seems to touch his back, then catapults his neck forward while he produces a seemingly painful *peent* sound. • Common Goldeneye females often lay their eggs in the nests of neighboring goldeneyes and other cavity-nesting ducks. Ducklings remain in the nest one to three days before jumping out of the tree cavity, often falling a long distance to the ground. • Common Goldeneyes breed around the world in northern forests, usually choosing to nest near lakes that have no fish. These lakes are well stocked with the goldeneye food of choice, aquatic invertebrates. • Common Goldeneyes are frequently called "Whistlers," because the wind whistles through their wings when they fly.

ID: steep forehead with peaked crown; black wings with large white patches; golden eyes; dives. *Male:* dark, iridescent green head; circular white patch in front of eye; dark bill; dark back; white sides and belly. *Female:* chocolate brown head; lighter breast and belly; rest of body gray brown; dark bill tipped with yellow in spring and summer.

Size: *L* 16–20 in; *W* 26 in. Male on average larger than female.

Status: common from March to November; many overwinter.

Habitat: *Breeding:* marshes, ponds, lakes and rivers. *In migration* and *winter:* open water of lakes, large ponds and rivers.

Nesting: in tree cavity, but will use nest box; cavity lined with wood chips and down; female incubates 6–10 blue green eggs 28–32 days; 2 females may each lay clutch in same nest if cavities in short supply.

Feeding: dives for crustaceans, mollusks and aquatic insect larvae; may also eat tubers, leeches, frogs and small fish.

Voice: *Male:* courtship calls a nasal *peent* and a hoarse *kraaagh. Female:* harsh croak.

Similar Species: *Barrow's Goldeneye:* male has large, white, crescent-shaped facial patch and purplish head; female has more orange on bill and more steeply sloped forehead.

Best Sites: *Breeding:* Glacier NP; Flathead Lake; Lee Metcalf NWR. *In migration* and *winter:* any reasonably deep waters in western Montana.

COMMON MERGANSER

Mergus merganser

Straining like a jumbo jet in takeoff, the Common Merganser runs along the surface of the water, beating its wings until it gains enough speed to become airborne. Once up and away, this great duck flies arrow-straight, low over the water, making broad, sweeping turns to follow rivers and shorelines. • These birds are highly social, often gathering in groups over winter and during migration. In winter, any open water with a fish-filled shoal may support good numbers of these skilled divers. • Widespread and abundant in North America, the Common Merganser also occurs in Eurasia, where it is called the "Goosander."

ID: large, elongated body; long, thin bill with serrated edges; dives. *Male:* glossy, green head without crest; blood red bill and feet; white body plumage; black stripe on back; dark eyes. *Female:* rusty neck and crested head; clean white "chin" and breast; orange bill; gray body; orangish eyes. *In flight:* shallow wingbeats; body compressed and arrowlike.

Size: *L* 22–27 in; *W* 34 in. Male on average larger than female.

Status: fairly common year-round; some overwinter.

Habitat: large, unpolluted rivers and deep lakes. *Breeding:* forest-edged waterways.

Nesting: often in tree cavity 15–20 ft above ground; occasionally under bush or log, on cliff ledge or in large nest box;

usually not far from water; female incubates 8–11 pale buff eggs 30–35 days.

Feeding: dives down to 30 ft for small fish; young eat aquatic invertebrates and insects before switching to fish.

Voice: *Male:* harsh *uig-a*, like a guitar twang. *Female:* harsh *karr karr*.

Similar Species: *Red-breasted Merganser:* uncommon migrant east of the Divide; male has shaggy green crest and spotted red breast; female lacks cleanly defined white throat. *Hooded Merganser:* much smaller; male has obvious white crest, brown body; female nearly all brown, with dark bill. *Mallard* (p. 23): dabbles for food from surface; male has chestnut brown breast and yellow bill. *Common Goldeneye* (p. 33): male has white facial patch and stubby, dark bill. *Common Loon* (p. 41): dark bill; white-spotted back.

Best Sites: Missouri River at Great Falls; Yellowstone River at Billings; Flathead Lake; Flathead River; Bitterroot River.

RUDDY DUCK
Oxyura jamaicensis

The small male Ruddy Duck displays energetic courtship behavior with comedic enthusiasm. He vigorously pumps his bright blue bill, almost touching his breast. The *plap, plap, plap-plap-plap* of the display increases in speed to its hilarious climax: a spasmodic jerk and sputter. • The male's dull "eclipse" plumage is worn throughout winter and well into spring, unlike most ducks, which regain breeding plumage by late fall. • Female Ruddies commonly lay up to 10 eggs at a time. This feat is remarkable considering that their eggs are bigger than those of a Mallard, a significantly larger bird. Ruddy Duck females sometimes dump eggs in a communal "dummy" nest, which may accumulate as many as 60 eggs that will receive no motherly care. • Although perhaps not the most appealing location, a local sewage lagoon is often a desirable place for birders who wish to see Ruddy Ducks.

breeding

eclipse

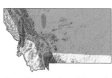

ID: large bill and head; short neck; long, stiff tail feathers (often held upward); dives. *Breeding male:* white "cheek"; chestnut red body; blue bill; black tail and crown. *Female:* brown overall; long, horizontal, dark "cheek" stripe beneath eye; darker crown and back. *Nonbreeding male:* similar to female but with large white "cheek." **Size:** *L* 15–16 in; *W* 18½ in. Male on average larger than female.
Status: common from April to October; rare in winter.
Habitat: *Breeding:* prairie potholes, shallow marshes with dense emergent vegetation (such as cattails or bulrushes) and muddy bottoms. *In migration* and *winter:* sewage lagoons, marshes and lakes with open, shallow water.

Nesting: in cattails, bulrushes or other emergent vegetation; female suspends woven platform nest over water; may use abandoned duck or coot nest, muskrat lodge or exposed log; female incubates 5–10 rough, whitish eggs 23–26 days; common brood parasite as well as "dummy" nester.
Feeding: dives to bottom of wetlands for seeds of pondweeds, sedges and bulrushes and for leafy parts of aquatic plants; also eats a few aquatic invertebrates.
Voice: *Male: chuck-chuck-chuck-chur-r-r-r* during courtship display. *Female:* generally silent.
Similar Species: male distinctive; no other female duck in Montana has long, horizontal dark stripe beneath eye.
Best Sites: Ninepipe NWR; Freezout Lake WMA; Medicine Lake NWR.

RUFFED GROUSE

Bonasa umbellus

E very spring, and occasionally in fall, mysterious drumbeats reverberate through the forest. The "drumming" is the sound of a male Ruffed Grouse proclaiming his territory. He struts along a fallen log with his tail fanned and his neck feathers ruffed, periodically beating the air with accelerating wing strokes. • The Ruffed Grouse is the common forest grouse of Montana, found in a wide variety of treed habitats ranging from small deciduous woodlots and suburban riparian woodlands to vast expanses of montane conifer forest. • Populations of Ruffed Grouse seem to fluctuate over a 10-year cycle. Many predators rely on this bird as a food source and show population fluctuations that closely track those of the Ruffed Grouse. • In winter, scales grow out along the sides of this bird's feet, giving the Ruffed Grouse temporary "snowshoes."

gray morph

rufous morph

ID: small, crested head; mottled, gray brown overall; black on sides of lower neck; gray- or reddish-barred tail has broad, dark, subterminal band and white tip. *Female:* incomplete subterminal tail band.
Size: *L* 15–19 in; *W* 22 in. Male on average larger than female.
Status: common year-round.
Habitat: forests and riparian woodlands; in many areas favors young second-growth with birch, poplar and especially aspen.
Nesting: female creates shallow depression in leaf litter, often beside boulder, under log or at base of tree; female incubates 9–12 buff-colored eggs 23–25 days.

Feeding: omnivorous diet includes seeds, flowers, berries, catkins, leaves, insects, spiders and snails; may take small frogs; in winter perches in deciduous trees to eat buds.
Voice: *Male:* uses wings to produce hollow, drumming courtship sound of accelerating, deep booms. *Female:* clucks and hisses around chicks.
Similar Species: *Spruce Grouse:* dark tail lacks black subterminal band and white tip; lacks head crest; male has red eye combs. *Sharp-tailed Grouse* (p. 39): unforested habitats; lacks fan-shaped tail and black feathers on lower neck.
Best Sites: wooded forest service roads and trails anywhere in western Montana; Glacier NP; Missoula; Bitterroot Valley; Helena.

GREATER SAGE-GROUSE

Centrocercus urophasianus

B eginning in March and April, groups of Greater Sage-Grouse assemble at their courtship areas (leks) to perform a traditional springtime dance. At dawn, males enter a flat, short-grass arena, inflate their pectoral sacs, spread their pointed tail feathers and strut with vigor to intimidate their peers and attract prospective mates. The most fit and experienced males claim positions at the center of the circular lek; immature males are generally poor strutters, and are forced to the periphery. The females wield the power, however, acting as the judges of this important competition. An impressive male can mate with up to 75 percent of the nearby females. • By late summer, sage-grouse often migrate to higher elevations, but this bird is always found in large tracts of sagebrush. • Road construction, mining operations, off-road vehicle use, overgrazing and West Nile virus have all contributed to steep declines in Montana's Greater Sage-Grouse population, threatening its long-term survival.

ID: *Male:* large grouse; black belly and "bib"; white breast; long, spiked tail; mottled brown back; yellow comb. *Female:* black belly; mottled brown plumage; very faint yellowish comb.
Size: *Male:* L 27–34 in; W 38 in. *Female:* L 18–24 in; W 33 in.
Status: rare to uncommon year-round.
Habitat: treeless plains and rolling hills dominated by sagebrush, grasses and forbs.
Nesting: usually under sagebrush, in shallow depression lined sparsely by female with leaves and grass; female incubates 6–9 finely spotted, yellowish to olive eggs up to 27 days.

Feeding: eats mostly sagebrush leaves; in summer also takes flowers, buds and terrestrial insects.
Voice: generally silent. *Male:* on lek makes unique, hollow *opp-la-boop*, like dripping water, as air is released from jiggling air sacs. *Female: quak-quak* call on lek. Flocks flush close by with startling burst of wingbeats.
Similar Species: *Ring-necked Pheasant:* smaller and slimmer; female lacks black belly and has unfeathered legs. *Blue Grouse* (p. 38): forest habitat; fan-shaped tail; lacks black belly. *Sharp-tailed Grouse* (p. 39): much smaller; white outer tail feathers; lacks black belly.
Best Sites: Bannack; Powder River and Tongue River valleys; Charles M. Russell NWR; Billings.

BLUE GROUSE

Dendragapus obscurus

The low, owl-like hoots of the male Blue Grouse carry indistinctly through high forests that have yet to be visited by most northbound migrants. Males sometimes begin their breeding calls while patches of snow still remain, making their deep courting notes one of the earliest signs of spring. The male's voice is so deep that the human ear can detect only a fraction of the sounds produced. • Hormonal changes and food availability cause these birds to make seasonal migrations, but rather than moving latitudinally, Blue Grouse simply move altitudinally. During late summer, some birds move upslope to timberline, where they spend the winter. • Although these birds roost in coniferous trees, they spend much time on the ground. There they are often easily approached— a characteristic that explains their nickname "Fool Hen."

ID: overall mottled, brownish gray coloration; white undertail coverts; tail nearly all dark, or with faint gray subterminal band; feathered legs. *Male:* blue gray crown, nape, upper back and tail feathers; orangish comb above eye; when displaying, shows inflated red throat patches surrounded by white feathers. *Female:* blue gray lower breast and belly; faint yellow comb.
Size: *L* 17–22 in; *W* 24–28 in. Male on average larger than female.
Status: uncommon year-round.
Habitat: coniferous forests of higher foothills and mountains; often found in burns or other forest clearings.
Nesting: often near fallen log or under shrub; female lines shallow depression with vegetation, such as leaves, twigs and needles; female incubates 7–10 buff-colored eggs 25–28 days.
Feeding: eats mainly leaves, berries, seeds and flowers; also takes conifer needles and buds in winter; young birds eat grasshoppers and beetles.
Voice: 5–8 extremely deep, ventriloquial hoots, the first or second hoot loudest, then trailing off.
Similar Species: *Spruce Grouse:* smaller; male has red eye combs; tail lacks gray band. *Ring-necked Pheasant:* unforested habitat; female has lighter undersides and longer, pointed tail. *Ruffed Grouse* (p. 36): smaller and paler; crested head; gray tail with black subterminal band.
Best Sites: remote roads and trails in montane conifer or mixed forest in western Montana; Glacier NP; Beartooth Mountains; Bridger Range.

SHARP-TAILED GROUSE
Tympanuchus phasianellus

The courtship display of the male Sharp-tailed Grouse has been emulated in traditional dances of many native cultures on the prairies. In spring, Sharp-tails gather at traditional dancing grounds (leks). With wings drooping at their sides, tails pointing skyward and purple air sacs inflated, males furiously pummel the ground with their feet, cooing and cackling for prospective mates. Each male has a small stage within the lek that he defends against rivals. • The Sharp-tailed Grouse is a fairly common resident of eastern Montana's prairies and grasslands. A separate population formerly found in valleys west of the Continental Divide, the "Columbian" Sharp-tailed Grouse, is now nearing extirpation in Montana. • As with other grouse, Sharp-tail numbers fluctuate dramatically. In years of high abundance, large numbers of Sharp-tails move great distances, often colonizing new areas of suitable habitat.

ID: mottled brown and black neck, breast and upperparts; dark crescents on white belly; white undertail coverts and outer tail feathers; long central tail feathers; yellow eye combs; feathered legs. *Male:* purplish pink air sacs on neck are inflated during courtship displays.
Size: *L* 17 in; *W* 25–26 in. Male on average larger than female.
Status: locally common year-round.
Habitat: open areas: grasslands, mid-grass prairie, sagebrush and woodland edges.
Nesting: usually under cover near lek, female lines depression with grass and feathers; female incubates 10–13 light brown eggs dotted with reddish brown for about 24 days.
Feeding: eats buds, seeds, flowers, green shoots and berries; also eats insects when available.
Voice: male gives mournful *coo-oo* call and cackling *cac-cac-cac-cac* during courtship; both sexes cluck.
Similar Species: *Ring-necked Pheasant:* unfeathered legs; paler markings on underparts; female has longer tail lacking white. *Greater Sage-Grouse* (p. 37): much larger; black belly; tail longer, lacking white. *Ruffed Grouse* (p. 36): forested habitat; head crest; broad, gray tail with dark subterminal band; black patches on neck. *Spruce Grouse:* forested habitat; black, fan-shaped tail; black or mottled throat; male has red eye combs.
Best Sites: Bowdoin NWR; Medicine Lake NWR; Benton Lake NWR.

WILD TURKEY

Meleagris gallopavo

The Wild Turkey was common in western North America until 20th-century habitat loss and overharvesting took a toll. It has now been reestablished across much of its former range, and has been introduced to Montana and other areas it did not formerly inhabit. • Although turkeys prefer to feed on the ground and travel by foot—they can run faster than 19 miles per hour—they are able to fly short distances and they roost in trees at night. • This charismatic bird is the only native North American animal that has been widely domesticated. The wild ancestors of most other domestic animals came from Europe. • The Wild Turkey is a wary bird with acute senses and a highly developed social system. Early in life both male and female turkeys gobble. The females eventually outgrow this practice, leaving males to gobble competitively for the honor of mating. • If Congress had taken Benjamin Franklin's advice in 1782, our national emblem would be the Wild Turkey instead of the majestic Bald Eagle.

ID: dark, glossy body plumage; barred, copper-colored tail; largely unfeathered legs. *Male:* naked, blue and red head; long central breast tassel; colorful head and iridescent body; red wattles. *Female:* smaller; blue gray head; less iridescent body.

Size: *Male: L* 3–3½ ft; *W* 5½ ft. *Female: L* 3 ft; *W* 4 ft.

Status: uncommon year-round.

Habitat: deciduous, mixed and riparian woodlands with large openings.

Nesting: under thick cover in woodland or at field edge; female lines depression with grass and leaves; female incubates 10–12 brown-speckled, pale buff eggs up to 28 days.

Feeding: forages on ground for seeds, fruits, bulbs and sedges; occasionally eats waste grain in late fall and winter; also eats insects, especially beetles and grasshoppers; may take small vertebrates.

Voice: wide array of sounds; courting male gobbles loudly; alarm call is loud *pert;* gathering call is cluck; contact call is loud *keouk-keouk-keouk.*

Similar Species: all other grouse and grouselike birds are much smaller, with feathered heads.

Best Sites: Kalispell; Bigfork; Ekalaka; Missoula Valley.

COMMON LOON

Gavia immer

The Common Loon is a classic symbol of pristine wilderness lakes; indeed, breeding loons are a sure sign of clean, healthy water. Though Montana hosts only about 65 pairs during the summer breeding season, this species is widespread throughout the state during spring and fall migration. • These well-adapted divers have nearly solid bones that make them less buoyant (most birds have hollow bones), and their feet are placed well back on their bodies for underwater propulsion. Small bass, perch, sunfish, pike and whitefish are all fair game for these skilled underwater hunters. • Breeding loons are sensitive to disturbance by watercraft and shoreline development, quickly deserting a preferred breeding lake. Recent conservation efforts by "loon rangers" are helping protect Montana's breeding population.

nonbreeding

breeding

ID: *Breeding:* green black head; stout, black bill; white "necklace"; white breast and underparts; black-and-white-checkered upperparts; red eyes. *Nonbreeding:* duller plumage; sandy brown back. *In flight:* long wings beat constantly; hunchbacked appearance; legs trail behind tail.

Size: *L* 28–35 in; *W* 4–5 ft. Male on average larger than female.

Status: *Breeding:* uncommon from June to July. *In migration:* common from April to May and August to October. Rarely overwinters.

Habitat: *Breeding:* large, deep glacial lakes, often with islands that provide undisturbed shorelines for nesting. *In migration:* lakes, reservoirs and large rivers with open water.

Nesting: on muskrat lodge, small island or projecting shoreline; always near water; pair builds nest mound from aquatic vegetation; pair incubates 1–3 dark-spotted, olive eggs 24–31 days; pair shares all parental duties.

Feeding: pursues small fish underwater to depths of 180 ft; occasionally eats large aquatic invertebrates and larval and adult amphibians.

Voice: alarm call is quavering tremolo, often called "loon laughter"; contact call is long but simple wailing note *(where aaare you?);* breeding notes are soft, short hoots; male territorial call is undulating, complex yodel.

Similar Species: *Double-crested Cormorant* (p. 46): thinner, longer neck; orange "chin" and throat; hooked bill. *Western Grebe* (p. 44): smaller; much slimmer neck; yellow bill. *Red-necked Grebe* (p. 42): smaller; rufous breast; contrasting gray "cheek."

Best Sites: *Breeding:* Seeley Lake; Glacier NP. *In migration:* Fort Peck; Flathead Lake; Lake Helena; East Front Reservoirs.

RED-NECKED GREBE

Podiceps grisegena

The enthusiastic laughing calls of courting Red-necked Grebes punctuate the beginning of a new breeding season on Montana's intermountain wetlands. Although Red-necked Grebes are not as vocally refined as loons, few loons can match the verbal vigor of a pair of Red-necks in the throes of spring passions. Typically, their wild laughter lasts through the nights in late May. Although their whinnylike calls are a raucous part of springtime evenings, Red-necks are usually quiet and retiring when they are away from their breeding grounds. • All grebes feed, sleep and court on water, and they carry their newly hatched young on their backs. The striped young are able to stay aboard even when their parents dive underwater. • The scientific descriptor *grisegena* means "gray cheek"—a distinctive field mark of adults.

nonbreeding

breeding

ID: *Breeding:* rusty neck; gray "cheek"; black crown; straight, heavy bill is dark above and yellow underneath; black upperparts; light underparts; dark eyes. *Nonbreeding:* grayish white foreneck, "chin" and "cheek."
Size: *L* 17–22 in; *W* 24 in.
Status: *Breeding:* locally uncommon to common from May to July. *In migration:* uncommon from April to May and July to October. Very rare in winter.
Habitat: open, deep lakes, reservoirs and large settling ponds.
Nesting: pair constructs floating platform nest of aquatic vegetation anchored to submerged plants; pair incubates 4–5 white

eggs 20–23 days; eggs often become stained by wet vegetation.
Feeding: dives and gleans water's surface for small fish, aquatic invertebrates and amphibians.
Voice: agitated, rapid series of *ah-ah-ah-ah-ah* notes during breeding; also gull-like *caw* notes; silent in migration.
Similar Species: *Horned Grebe:* smaller; dark "cheek" and golden "horns" in breeding plumage; red eyes, all-dark bill and bright white "cheek" in nonbreeding plumage. *Eared Grebe* (p. 43): smaller; black neck in breeding plumage; black "cheek" in nonbreeding plumage. *Pied-billed Grebe:* smaller, mostly brown body; thicker, stubbier bill.
Best Sites: *Breeding:* Georgetown Lake. *In migration:* East Front Reservoirs; Flathead Lake; Ninepipe NWR.

EARED GREBE

Podiceps nigricollis

The Eared Grebe, a common summer resident of Montana's larger wetlands, also inhabits parts of Europe, Asia, Central Africa and South America. It is the most abundant grebe not only in North America, but also the world. • Eared Grebes undergo cyclical periods of atrophy and hypertrophy throughout the year, meaning that their internal organs and pectoral muscles shrink or swell, depending on whether or not the birds need to migrate. This strategy leaves Eared Grebes flightless for nine to ten months of the year—longer than any other flying bird. • Like other grebes, the Eared Grebe eats feathers. The feathers often pack the digestive tract and are thought to protect it from sharp fish bones or parasites, or perhaps to slow the passage of food, allowing more time for digestion.

nonbreeding

breeding

ID: *Breeding:* black neck, forehead and back; red flanks; fanned-out, golden "ear" tufts; white underparts; thin, straight bill; red eyes; slightly raised crown. *Nonbreeding:* dark "cheek" and upperparts; light underparts; dusky upper foreneck and flanks. *In flight:* rarely seen; wings beat constantly; hunchbacked appearance; legs trail behind tail.

Size: *L* 11½–14 in; *W* 16 in.

Status: common from mid-April to November.

Habitat: wetlands, larger lakes, reservoirs and sewage ponds.

Nesting: usually colonial; pair builds shallow, flimsy, floating platform nest of wet and decaying plants anchored or placed among thick emergent vegetation;

pair incubates 3–5 white eggs 20–22 days and raises young together.

Feeding: makes shallow dives and gleans water's surface for aquatic insects, crustaceans, mollusks, small fish and larval and adult amphibians.

Voice: an oft-heard *poo-ee-chk* during courtship; usually quiet outside breeding season.

Similar Species: *Horned Grebe:* rufous neck in breeding plumage; yellow "ear" tufts higher than level of eye; white "cheek" in nonbreeding plumage. *Pied-billed Grebe:* thicker, stubbier bill with black ring in breeding season; mostly brown body. *Red-necked Grebe* (p. 42): larger; longer; yellowish bill; red neck and gray "cheek" in breeding plumage; dusky white "cheek" in nonbreeding plumage.

Best Sites: any large wetland, especially in eastern Montana; Bowdoin NWR; Medicine Lake NWR; Benton Lake NWR.

WESTERN GREBE

Aechmophorus occidentalis

The courtship displays of the Western Grebe are among the most elaborate and beautiful rituals in the bird world. During the "weed dance," the male and female swim with torsos and heads held high, caressing each other with aquatic vegetation held in their bills. The "rushing" display, which Western Grebes are most famous for, involves two or more individuals exploding into a paddling sprint side by side, so that they literally "walk on water." The grebes stand high, feet paddling furiously, with their wings stretched back and heads and necks held rigid, until the race ends with the pair breaking the water's surface in a graceful dive. • Like those of most grebes, Western Grebe eggs hatch at regular intervals instead of all at once. Parental duties are often divided, with each parent feeding half the fledged young. • Another species, the Clark's Grebe, is nearly identical in plumage to the Western Grebe and is present in Montana in small numbers. Look for it among groups of Westerns, especially at Freezout Lake.

ID: long, slender neck; black upperparts from base of bill to tail; white under-parts from "chin" to belly; long, thin, yellow bill; white "cheek"; black on face extends below red eyes.

Size: *L* 25 in; *W* 24 in.

Status: common from April to October; rare in winter.

Habitat: large, deep lakes with emergent vegetation for nesting. *In migration:* also uses reservoirs.

Nesting: usually in colonies; pair builds floating nest of fresh and decaying vegetation anchored or placed among emergent vegetation; pair incubates 2–7 bluish green to buffy eggs (becoming stained brown) for about 23 days.

Feeding: gleans water's surface and dives for small fish, some amphibians and aquatic invertebrates.

Voice: high-pitched, scraping *crreeet-crreeet*; call sounds like a squeaky wheel when repeated in series.

Similar Species: *Clark's Grebe:* nearly identical but white of face extends above eyes; orange yellow bill; single-note call. *Red-necked Grebe* (p. 42): shorter, stockier neck; dark eyes; darker sides and neck in nonbreeding plumage.

Best Sites: Freezout Lake WMA; Medicine Lake NWR; Canyon Ferry Lake; Ninepipe NWR.

AMERICAN WHITE PELICAN
Pelecanus erythrorhynchos

Pelicans are majestic wetland inhabitants with a wingspan only a foot shy of the height of a basketball hoop. Their huge, bucketlike bills are dramatically adapted to their unusual feeding habits. Groups of swimming pelicans herd fish into schools, then scoop up the prey. As a pelican lifts its bill from the water, the fish are held within its flexible pouch while the water drains out. In a single scoop, a pelican can hold over three gallons of water and fish—about two to three times as much as its stomach can hold. This impressive feat confirms Dixon Lanier Merritt's quotation: "A wonderful bird is a pelican. His bill will hold more than his belican!" American White Pelicans eat about four pounds of fish per day. • This species is commonly seen soaring on midday thermals, and in-flight identification is straight-forward. It flies with its neck pulled back toward its wings, rather than extended, and it is the only large, white bird with black wing tips to do so.

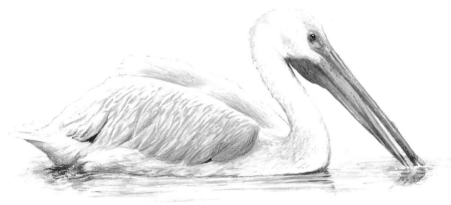

nonbreeding

Nesting: colonial; on bare, low-lying island; pair creates nest scrape lined with pebbles and debris or left completely unlined; pair incubates 2 dull white eggs 29–36 days; young hatch at different times and differ in size; young are fed by regurgitation.

Feeding: surface dips for small fish and amphibians; small groups of pelicans feed cooperatively by herding fish into large concentrations.

Voice: generally quiet; adults rarely issue piglike grunts.

Similar Species: no other large, white bird has a long bill with a throat pouch.

Best Sites: breeds regularly at only 5 sites in Montana: Medicine Lake NWR, Bowdoin NWR, Freezout Lake WMA, Arod Lake and Canyon Ferry Lake; commonly seen at many other wetlands statewide, even in breeding season.

ID: large, stocky, white bird; long, orange bill and throat pouch; black primary and secondary wing feathers; short tail; naked, orange skin patch around eye. *Breeding:* small, keeled plate develops on upper mandible; pale yellow crest on back of head. *Nonbreeding* and *immature:* white plumage is tinged with brown.

Size: *L* 4½–6 ft; *W* 9 ft. Male on average larger than female.

Status: common from April to October.

Habitat: large lakes, wetlands, reservoirs and rivers.

DOUBLE-CRESTED CORMORANT
Phalacrocorax auritus

You may find it difficult to appreciate the Double-crested Cormorant's beauty—until you see one up close. With its startling green iris, orange throat and beautiful iridescent sheen, this cormorant appeals to even the most cynical of birders. Still, the bird sometimes appears disheveled, especially after long periods of feeding. It lacks oil glands, and the resulting poor waterproofing helps it during dives by decreasing its buoyancy. But because its feathers become waterlogged, the cormorant is forced to air dry. It is often seen perched in a tree, wings fully spread, in the strong sunlight of midday. • The Double-crested Cormorant's mastery of the aquatic environment is virtually unsurpassed, with its long, rudderlike tail, fully webbed feet, excellent underwater vision and sealed nostrils. • Populations of this cormorant have increased greatly in Montana over the past few decades, and it is now a common summer resident throughout much of the state.

juvenile

breeding

ID: all-black body; long, crooked neck; thin, hooked bill; green eyes. *Breeding:* throat pouch becomes intense orange yellow; fine black or white plumes trail from "eyebrows." *Immature:* brown upperparts; whitish throat and breast; yellowish throat patch. *In flight:* rapid wingbeats; kinked neck.
Size: *L* 26–32 in; *W* 4½ ft. Male on average larger than female.
Status: common from April to October; rare in winter.
Habitat: large lakes, reservoirs and rivers; breeds on small treed islands.

Nesting: colonial; high in tree, often with Great Blue Herons; pair constructs nest platform of sticks, aquatic vegetation and guano; pair incubates 3–6 bluish white eggs 25–33 days; young are fed by regurgitation.
Feeding: long underwater dives to depths of 30 ft or more for small schooling fish; rarely eats amphibians and invertebrates.
Voice: generally quiet; may issue piglike grunts or croaks, especially near nesting colonies.
Similar Species: *Common Loon* (p. 41): thicker neck; unhooked bill; lacks orange or yellow on throat and face. *Western Grebe* (p. 44): unhooked bill; lacks orange on throat; very slim neck.
Best Sites: Ninepipe NWR; Freezout Lake WMA; Canyon Ferry Lake; Bowdoin NWR.

GREAT BLUE HERON

Ardea herodias

The sight of a majestic Great Blue Heron is always memorable, whether you are observing its stealthy, often nearly motionless hunting strategy or tracking its graceful wingbeats. The Great Blue Heron nests in large colonies known as rookeries, which may contain well over 50 treetop nests in a small area. Rookeries are sensitive to human disturbance, so it is best to observe the birds' behavior from a distance. • Great Blue Herons winter farther north than other herons, and thus are vulnerable to freeze-up. Spotting one would highlight your local Christmas bird count. • This heron is often mistaken for a crane, but unlike a crane, which holds its neck outstretched in flight, the Great Blue folds its neck back over its shoulders in an S-shape. • Though mostly a fish eater, this bird may also be found stalking fields and meadows in search of young Richardson's ground squirrels and other rodents.

breeding

ID: large, blue gray bird; long, curving neck; long, dark legs; blue gray back and wing coverts; straight, yellow bill; chestnut brown thighs. *Breeding:* richer colors; plumes streak from crown and throat. *In flight:* neck folds back over shoulders; legs trail behind body; slow, steady wingbeats on bowed wings.
Size: *L* 4–4½ ft; *W* 6 ft. Male on average larger than female.
Status: common from March to November; a few overwinter each year.
Habitat: forages along edges of streams, lakes, marshes, fields and wet meadows; also dry fields with rodent burrows.

Nesting: colonial; nest placed high in tree; pair builds flimsy to elaborate stick-and-twig platform up to 4 ft in diameter, often added onto over years; pair incubates 4–7 pale blue eggs about 28 days.
Feeding: patient stand-and-wait predator; strikes at small fish, amphibians, small mammals, aquatic invertebrates and reptiles; rarely scavenges.
Voice: usually quiet away from nest; occasionally a deep, harsh *frahnk frahnk frahnk,* usually during takeoff.
Similar Species: *Sandhill Crane* (p. 61): red "cap"; flies with neck outstretched.
Best Sites: Lee Metcalf NWR; Ninepipe NWR; Medicine Lake NWR; Bowdoin NWR; Freezout Lake WMA.

TURKEY VULTURE

Cathartes aura

The Turkey Vulture is unmatched at using updrafts and thermals. It can tease lift from the slightest pocket of rising air and patrol the skies when other soaring birds are grounded. • This birds eats primarily carrion, so its bill and feet are not as powerful as those of predatory raptors. Its red, featherless head allows it to remain relatively clean while feeding on messy carcasses. • Vultures have mastered the art of regurgitation. This ability allows parents to transport food over long distances to their young and also enables engorged birds to repulse an attacker or "lighten up" for an emergency takeoff. • Recent studies have shown that American vultures are most closely related to storks, not to hawks and falcons as was previously thought. Supporting this reclassification are molecular similarities with storks, lack of a syrinx (the avian "voicebox"), and the shared tendency to defecate on their own legs to cool down.

ID: all black; bare, red head. *Immature:* gray head. *In flight:* head appears small; two-toned underwing with silvery gray flight feathers and black wing linings; wings are held in a shallow "V"; rocks from side to side when soaring.
Size: *L* 26–32 in; *W* 5½–6 ft.
Status: uncommon from April to September.
Habitat: usually seen flying over open country, shorelines, roads or woods with sizeable open areas.
Nesting: in cave crevice or among boulders; sometimes in hollow stump or log; no nest material used; pair incubates 2 dull white eggs, blotched with reddish brown, for up to 41 days; young are fed by regurgitation.
Feeding: entirely on carrion (mostly mammalian).
Voice: generally silent; occasional hiss or grunt if threatened.
Similar Species: *Golden Eagle* (p. 56) and *Bald Eagle* (p. 50): lack silvery gray flight feathers; wings held flat in flight; do not rock when soaring; head more visible in flight. Dark morphs of *Red-tailed Hawk* (p. 54), *Ferruginous Hawk*, *Swainson's Hawk* (p. 55): smaller; larger heads; tail with barring or some amount of white or red (not uniformly dark).
Best Sites: Billings; Pryor Mountains; Bitterroot Valley.

OSPREY
Pandion haliaetus

The Osprey eats fish exclusively and is found near water, especially where humans have erected nesting platforms. While hunting, an Osprey hovers far above the water, its white belly hard for fish to see. The Osprey's dark eye line blocks glare from the water, enabling it to spot a slowly moving shadow or a flash of silver near the water's surface. Folding its wings, the Osprey hurls itself in a headfirst dive toward its target. An instant before striking the water, the bird rights itself and thrusts its feet forward to grasp its slippery prey. The Osprey's feet prevent its catch from squirming free—two toes face forward and two backward, and the toes have sharp spines for extra grip.

• The Osprey is found on every continent except Antarctica.

ID: dark brown upperparts; white underparts; dark eye line; yellow eyes; light crown. *Male:* all-white breast. *Female:* fine, dark "necklace." *In flight:* shape unique: long wings are held in shallow "M"; regularly hovers over water; dark "wrist" patches; brown-and-white-banded tail.
Size: *L* 22–25 in; *W* 4½–6 ft.
Status: locally common from April to September.
Habitat: lakes, marshes and slowly flowing streams and rivers.
Nesting: on treetop, usually near water; uses specially made platform placed atop utility pole or tower up to 100 ft high; pair builds massive stick nest, reused over many years; pair incubates 2–4 yellowish eggs,

blotched with reddish brown, about 38 days; both adults feed young, but male hunts more.
Feeding: dramatic, feet-first dives; fish, averaging 2 lbs per day, make up almost whole diet.
Voice: series of melodious ascending whistles, *chewk-chewk-chewk;* also an often-heard *kip-kip-kip.*
Similar Species: *Bald Eagle* (p. 50): larger; holds its wings straight out while soaring; larger bill with yellow base; yellow legs; adult has clean white head and tail on otherwise dark body; lacks white underparts and dark "wrist" patches. *Rough-legged Hawk* (p. 55): winter resident; smaller; hovers over fields with wings in open "V"; light phase has whitish wing linings and light tail band.
Best Sites: Lee Metcalf NWR; Clark Fork River; Flathead Lake; Charles M. Russell NWR.

BALD EAGLE

Haliaeetus leucocephalus

adult

Bald Eagle pairs perform dramatic aerial displays. In one impressive maneuver, the two birds fly up to a great height, locking talons and then tumbling perilously toward the earth. The birds break off at the last second, just before crashing into the ground. • Bald Eagles do not mature until their fourth or fifth year, only then developing the characteristic white head and tail plumage. Immatures can often be identified by their mottled brown and white plumage and white wing linings. • Bald Eagles generally mate for life. They renew their pair bonds each year by adding new sticks and branches to their massive nests, the largest of any North American bird.

immature

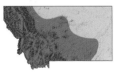

ID: white head and tail; dark brown body; yellow bill and feet. *1st year:* dark overall; dark bill; some white in underwings. *2nd year:* dark "bib"; white in underwings. *3rd year:* mostly brown plumage; largely white head and tail; yellow at base of bill; yellow eyes. *4th year:* like adult but with remnants of immature mottling on head, tail and body. *In flight:* broad wings held flat; large head.
Size: *L* 30–43 in; *W* 5½–8 ft. Female on average larger than male.
Status: uncommon to fairly common year-round.
Habitat: large lakes and rivers; also fields and pastures, especially in winter.
Nesting: usually in tree near lake or large river, but may be far from water; huge stick nest, up to 15 ft across, is built by pair and often reused for many years; pair incubates 1–3 white eggs 34–36 days; pair feeds young.
Feeding: eats waterbirds, small mammals and fish captured at water's surface; frequently feeds on carrion; sometimes pirates fish from Ospreys; commonly eats cattle afterbirth during winter.
Voice: thin, weak squeal or gull-like cackle: *kleek-kik-kik-kik* or *kah-kah-kah.*
Similar Species: adult is distinctive. *Golden Eagle* (p. 56): smaller head; wings held in shallow "V" when soaring; adult dark overall, except for golden nape; tail may appear faintly banded with white; immature lacks extensive white wing linings but usually have prominent white patches on outer wing and at base of tail. *Osprey* (p. 49): like 3rd-year Bald Eagle, but much whiter; dark "wrist" patches; dark bill; M-shaped wings in flight.
Best Sites: *Breeding:* along large rivers in western Montana—Missouri, Kootenai, Clark Fork, Bitterroot. *In migration* and *winter:* Mission Valley; Canyon Ferry Lake.

NORTHERN HARRIER

Circus cyaneus

The Northern Harrier may be the easiest raptor to identify on the wing because no other daytime raptor routinely flies so close to the ground. It cruises low over fields and marshes, grazing the tops of long grasses and cattails, hunting by surprise attack. Its owl-like, parabolic facial disc allows it to hunt easily by sound as well. • The Northern Harrier was once called "Marsh Hawk" in North America, and it is still called "Hen Harrier" in Europe. Britain's Royal Air Force was so impressed by the bird's maneuverability that it named its Harrier aircraft after it. • In spring courtship, the male Northern Harrier climbs almost vertically and then stalls, sending himself into a reckless dive. At the last second he saves himself with a flight course that sends him skyward again. • This bird has declined in numbers, owing to loss of its wetland and native prairie habitats.

ID: lanky; long wings and tail; white rump; black wing tips. *Male:* blue gray to silver gray upperparts; white underparts; indistinct tail bands, except for 1 dark subterminal band. *Female:* dark brown upperparts; streaky brown and buff underparts. *Immature:* rich reddish brown plumage; dark tail bands; streaked breast, sides and flanks.
Size: *L* 16–24 in; *W* 3½–4 ft. Female on average larger than male.
Status: fairly common from April to October; uncommon in winter.
Habitat: open country, including wet meadows, marshes, bogs and croplands.
Nesting: on ground, often on slightly raised mound; usually in tall grass or cattails; primarily female lines shallow depression or platform nest with grass, sticks and cattails; female incubates 4–6 bluish white eggs 30–32 days.
Feeding: hunts in low, rising and falling flights, often skimming tops of vegetation; eats small mammals, birds, amphibians, reptiles and some invertebrates.
Voice: most vocal near nest and during courtship, but generally quiet; high-pitched *ke-ke-ke-ke-ke-ke* near nest.
Similar Species: *Short-eared Owl* (p. 78): moth-like flight; lacks white uppertail coverts; dark "wrist" mask on underwings; nocturnal but occasionally active during day. *Rough-legged Hawk* (p. 55): broader wings; dark "wrist" patches; black tail with wide, white base; dark belly.
Best Sites: Freezout Lake WMA; National Bison Range; Benton Lake NWR; Bowdoin NWR; Medicine Lake NWR.

SHARP-SHINNED HAWK

Accipiter striatus

When delivering food to his nestlings, the male Sharp-shinned Hawk is cautious around his mate: she is typically one-third larger than he is. The two sexes often prey on different-sized animals, helping to reduce competition and maximize the available food base. • The accipiters (Sharp-shinned Hawk, Cooper's Hawk and Northern Goshawk) are woodland hawks. Their short, rounded wings and long, rudder-like tails allow these birds to negotiate a maze of tree trunks and foliage at high speeds. A typical sighting might last only a few seconds as the raptor darts through the forest. • Rural feeders often attract "Sharpies," who come not for the seeds, but for the small birds.

immature

ID: small, slender hawk; short, rounded wings; long, straight tail; blue gray back; fine, red horizontal bars on underparts; red eyes. *Immature:* brown overall; brown eyes; lengthwise rusty brown streaking on breast and belly. *In flight:* flap-and-glide flier; tail heavily barred and squared or notched at tip, with narrow white terminal band.
Size: *Male: L* 10–12 in; *W* 20–24 in. *Female: L* 12–14 in; *W* 24–28 in.
Status: fairly common from April to October; uncommon in winter.
Habitat: dense to semi-open forest; occasionally riparian areas. *In migration* (especially in fall): usually seen soaring on thermals or hunting in alpine areas.

Nesting: stick or twig nest usually built each year, normally about 2 ft across; may remodel abandoned crow nest; female incubates 4–5 white or bluish white, often speckled eggs up to 35 days; male feeds female during incubation.
Feeding: pursues small birds in high-speed chases; takes more birds than other accipiters; rarely takes small mammals, amphibians and insects.
Voice: silent, except during breeding season, when an intense and often repeated *kik-kik-kik-kik* greets intruders at nest sites.
Similar Species: *Cooper's Hawk:* larger but extremely similar; rounded "spoony" tail with thicker white terminal band; larger head; perches on utility poles. *American Kestrel* (p. 57): long, pointed wings; vividly patterned; 2 dark "sideburns"; usually seen perched or flying in open country. *Merlin:* pointed wings; rapid wingbeats; lacks red breast streaks.
Best Sites: *Breeding:* any forested setting in western Montana: Missoula Valley; Glacier NP. *In migration:* found statewide virtually anywhere.

SWAINSON'S HAWK
Buteo swainsoni

The beautiful Swainson's Hawk typifies the mid-grass prairie of the eastern half of Montana, especially where ground squirrels are abundant. Twice a year, this hawk undertakes a long migration that may lead it as far south as the southern tip of South America and as far north as Alaska. Traveling up to 12,500 miles in a single year, the Swainson's Hawk is second only to the arctic-breeding Peregrine Falcon for long-distance travel among birds of prey. • The massive "kettles" of Swainson's Hawks migrating through Central America have been likened to the legendary flocks of Passenger Pigeons that once blackened the sky. Unfortunately, many hawks are killed by the incautious use of insecticides in Argentina, reminding us that conservation of migratory species requires international cooperation.

light morph

dark morph

ID: long wings with pointed tips; wing tips reach tail tip at rest; narrowly banded tail; dark flight feathers. *Dark morph:* dark brown overall; only significant pale area is undertail coverts; juvenile has whitish head and white streaking on body. *Light morph:* dark "bib"; white belly; white wing linings contrast with dark flight feathers; juvenile has incomplete "bib." *In flight:* holds wings in shallow "V."
Size: *L* 19–22 in; *W* 4½ ft. Female on average larger than male.
Status: common from late April to September.
Habitat: open fields, grasslands, sagebrush, agricultural areas.

Nesting: in tree or shrub adjacent to open habitat; rarely on cliffs; nest of sticks, twigs and forbs is lined with bark and fresh leaves; nest often reused; pair incubates 2–4 brown-spotted, whitish eggs 28–35 days.
Feeding: dives for mice and ground squirrels; also eats snakes, small birds and large insects, such as grasshoppers and crickets.
Voice: typical hawk call, *keeeaar,* is higher pitched than Red-tail's.
Similar Species: *Red-tailed Hawk* (p. 54): more rounded wing tips; holds wings flat in flight; wing tips usually fall short of tail tip at rest. *Ferruginous Hawk, Rough-legged Hawk* (p. 55): flight feathers paler than wing lining. *Golden Eagle* (p. 56): much larger; golden nape; massive bill.
Best Sites: Medicine Lake NWR; Billings; Hwy 87 between Great Falls and Havre.

RED-TAILED HAWK
Buteo jamaicensis

The Red-tailed Hawk is the most commonly seen hawk in many areas of North America. An afternoon drive through the country often reveals resident Red-tails perching on fence posts or utility poles overlooking open fields and roadsides. During spring courtship, excited Red-tailed Hawks dive at each other, sometimes locking talons and tumbling through the air together. • Montana's Red-tails come in a dazzling array of color morphs from nearly all dark to very pale. Paler morphs have a dark leading edge on the underwing, easily visible in flight and diagnostic for this species. • The Red-tailed Hawk's famous piercing call is often wrongly paired with the image of an eagle in TV commercials and movies.

intermediate morph

light morph

ID: extremely variable; most adults have red tail; dark upperparts usually with some white highlights; dark brown streaks across mid-belly; wing tips usually fall short of tail tip at rest. *Immature:* variable; multibanded tail lacking red; generally darker; streaks on mid-belly. *In flight:* fan-shaped tail; white or occasionally tawny brown underside and underwing linings; dark leading edge on underwing; light flight feathers with faint barring; holds wings flat or occasionally in very shallow "V."
Size: *L* 18–25 in; *W* 4–5 ft. Female on average larger than male.
Status: common year-round but less so in winter.

Habitat: open country with some trees; also roadsides, fields, woodlots, hedgerows, mixed forests and moist woodlands.
Nesting: in woodland adjacent to open habitat; usually in deciduous tree, rarely on cliff or in conifer; pair builds bulky stick nest, usually added to each year; pair incubates 2–4 brown-blotched, whitish eggs 28–35 days; male brings food to female and young.
Feeding: scans for food while perched or soaring; drops to capture prey; rarely stalks prey on foot; eats mice, rabbits, chipmunks, birds, amphibians and reptiles; rarely takes large insects.
Voice: powerful, descending scream, *keeearrrr.*
Similar Species: *Rough-legged Hawk* (p. 55): winter resident; black and white tail; dark "wrist" patches on underwings. *Swainson's Hawk* (p. 53): more pointed wing tips; wing tips reach tail tip at rest; dark flight feathers and pale wing linings in flight; holds wings in shallow "V."
Best Sites: Bitterroot Valley; Mission Valley; Benton Lake NWR.

ROUGH-LEGGED HAWK

Buteo lagopus

Numbers of the Rough-legged Hawk, a winter inhabitant of Montana, change in relation to fluctuating densities of voles and northern lemmings in their Arctic breeding grounds. When lemming and vole numbers are high, Rough-legs can produce up to seven young; in lean years a pair is fortunate to raise a single chick. • While hunting, the Rough-legged Hawk often "wind-hovers" to scan the ground below, flapping to maintain a stationary position while facing upwind. This hunting technique serves as an excellent long-distance identification tool for birders. The Rough-legged Hawk hovers because its open-country breeding habitat has generally lacked high perches, though fence posts and telephone poles are now often exploited in Montana. • These hawks range from light morphs with dark patterning to birds that are almost entirely dark but with distinctive whitish foreheads. • Montana lays claim to the world's largest known communal roost of Rough-legs: over 150 individuals in the Mission Valley in the mid-1990s.

immature

ID: unusually small feet; legs feathered to toes; tail white underneath with 1 wide, dark subterminal band; dark brown upperparts; light flight feathers. *Dark morph:* entirely dark wing linings, head and underparts; white forehead. *Light morph:* dark belly; dark streaks on breast and head; dark "wrist" patches on underwing; light underwing linings. *Immature:* lighter streaking on breast; bold belly band; buff leg feathers. *In flight:* most show dark "wrist" patches; frequently hovers.
Size: *L* 19–24 in; *W* 4–4½ ft. Female on average larger than male.

Status: fairly common from October to April.
Habitat: fields, mountainsides, croplands.
Nesting: does not nest in Montana.
Feeding: soars and hovers while searching for prey; eats primarily small rodents, occasionally birds, amphibians and large insects.
Voice: usually silent in Montana; alarm call is catlike *kee-eer,* usually dropping at the end.
Similar Species: *Other buteos* (pp. 53–54): rarely hover; lack dark "wrist" patches and white tail base; dark morphs lack white forehead. *Northern Harrier* (p. 51): courses low over fields; owl-like facial disc; lacks dark "wrist" patches and dark belly; longer, thinner tail lacks broad, dark subterminal band.
Best Sites: Mission Valley; Great Falls; East Front of Rockies.

GOLDEN EAGLE

Aquila chrysaetos

The Golden Eagle is actually more closely related to the buteos than it is to the Bald Eagle. Unlike the Bald Eagle, the Golden Eagle hunts prey as large as foxes, geese and newborn pronghorns. • The Golden Eagle can soar high above mountain passes for hours, sometimes stooping at great speeds—150 to 200 miles per hour—for prey or for fun. • This giant raptor is found throughout Montana's extensive openlands. Previously thought to be nonmigratory, its migration route along the Rockies was discovered in 1992. • Few people forget the sight of a Golden Eagle soaring overhead— the average wingspan of an adult exceeds 6 feet! Unfortunately, these noble birds were once perceived as a threat to livestock and were shot and poisoned for bounties. Today, the species is protected under the Migratory Bird Treaty Act.

immature

adult

ID: very large; brown overall with golden nape; brown eyes; dark bill; brown tail has grayish white bands; yellow feet; fully feathered legs. *Immature:* 3 obvious white patches in flight, under tail and under each outer wing. *In flight:* wings held in shallow "V"; relatively small head; long tail; large, rectangular wings.
Size: *L* 30–40 in; *W* 6½–7½ ft. Female on average larger than male.
Status: locally common year-round, but less so in winter.
Habitat: *Breeding:* arid prairies, foothills, canyons, mountainsides and other areas with cliffs or large trees for nesting. *In migration:* along escarpments, mountain ridges and hillsides. *Winter:* semi-open woodlands and fields.

Nesting: on bluff or sometimes tall tree; pair builds large basket of sticks lined with grass and leaves; nest reused for years, with new material added and often becoming very large; pair incubates 1–4 whitish, often spotted eggs 40–45 days.
Feeding: swoops on prey from soaring flight; eats hares, grouse, rodents, foxes and occasionally young ungulates; often eats carrion.
Voice: generally quiet; rarely a short bark.
Similar Species: *Bald Eagle* (p. 50): larger head without golden nape; shorter tail; immature lacks distinct white underwing and undertail patches, often has extensive white wing linings. *Turkey Vulture* (p. 48): naked, pink head; pale flight feathers; dark wing linings; teeters while soaring. *Dark morph buteos* (pp. 53–55): much smaller; pale flight feathers; lack golden napes.
Best Sites: East Front of Rockies; Livingston. *In migration:* Rogers Pass.

AMERICAN KESTREL

Falco sparverius

The American Kestrel is the smallest and most common of Montana's five falcons. It hunts small rodents and insects in open areas, and it is a familiar sight atop roadside poles and wires in summer. A helpful identification tip for viewing from afar: the American Kestrel repeatedly lifts its tail while perched and scouting for prey. • The Eurasian Kestrel, a close relative, can detect ultraviolet reflections from rodent urine on the ground. It is not known whether the American Kestrel has this same ability, but it is frequently seen hovering above the ground while looking for small ground-dwelling prey. • This diminutive raptor can nest in tree cavities; these excellent locations help protect nestlings from hungry predators. • Old field guides refer to this bird as "Sparrow Hawk," and the scientific descriptor *sparverius* means "pertaining to a sparrow."

ID: 2 distinctive vertical facial stripes; typical pointed wing tips of a falcon. *Male:* rusty back; blue gray wings; blue gray crown with rusty "cap"; lightly spotted underparts. *Female:* rusty back, wings and breast streaking. *In flight:* frequently hovers; long, rusty tail; buoyant, indirect flight style.
Size: *L* 7½–9 in; *W* 20–24 in. Female on average larger than male.
Status: common from April to October; small numbers overwinter each year.
Habitat: open fields, riparian woodlands, forest edges, roadside ditches, grassy highway medians.
Nesting: in tree cavity (usually abandoned woodpecker or flicker cavity); may use nest box; mostly female incubates 4–6 white to pale brown eggs, spotted with brown and gray, for 29–30 days; both adults raise young.
Feeding: swoops from perch (tree, fenceline, post, road sign or power line) or from hovering flight; eats mostly insects and some small rodents, birds, reptiles and amphibians.
Voice: loud, often repeated, shrill *killy-killy-killy* when excited; female's voice is lower pitched.
Similar Species: *Mourning Dove* (p. 74): surprisingly similar when perched; small head; thinner, pointed tail; uniform grayish plumage. *Merlin:* similar size but much darker overall; only 1 facial stripe; does not hover; flight more powerful and direct. *Sharp-shinned Hawk* (p. 52): rounded wings; reddish barring on underparts; lacks facial stripes; flap-and-glide flight.
Best Sites: Mission Valley; Bitterroot Valley; Bozeman; Billings.

PRAIRIE FALCON

Falco mexicanus

Rocketing overhead like a fighter jet, the Prairie Falcon often seems to appear out of nowhere. This western raptor of arid openlands is best identified by its brown plumage and dark "armpits." • In spring and summer, Prairie Falcons often concentrate their hunting efforts on ground squirrel colonies, swooping over windswept grass to pick off naive youngsters. As summer fades to fall, large flocks of migrating songbirds often capture the attention of these pallid "ghosts of the plains." • Inexperienced and over-eager, newly fledged falcons risk serious injury or death when pushing their limits in early hunting forays. Swooping falcons sometimes misjudge their flight speed or their ability to pull out of a dive. • Prairie Falcons commonly soar for long periods on updrafts or along ridgelines.

ID: brown upperparts; pale face with dark brown, narrow "mustache" stripe; white underparts with brown spotting; often perches on crossbar of utility poles. *In flight:* diagnostic dark "wing pits"; pointed wings; long, narrow, banded tail; quick wingbeats and direct flight.

Size: *Male: L* 14–15 in; *W* 37–39 in. *Female: L* 17–18 in; *W* 41–43 in.

Status: uncommon year-round.

Habitat: *Breeding:* river canyons, cliffs, rimrocks or rocky promontories in arid, open lowlands or high intermontane valleys. *In migration* and *winter:* open, treeless country, such as fields, pastures and sagebrush flats.

Nesting: on cliff ledge or in crevice; rarely in abandoned nest of other raptor or crow; usually without nesting material; mostly female incubates 3–5 brown-spotted, whitish eggs about 30 days; male brings food to female and young.

Feeding: high-speed strike-and-kill from diving swoops, low flights or chases on the wing; eats ground squirrels and small birds; also takes some lizards and large insects; female consumes more mammalian prey than male.

Voice: generally silent; alarm call near nest is a rapid, shrill *kik-kik-kik-kik*.

Similar Species: *Peregrine Falcon:* lacks dark "wing pits"; dark, distinctive "helmet." *Merlin:* tends toward more wooded habitats; much smaller; no contrasting "wing pits." *American Kestrel* (p. 57): smaller; much more colorful; 2 bold facial stripes; often hovers; lacks dark "wing pits."

Best Sites: Bighorn Canyon NRA; East Front of Rockies; Ekalaka. *Winter:* Mission Valley.

SORA

Porzana carolina

Two ascending whistles followed by a strange, descending whinny abruptly announce the presence of the otherwise hard-to-detect Sora. The Sora is the most common and widespread rail in North America, and like most rails is seldom seen by birders. Its elusive habits and preference for dense marshlands force most would-be observers to settle for a quick look at this small bird. On occasion, it has been known to parade around, unconcerned with onlookers, while it searches the shallows for food. Look for it especially when it is accompanying chicks or during periods of freeze-up. • Even though its feet are not webbed or lobed, the Sora swims quite well over short distances. It may appear to be a weak and reluctant flier, but the Sora migrates hundreds of miles each year between its breeding and wintering wetlands.

breeding

ID: short, yellow bill; black face, throat and fore-neck; gray neck and breast; long, greenish legs. *Immature:* no black on face; buffier with paler underparts; greenish bill.
Size: *L* 8–10 in; *W* 14 in. Male on average larger than female.
Status: common from May to September.
Habitat: wetlands with abundant emergent cattails, bulrushes, sedges and grasses.
Nesting: usually over water, but occasionally in wet meadow under concealing vegetation; well-built basket nest made by pair of grass and aquatic vegetation; pair incubates 10–12 buff or olive buff, darkly speckled eggs 18–20 days.
Feeding: gleans and probes for seeds, plants, aquatic insects and mollusks.
Voice: usual call is clear, 2-note *coo-wee;* alarm call is sharp *keek;* courtship song begins *or-Ah or-Ah*, exploding into distinctive series of descending *weee-weee-weee* notes.
Similar Species: *Virginia Rail:* slightly larger; long, downcurved, orangy bill; chestnut brown wing patch; rufous breast.
Best Sites: Lee Metcalf NWR; Freezout Lake WMA; Benton Lake NWR; Medicine Lake NWR.

AMERICAN COOT

Fulica americana

The American Coot is truly an all-terrain bird: in its quest for food it dives, dabbles and swims skillfully, and it grazes confidently on land. • American Coots squabble constantly during the breeding season, not just among themselves, but also with any waterbird that has the audacity to intrude on their waterfront property. These odd birds can often be seen scooting across the surface of the water, charging rivals with flailing, splashing wings in an attempt to intimidate. Outside the breeding season, coots gather amicably in large groups. During spring and fall, thousands congregate at select staging sites such as Flathead Lake, where they are sometimes seen on open water throughout the winter. These numerous waterbirds are easy to spot because of their chunky proportions and pendulous head movements while swimming. • The American Coot is colloquially known as "Mud Hen," and many people mistake it for a species of duck (it is actually a rail).

ID: gray black overall; white, chickenlike bill with dark ring around tip; reddish spot on white forehead "shield"; long, greenish yellow legs; lobed toes; red eyes. *Immature:* lighter body color; darker bill and legs; lacks prominent forehead "shield."
Size: *L* 13–16 in; *W* 24 in. Male on average larger than female.
Status: common from April to October; some to many overwinter on open water.
Habitat: shallow marshes, ponds and wetlands with open water and emergent vegetation. *In migration* and *winter:* also sewage lagoons and lakes.

Nesting: in emergent vegetation; pair builds floating nest of cattails and grass; pair incubates 6–11 brown-spotted, buffy white eggs 21–25 days.
Feeding: gleans water's surface; sometimes dives, tips up or even grazes on land; eats aquatic vegetation, insects, snails, crayfish, worms, tadpoles and fish; may steal food from ducks.
Voice: calls frequently in summer, day and night: *kuk-kuk-kuk-kuk-kuk;* also grunts.
Similar Species: *Ducks* (pp. 23–35): all lack chickenlike, white bill and uniformly black body with white undertail coverts. *Grebes* (pp. 42–44): lack white forehead "shield" and all-dark plumage.
Best Sites: nearly any wetland: Freezout Lake WMA; Bowdoin NWR; Medicine Lake NWR; Red Rock Lakes NWR.

SANDHILL CRANE
Grus canadensis

D eep, resonant, rattling calls announce the approach of Sandhill Cranes long before they pass overhead. These stately creatures grace the wetlands of western Montana during the breeding season, their prehistoric sounds echoing over the landscape. The bird's coiled trachea adds harmonies to the calls, allowing the notes to travel farther. • Although the large, V-shaped flocks of migrating cranes look very similar to flocks of Canada Geese, cranes circle upward on thermal rises, then slowly soar downward until they find another rise, much in the pattern of a raptor. Migrating flocks of Sandhills consist mainly of mated pairs and close family members. • Cranes mate for life. They reinforce their pair bonds each spring with an elaborate courtship dance, which involves some leaps over six feet high. It has often been likened to human dancing—a seemingly strange comparison until you see the ritual firsthand. • Sandhill Cranes are sensitive nesters, preferring to raise their young in areas that are isolated from human disturbance.

ID: very large, all-gray bird with long neck and legs; naked, red crown; long, straight bill; plumage often stained rusty red from iron oxides in water. *Immature:* lacks red crown; reddish brown plumage may appear patchy. *In flight:* extends neck and legs; often glides, soars and circles.
Size: *L* 3½–4 ft; *W* 6–7 ft. Male on average larger than female.
Status: fairly common from late March to October.
Habitat: *Breeding:* isolated, open marshes, riverine islands and wetlands surrounded by forest or shrubs. *In migration:* also uses agricultural fields.
Nesting: pair builds nest on large mound of aquatic vegetation in water or along shoreline; pair incubates 2 brown-splotched, olive buff eggs 29–32 days; egg hatching is staggered; young fly at about 50 days.
Feeding: probes and gleans ground for insects, soft-bodied invertebrates, waste grain, shoots and tubers; frequently eats small vertebrates.
Voice: loud, resonant, rattling *gu-rrroo gu-rrroo gu-rrroo.*
Similar Species: *Great Blue Heron* (p. 47): lacks red forehead patch; neck folds back over shoulders in flight.
Best Sites: Lee Metcalf NWR; Red Rock Lakes NWR; Wisdom; Choteau.

61

KILLDEER

Charadrius vociferus

The ubiquitous Killdeer is often the first shorebird a birder learns to identify. Its boisterous calls rarely fail to catch the attention of people passing through its wide variety of nesting environments. The Killdeer's preference for open fields, gravel driveways, beach edges, golf courses and abandoned industrial areas has allowed it to thrive throughout our rural and suburban landscapes. • If you happen to wander too close to a Killdeer nest, the parent will try to lure you away by issuing loud alarm calls and feigning a broken wing. Most predators take the bait and are led far enough away for the parent to suddenly recover from its injury and fly off, sounding its piercing calls. Similar distraction displays are widespread in the bird world, but in our region, the Killdeer's broken wing act is unquestionably the gold medal winner. • The scientific descriptor *vociferus* aptly describes this vocal bird, but double-check all calls in spring, when the Killdeer is often imitated by frisky European Starlings.

ID: long, dark yellow legs; white upper-parts with 2 black breast bands; brown head and back; white underparts; white "eyebrow"; white face patch above bill; black forehead band; rufous rump; tail projects beyond wing tips. *Immature:* downy; only 1 breast band.
Size: *L* 9–11 in; *W* 24 in. Female on average larger than male.
Status: very common from April to October; a few overwinter.
Habitat: open ground, fields, lakeshores, sandy beaches, mudflats, gravel streambeds, wet meadows, marshes and grasslands.

Nesting: on open ground; male scrapes out shallow depression; pair incubates 4 darkly spotted and blotched, pale buff eggs 24–28 days; may raise 2 broods.
Feeding: run-and-stop foraging technique; eats mostly insects; also takes spiders, snails, earthworms and crayfish.
Voice: loud, distinctive *kill-dee kill-dee kill-deer* and variations, including *deer-deer*.
Similar Species: *Semipalmated Plover:* spring and fall migrant on open mudflats; smaller; only 1 breast band. *Piping Plover:* northeastern Montana only; smaller; lighter brown upperparts; 1 often incomplete breast band.
Best Sites: Ninepipe NWR; Lee Metcalf NWR; Freezout Lake WMA; Bowdoin NWR; Medicine Lake NWR.

AMERICAN AVOCET

Recurvirostra americana

An American Avocet in full breeding plumage is a strikingly elegant bird, with its long, peachy red neck accentuating the length of its slender bill and stiltlike legs. Often by August, the peach-colored "hood" has been replaced by a more subdued winter gray, which the bird will wear for the greater part of the year. It is the only avocet in the world that undergoes a yearly color change. • The American Avocet's upcurved bill looks bent out of shape, but it is ideal for efficiently skimming aquatic vegetation and invertebrates off the surface of shallow water. Avocets will walk rapidly or run about in fairly deep water, swinging their bills from side to side along the muddy bottom. At other times, they use their webbed feet to swim, then feed by tipping up like dabbling ducks. • If an American Avocet is disturbed while standing in its one-legged resting position, it will take off, switch legs in midair, and land on the rested leg.

nonbreeding

♀

breeding

♂

ID: long, upcurved, black bill; long, pale blue legs; black wings with wide white patches; white underparts; female's bill more upcurved and shorter than male's. *Breeding:* peachy red head, neck and breast. *Nonbreeding:* gray head, neck and breast. *In flight:* long, skinny legs and neck; black and white wings.
Size: *L* 17–18 in; *W* 31 in. Male on average larger than female.
Status: fairly common from late April to September.

Habitat: lakeshores, alkaline wetlands and exposed mudflats.
Nesting: semicolonial; in shallow depression along dried mudflat, exposed shoreline or open area, always near water; pair creates shallow scrape or mound of vegetation lined with pebbles or other debris; pair incubates 4 darkly blotched eggs 23–25 days.
Feeding: sweeps bill, slightly opened, from side to side just beneath water's surface, picking up minute crustaceans, aquatic insects and occasionally seeds; male sweeps lower in water than female; occasionally swims and tips up like a duck.
Voice: harsh, shrill *plee-eek plee-eek*.
Similar Species: *Willet* (p. 64): grayish overall; straight, thicker bill.
Best Sites: Bowdoin NWR; Freezout Lake WMA; Benton Lake NWR; Medicine Lake NWR.

WILLET

Catoptrophorus semipalmatus

On the ground, the Willet cuts a rather dull figure. The moment it takes flight or displays, however, its black and white wings add sudden contrast. The sensory experience is enhanced by its call: a loud, rhythmic *will-will willet, will-will-willet!* The bright, bold flashes of the Willet's wings may alert other shore-birds to imminent danger. If you look closely, you may notice that the white markings across the Willet's wingspan form a rough "W" as it flies away. • Willets breed along the margins of lakes and wetlands in central and eastern Montana, usually in wet, grassy areas. When faced with the close approach of a human near its nest, these intrepid birds will launch an all-out airborne attack until the intruder retreats to a safe distance. • Willets are loud, social, easily identified birds—a nice change when dealing with sandpipers. The cumbersome genus name *Catoptrophorus* translates as "mirror-bearing," a reference to the black and white wings.

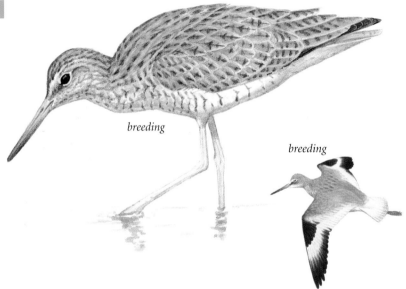

breeding

breeding

ID: plump bird; heavy, straight, black bill; light throat and belly. *Breeding:* dark streaking and barring overall. *In flight:* black and white wing pattern.

Size: *L* 14–16 in; *W* 26 in. Female on average larger than male.

Status: locally common from mid-April to August.

Habitat: wet fields and shorelines of marshes, lakes and ponds.

Nesting: in shallow depression lined with grass, usually in fields and pastures several hundred yards from water; pair incubates 4–5 brown-spotted, olive eggs 22–30 days.

Feeding: probes muddy areas; also gleans ground for insects; occasionally eats shoots and seeds.

Voice: loud, rolling *will-will willet, will-will-willet.*

Similar Species: *Marbled Godwit* (p. 67): much longer, bicolored bill with dark, slightly upturned tip; larger body; lacks black and white wing pattern.

Best Sites: Bowdoin NWR; Medicine Lake NWR; Benton Lake NWR; Freezout Lake WMA.

SPOTTED SANDPIPER

Actitis macularius

Researchers made an unexpected discovery in 1972 about the Spotted Sandpiper's breeding activities. The female Spotted Sandpiper defends a territory and mates with more than one male in a single breeding season, leaving the male to tend the nest and eggs. This unusual reproductive behavior, known as polyandry, is found in only about one percent of all bird species. • Even though its breast spots are not noticeable from a distance, the Spotted Sandpiper's stiff-winged, quivering flight pattern, strident calls and tendency to burst from the shore are easily recognizable. This bird is also known for its continuous "teetering" behavior as it forages. • The scientific descriptor *macularius* is Latin for "spotted," referring to the spots on this bird's underparts in breeding plumage.

breeding

nonbreeding

ID: teeters almost continuously. *Breeding:* white underparts heavily spotted with black; yellow orange legs; black-tipped, yellow orange bill; white "eyebrow." *Nonbreeding* and *immature:* pure white breast, foreneck and throat; brown bill; dull yellow legs. *In flight:* flies close to water with rapid, shallow wingbeats on noticeably bowed wings; white upperwing stripe.

Size: *L* 7–8 in; *W* 15 in.

Status: common from May to September.

Habitat: shorelines, gravel beaches, ponds, marshes, alluvial wetlands, rivers, streams, swamps and sewage lagoons; occasionally seen in cultivated fields.

Nesting: usually near water; often under overhanging vegetation among logs or under bushes; pair lines shallow depression with grass; almost exclusively male incubates 4 creamy buff, heavily blotched and spotted eggs for 20–24 days and raises young.

Feeding: picks and gleans along shorelines for terrestrial and aquatic invertebrates; also snatches flying insects from air.

Voice: sharp, crisp *eat-wheat, eat-wheat, wheat-wheat-wheat-wheat.*

Similar Species: *Other sandpipers* (pp. 64–68): do not teeter; black bills and legs; lack spotting on breast.

Best Sites: Bowdoin NWR; Medicine Lake NWR; Freezout Lake WMA; Bitterroot River; Missouri River.

LONG-BILLED CURLEW
Numenius americanus

These stunning birds breed in many areas of Montana, but they are most common along the East Front of the Rockies. Long-billed Curlews are fun to watch during the breeding season. Males put on spectacular displays over their nesting territories, issuing loud ringing calls as they flutter higher and higher, and then glide down again in an undulating flight. • The Long-billed Curlew spends the summer in arid grasslands, but during migration it is more often found in wetlands, grazed pastures and stubble fields. Its long, downcurved bill is a wonderfully dexterous tool for picking up invertebrates while it keeps a watchful eye above the prairie grass. • Populations of many of our curlews, including the Long-billed, have declined dramatically since pre-settlement times, mainly because of habitat loss and fragmentation. • The genus name *Numenius* means "new moon" and refers to the crescent-shaped bill shared by all curlews.

ID: very long, downcurved bill (female's bill is distinctly longer); buff brown under-parts; brown upperparts; mottled back; unstriped head; long legs. *In flight:* obvious cinnamon tinge to wings.
Size: *L* 23 in; *W* 35 in. Female on average larger than male.
Status: uncommon from mid-April to August.
Habitat: *Breeding:* short-grass prairie and mid-grass prairie, sage-steppe, prairie potholes. *In migration:* agricultural fields, grazed pastures, wetlands, mudflats.

Nesting: usually on dry prairie, often with water nearby; in slight depression sparsely lined with grass and debris; pair incubates 4 brown-spotted, olive eggs 27–30 days.
Feeding: *Breeding:* picks grasshoppers and other invertebrates from grass and sloughs; also feeds on nestlings of grassland song-birds. *In migration:* probes shorelines and mudflats for soft-bodied invertebrates.
Voice: most common call in summer is loud whistle, *cur-lee cur-lee cur-lee*; also melodi-ous, rolling *cuurrleeeuuu*.
Similar Species: *Marbled Godwit* (p. 67): slightly upturned, bicolored bill.
Best Sites: *Breeding:* East Front of Rockies; Dillon. *In migration:* Freezout Lake WMA.

MARBLED GODWIT

Limosa fedoa

During the breeding season, Marbled Godwits are as much grassland birds as they are shorebirds. Godwits are found primarily in north-central Montana, where they have access to a great number of prairie potholes and native prairies for nesting. In migration, however, these birds again become shorebirds proper, and large numbers congregate at mudflats and lakeshores. During this time they prefer muddy shorelines, sometimes wandering into deep water and dipping their heads beneath the water's surface, probing deep into soil and mud. The godwit's bill is sensitive to underground movements, so it is adept at locating and extracting worms and mollusks. • Godwits draw attention to themselves with their loud, incessant calls, so they are often easy birds to find. Next to the Long-billed Curlew, the Marbled Godwit is the largest shorebird in Montana.

nonbreeding

breeding

ID: large bird; long, slightly upcurved, bicolored bill; long neck; mottled buff brown plumage darkest on upperparts; long, blackish blue legs. *In flight:* obvious cinnamon wing linings.

Size: *L* 16–20 in; *W* 31 in. Female on average larger than male.

Status: locally common from late April to September.

Habitat: *Breeding:* prairie potholes, short-grass prairie, marshes, alkali lakes. *In migration:* mudflats, marshes, flooded fields, wet meadows, lakeshores.

Nesting: often in loose colonies; on dry ground in short grass, usually near water; slight depression is lined with dry grass, may have canopy; pair incubates 4 brown-spotted, olive brown eggs 21–23 days.

Feeding: probes deeply in soft substrates for worms, insect larvae, crustaceans and mollusks; picks insects from grass.

Voice: loud, gull-like squawks and squeals: *co-rect co-rect* or *god-wit god-wit*; also *raddica-raddica-raddica*.

Similar Species: *Long-billed Curlew* (p. 66): shares cinnamon wing linings and large size, but has long, downcurved bill.

Best Sites: *Breeding:* Bowdoin NWR; Benton Lake NWR; Medicine Lake NWR; Westby. *In migration:* Freezout Lake WMA.

WILSON'S PHALAROPE

Phalaropus tricolor

The Wilson's Phalarope is the only one of the three phalarope species that does not feed at sea in winter. It is also the only phalarope that breeds in Montana, where it is a common summertime inhabitant of wetlands and marshes. • Phalaropes are among the most colorful and unusual shorebirds. Like Spotted Sandpipers, they practice an uncommon mating strategy known as polyandry: each female mates with several males and often produces a clutch of eggs with each one. After laying a clutch, the female usually abandons her mate, leaving him to incubate the eggs and tend the precocial young. This reversal of gender roles includes a reversal of the usual plumage characteristics—here the female is more brightly colored. Even John James Audubon was fooled; he mislabeled the male and female birds in all of his phalarope illustrations.

breeding

ID: dark, needle-like bill; white "eyebrow," throat and nape; light underparts; black legs; swims more than other sandpipers. *Breeding female:* very sharp colors; gray "cap"; chestnut brown on side of neck; black eye line extends down side of neck and onto back. *Breeding male:* duller overall; dark "cap." *Nonbreeding:* all-gray upperparts; white "eyebrow" and gray eye line; white underparts; dark yellowish or greenish legs. *Juvenile:* plain face; yellow legs; darker crown than adult.
Size: *L* 9–9½ in; *W* 17 in. Female on average larger than male.
Status: common from May to early September.
Habitat: *Breeding:* cattail marshes, saline wetlands, wet meadows, sloughs.

In migration: lakeshores, marshes, mudflats and sewage lagoons.
Nesting: often near water; well concealed in depression lined by male with grass and other vegetation; male incubates 4 brown-blotched, buff eggs 18–27 days; male rears young.
Feeding: often spins in tight circles while swimming to stir up prey, then picks aquatic invertebrates from water's surface or just below; on land makes short jabs to pick up invertebrates.
Voice: deep, grunting *work work* or *wu wu wu*, usually heard on breeding grounds.
Similar Species: *Red-necked Phalarope:* in migration only; rufous stripe down side of neck in breeding plumage; dark nape and line behind eye in nonbreeding plumage.
Best Sites: Bowdoin NWR; Medicine Lake NWR; Freezout Lake WMA; Benton Lake NWR.

FRANKLIN'S GULL

Larus pipixcan

The Franklin's Gull is not a typical "seagull." A large part of its life is spent inland, and on its traditional nesting territory on the prairies, it is affectionately known as "Prairie Dove." It has a dovelike profile and often follows tractors across agricultural fields, snatching up insects from the tractor's path in much the same way its cousins follow fishing boats. Large nesting colonies are found in a few select areas of Montana; elsewhere in the state it occurs only as a migrant. • The Franklin's Gull is one of only two gull species that migrate long distances between breeding and wintering grounds—most Franklin's Gulls winter along the Pacific coast of Peru and Chile.

breeding

ID: dark gray mantle; broken white eye ring; white underparts. *Breeding:* black head; orange red bill and legs; breast might have pinkish tinge. *Nonbreeding:* white head with dark partial "hood"; all-black bill. *Immature:* like nonbreeding adult but with brownish upperparts. *In flight:* white crescent on black wing tips.
Size: *L* 13–15 in; *W* 3 ft. Male on average larger than female.
Status: locally common from mid-April to September.
Habitat: large cattail and bulrush marshes and wetlands, agricultural fields, river and lake shorelines, rivermouths and landfills.

Nesting: colonial, in marsh; pair builds large floating platform from cattails and bulrushes; pair incubates 2–4 blotched and spotted, greenish to buff-colored eggs 23–26 days.
Feeding: very opportunistic; gleans agricultural fields and meadows for grasshoppers and insects; often catches dragonflies, mayflies and other flying invertebrates in midair; also eats small fish and some crustaceans.
Voice: mewing, shrill *weeeh-ah weeeh-ah* while feeding and in migration.
Similar Species: dark gray mantle and presence of significant black on head unique, except for *Bonaparte's Gull:* migrant only; black bill; conspicuous white wedge on forewing.
Best Sites: Freezout Lake WMA; Bowdoin NWR; Medicine Lake NWR.

RING-BILLED GULL
Larus delawarensis

Ring-billed Gulls nest in large colonies on Montana's wetlands, often in close association with other gull species. This familiar bird is probably as well known to nonbirders as it is to birders, and it is the species most people think of when they use the word "seagull." The Ring-billed Gull's numbers have greatly increased in recent years, and its tolerance for humans has made it a part of our everyday lives—a connection that often involves Ring-bills scavenging our litter or fouling the windshields of our automobiles. Some people feel that Ring-billed Gulls have become pests; many parks, beaches, golf courses and even fast-food restaurant parking lots are inundated with marauding gulls looking for food handouts. Few species, however, have fared as well as the Ring-billed Gull in the face of human development, which, in itself, is something to appreciate.

breeding

ID: white head; yellow eyes, legs and bill; black ring around bill tip; pale gray mantle; white underparts. *Nonbreeding:* brown-streaked head. *Immature:* gray back; brown wings and breast; bicolored pink and black bill. *In flight:* black wing tips with a few white spots.
Size: *L* 18–20 in; *W* 4 ft. Male on average larger than female.
Status: very common from March to November; many overwinter at dumps and areas of open water.
Habitat: *Breeding:* sparsely vegetated islands, open beaches, breakwaters and dredge-spoil areas. *In migration* and

winter: lakes, rivers, landfills, golf courses, fields and parks.
Nesting: colonial; pair lines shallow scrape on ground with plants, debris and sticks; pair incubates 2–4 brown-blotched, gray to olive eggs 23–28 days.
Feeding: gleans ground for human food waste, spiders, insects, rodents, earthworms, grubs and some waste grain; scavenges for carrion; surface-tips for aquatic invertebrates and fish.
Voice: high-pitched *kakakaka-akakaka;* also low, laughing *yook-yook-yook.*
Similar Species: *California Gull* (p. 71): darker gray mantle; no bill ring; black and red spots near tip of lower mandible; dark eyes. *Herring Gull:* in migration and winter only; larger; pinkish legs; no bill ring; red spot near tip of lower mandible.
Best Sites: nearly any wetland or lake. *Winter:* landfills.

CALIFORNIA GULL

Larus californicus

California Gulls are intermediate in size between the larger Herring Gull and the slightly smaller Ring-billed Gull. When all three are present, it's a test of a birder's skill to identify them correctly. It takes a keen eye to recognize a California Gull as it roosts among Ring-bills, but once you learn how, you'll see them all the time. For those people who come to love gull watching, spotting a California Gull might be their first assurance that it is in fact possible to see something other than Ring-bills in your average gang of white-headed gulls. • California Gulls breed on the northern Great Plains, and most migrate to the Pacific coast for the winter. These birds tend to nest communally on low-lying islands. Their simple scrape nests are generally placed no closer than the distance two gulls can bridge with aggressive bill jabs from atop their eggs.

breeding

ID: dark eyes; yellow bill with red and black spots; yellow green legs; gray mantle; extensive black wing tips. *Breeding:* white head and underparts. *Nonbreeding:* dark spotting on head. *Immature:* mottled brown overall; pinkish legs; bill all dark or pale with black tip.

Size: *L* 18–20 in; *W* 4–4½ ft. Male on average larger than female.

Status: common from April to November; some overwinter.

Habitat: *Breeding:* large lakes and wetlands. *In migration* and *winter:* farmlands, landfills and parks.

Nesting: colonial; often on open beaches or shorelines; pair lines shallow scrape with plants, feathers and small sticks; pair incubates 2–3 brown-marked, olive or gray eggs 23–27 days.

Feeding: gleans ground for terrestrial invertebrates, especially grasshoppers, earthworms and cutworms; scavenges; surface-tips for aquatic invertebrates.

Voice: high-pitched, nasal *kiarr-kiarr,* most often heard at breeding colonies.

Similar Species: *Ring-billed Gull* (p. 70): lighter gray back; light eyes; black ring around bill. *Herring Gull:* in migration and winter only; larger; lighter gray back; light eyes; pink legs.

Best Sites: Freezout Lake WMA; Benton Lake NWR; Bowdoin NWR; Medicine Lake NWR.

BLACK TERN

Chlidonias niger

Wheeling about in foraging flights, Black Terns pick small minnows from the water's surface or catch flying insects in midair. Black Terns have dominion over the winds and these acrobats slice through the sky with grace even in a stiff wind. When they leave our region in August and September, these terns head for the warmer climates of Central and South America. • Black Terns are finicky nesters and refuse to return to nesting areas that show even slight changes in water level or in the density of emergent vegetation. This selectiveness, coupled with the degradation of marshes across North America, has contributed to a significant decline in populations of the species over recent decades. Commitment to restoring and protecting valuable wetland habitats will eventually help this bird to reclaim its once prominent place in the bird kingdom. • In order to spell the Black Tern's genus name correctly, one must misspell *chelidonias,* the Greek word for "swallow." This bird is named for its swallowlike, darting flight as it pursues insects.

breeding

breeding

ID: *Breeding:* black head, bill and underparts; gray back, tail and wings; white undertail coverts; reddish black legs. *Nonbreeding:* white underparts and forehead; molting fall birds may be mottled with brown. *In flight:* long, pointed wings; shallowly forked tail.
Size: *L* 9–10 in; *W* 24 in.
Status: locally common from May to September.

Habitat: shallow, freshwater cattail and bulrush marshes, wetlands, lake edges and sewage ponds with emergent vegetation.
Nesting: loosely colonial; pair builds flimsy nest of dead plant material on floating vegetation, muddy mound or muskrat house; pair incubates 3 darkly blotched, olive to pale buff eggs 21–22 days.
Feeding: snatches insects from air, tall grass and water's surface; also eats small fish.
Voice: greeting call is shrill, metallic *kik-kik-kik-kik-kik;* typical alarm call is *kreea.*
Similar Species: *Other terns:* all light in color.
Best Sites: Medicine Lake NWR; Bowdoin NWR; Red Rock Lakes NWR; Benton Lake NWR.

ROCK PIGEON

Columba livia

Formerly known as "Rock Dove" and introduced to North America in the early 17th century, Rock Pigeons have settled wherever cities, towns and farms are found. Most of these birds seem content to nest on buildings or farmhouses, but "wilder" individuals can occasionally be seen nesting on tall cliffs. • It is believed that Rock Pigeons were domesticated from Eurasian birds as a source of meat in about 4500 BC. Since their domestication, they have been used as message couriers (both Caesar and Napoleon used them), as scientific subjects and even as pets. Much of our understanding of bird migration, endocrinology and sensory perception derives from experiments involving Rock Pigeons. • All members of the pigeon family, including doves, feed "milk" to their young. Because birds lack mammary glands, it is not true milk, but a nutritious liquid produced by glands in the bird's crop. The chicks insert their bills down the adult's throat to eat the thick, protein-rich fluid. • No other "wild" bird varies as much in coloration—a result of semidomestication and extensive inbreeding.

ID: color highly variable (iridescent, blue gray, red, white or tan); usually has white rump and orange feet; dark-tipped tail. *In flight:* holds wings in deep "V" while gliding.
Size: *L* 12–13 in; *W* 28 in.
Status: very common year-round.
Habitat: urban areas, railroad yards and agricultural areas; high cliffs provide a more natural habitat for some.
Nesting: on ledge in barn or on cliff, bridge, building or tower; mainly female builds flimsy nest from sticks and assorted vegetation; pair incubates 2 white eggs 16–19 days; pair feeds young "pigeon milk"; may raise broods year-round.
Feeding: gleans ground for waste grain, seeds and fruits; occasionally eats insects.
Voice: soft, cooing *coorrr-coorrr-coorrr.*
Similar Species: *Mourning Dove* (p. 74): smaller; slimmer; pale brown plumage; long tail and wings. *Merlin, Prairie Falcon* (p. 58) and *Peregrine Falcon: In flight:* not as heavy bodied; longer tails; do not hold wings in "V"; wings do not clap on takeoff.
Best Sites: almost any city.

73

MOURNING DOVE

Zenaida macroura

The soft cooing of the Mourning Dove, heard filtering through our broken woodlands, farmlands and suburban parks and gardens, is often confused with the muted hoots of an owl. When birders track down the source of these calls, they usually discover one or two doves perched upon a fence, tree branch or utility wire. • The Mourning Dove is one of the most abundant and widespread native birds in North America and one of the most popular game birds. This species has benefited from human-induced changes to the landscape, and its numbers and distribution have increased since the continent was settled. It is encountered in both rural and urban habitats, but it avoids heavily forested areas. • Despite its fragile appearance, the Mourning Dove is a swift, direct flier whose wings often whistle as it cuts through the air at high speed. When this bird bursts into flight, its wings clap above and below its body. • The common name reflects the Mourning Dove's sad, cooing song. The genus name *Zenaida* honors Zenaïde, Princess of Naples and wife of Charles-Lucien Bonaparte, who was a naturalist and a nephew of the French emperor.

ID: buffy, gray brown plumage; small head; long, white-trimmed, tapering tail; sleek body; dark, shiny patch below ear; dull red legs; dark bill; pale rosy underparts; black spots on upperwing.
Size: *L* 11–13 in; *W* 18 in. Male on average larger than female.
Status: locally fairly common from April to October; rare in winter.
Habitat: open and riparian woodlands, woodlots, forest edges, agricultural and suburban areas and open parks.

Nesting: in fork of shrub or tree, occasionally on ground; female builds fragile, shallow platform nest from twigs supplied by male; pair incubates 2 white eggs 14 days; young are fed "pigeon milk."
Feeding: gleans ground and vegetation for seeds; visits feeders.
Voice: mournful, soft, slow *oh-woe-woe-woe.*
Similar Species: *Rock Pigeon* (p. 73): stockier; white rump; shorter tail; iridescent neck.
Best Sites: Lee Metcalf NWR; Charles M. Russell NWR; Giant Springs SP; Billings.

GREAT HORNED OWL

Bubo virginianus

The familiar *hoo-hoo-hoooo hoo-hoo* that resounds through campgrounds, suburban parks and farmyards is the call of the adaptable and superbly camouflaged Great Horned Owl. This formidable, primarily nocturnal hunter uses its acute hearing and powerful vision to hunt a wide variety of prey. Almost any small creature that moves is fair game. This bird apparently has a poorly developed sense of smell, which might explain why it is the only consistent predator of skunks. • Great Horned Owls often begin their courtship as early as January, at which time their hooting calls make them quite conspicuous. By February and March, females are already incubating their eggs, and by the time most migratory birds arrive in our region, Great Horned owlets have already fledged. • The large eyes of an owl are fixed in place, so to look up, down or to the side, the bird must move its entire head. As an adaptation to this situation, an owl can swivel its neck 180 degrees to either side and 90 degrees up and down.

ID: yellow eyes; tall "ear" tufts set wide apart on head; fine, horizontal barring on breast; facial disc outlined in black and often rusty orange in color; white "chin"; heavily mottled gray, brown and black upperparts; overall plumage varies from light gray to dark brown.

Size: *L* 18–25 in; *W* 3–5 ft. Female on average larger than male.

Status: common year-round.

Habitat: dense hedgerows, fragmented forests, agricultural areas, woodlots, meadows, riparian woodlands, wooded suburban parks and wooded edges of landfills.

Nesting: in abandoned stick nest of another bird; may also nest on cliff or on deserted Osprey platform; adds little or no material to nest; mostly female incubates 2–3 dull whitish eggs 28–35 days.

Feeding: mostly nocturnal, but also hunts at dusk in winter; usually swoops from perch; eats small mammals, birds, snakes, amphibians and even fish.

Voice: call during breeding season is 4–6 deep hoots: *hoo-hoo-hoooo hoo-hoo* or *Who's awake? Me too;* male also gives higher-pitched hoots.

Similar Species: *Long-eared Owl:* smaller; thinner; vertical breast streaks; "ear" tufts are close together. *Great Gray Owl* (p. 77) and *Short-eared Owl* (p. 78): lack prominent "ear" tufts.

Best Sites: Lee Metcalf NWR; Ninepipe NWR; Giant Springs SP; Benton Lake NWR.

BURROWING OWL
Athene cunicularia

Although Burrowing Owls do make frequent use of burrows for nesting, they do not usually excavate burrows themselves. These birds nest primarily in abandoned tunnels of black-tailed prairie-dogs and Richardson's ground squirrels in areas nearly devoid of vegetation. • Burrowing Owls were once common birds in Montana, but their numbers have declined significantly in recent years. The extermination of prairie-dogs and ground squirrels in many areas of our state has greatly reduced the number of suitable owl nesting sites. Other factors relating to their decline include poisonings, collisions with vehicles, the use of agricultural chemicals and the conversion of native grasslands to croplands and residential areas. • During the day, these ground-dwelling birds can be seen atop fence posts or rocks in open grassland habitat. When they perch at the entrance to their burrows, they look very similar to the ground squirrels with which they closely associate, especially from a distance.

ID: long legs unique among owls; short tail; rounded head; no "ear" tufts; white around eyes; yellow bill; bold, white "chin" stripe; horizontal barring on underparts; brown upperparts flecked with white. *Immature:* brownish band across breast; pale, unbarred underparts.
Size: *L* 8–9 in; *W* 21–24 in. Female slightly larger than male.
Status: uncommon to rare from April to September.
Habitat: large, active, black-tailed prairie-dog towns; open, short-grass haylands, pastures and prairies; occasionally lawns and golf courses.
Nesting: singly or in loose colonies; in abandoned natural or artificial burrow;

nest lined mainly by male with bits of dry manure, food debris, feathers and fine grass; female incubates 5–11 white eggs 21–28 days.
Feeding: eats mostly ground insects, such as grasshoppers, beetles and crickets; also eats small rodents, some birds, amphibians and reptiles.
Voice: call is harsh *chuk;* also chattering *quick-quick-quick;* rattlesnake-like warning call when inside burrow. *Male:* courtship call *coo-Hooo!* is higher than, but similar to, Mourning Dove's coo.
Similar Species: *Short-eared Owl* (p. 78): heavy vertical streaks on underparts; small "ear" tufts; long wings with dark "wrist" marks; black eye sockets; doesn't nest in burrows.
Best Sites: Charles M. Russell NWR; Molt (Big Lake area); Musselshell River area near Mosby.

GREAT GRAY OWL

Strix nebulosa

A face shaped like a satellite dish and an ensnaring cluster of talons may be the last look at life for a rodent scouted by a Great Gray Owl. This bird's great head swivels smoothly, focusing instantly on the slightest sound or movement beneath a carpet of snow or vegetation. When prey is detected, the owl launches itself in noiseless flight, gliding downward on fixed wings, punching through anything in the way of its meal. • Although this owl is the largest in North America, the Great Gray's apparent bulk is largely a mass of fluffy insulation—it is outweighed by about 15 percent by the Great Horned Owl. • Great Gray Owls are widespread across the boreal forests of the northern hemisphere, but are nowhere common. Following the cool conifer forests southward via the Rockies, they are found throughout western Montana south to Wyoming.

ID: very large size; gray plumage; large, rounded head; no "ear" tufts; small, yellow eyes; well-defined concentric rings in facial disc; black "chin" bordered by white "bow tie"; long tail.

Size: *L* 24–33 in; *W* 54–60 in. Female on average larger than male.

Status: uncommon to rare year-round.

Habitat: woodland edges, meadows and forest openings; also dense coniferous or mixed forests of Douglas-fir, subalpine fir, ponderosa pine and especially lodgepole pine.

Nesting: typically atop broken snag or abandoned hawk, raven or eagle nest; little nest material added; female incubates 2–4 white eggs up to 36 days.

Feeding: listens and watches from perch, then swoops to catch voles, mice, shrews, ground squirrels, squirrels and small hares.

Voice: slow, deep series of single hoots.

Similar Species: *Great Horned Owl* (p. 75): has "ear" tufts. *Barred Owl:* smaller; brown and white plumage; dark eyes.

Best Sites: Georgetown Lake; Flint Creek Range; Kleinschmidt Flat (east of Ovando); Red Rock Lakes NWR.

SHORT-EARED OWL

Asio flammeus

This unique raptor fills a niche in open country that has been left unoccupied by forest-dwelling owls, but is filled during daylight hours by the Northern Harrier. The Short-eared Owl courses low over the ground in search of rodent prey in treeless habitats such as wet meadows, marshes, hayfields and upland prairies. • These owls can be difficult to locate during the summer breeding season when females are sitting on their ground nests. During other times of the year, they may become active even during the daytime, perching on fenceposts and hunting actively. • In spring, courting Short-eared Owls fly together, and the male claps his wings together on each downstroke as he periodically performs short dives. • Short-eared Owl populations grow and decline over many years in response to dramatic fluctuations in prey. Cold weather and low small mammal numbers occasionally force many of these owls, especially immature birds, to become temporary nomads, moving well outside their usual breeding range.

ID: yellow eyes set in black sockets; heavy, vertical streaking on buff belly; short, inconspicuous "ear" tufts. *In flight:* flies like giant moth; dark "wrist" crescents; deep wingbeats; long wings.
Size: *L* 13–17 in; *W* 3–4 ft. Female on average larger than male.
Status: fairly common year-round.
Habitat: open areas, including grasslands, wet meadows, marshes, shrub-steppe, overgrown fields, airports and forest clearings.
Nesting: on ground in open area, tundra or hummocky marsh; female lines slight depression sparsely with grass; female

incubates 4–7 white eggs 24–37 days; male feeds female during incubation.
Feeding: forages mostly at dawn and dusk; flies low and pounces on prey from the air; eats mostly voles and other small rodents; also takes insects, small birds and amphibians.
Voice: generally quiet; squeals and barks like a small dog; also produces soft *toot-toot-toot* during breeding season.
Similar Species: *Northern Harrier* (p. 51): similar habits but active during daylight; white uppertail coverts. *Long-eared Owl* and *Great Horned Owl* (p. 75): long "ear" tufts; never hunt during day. *Burrowing Owl* (p. 76): much longer legs; shorter tail and shorter wings.
Best Sites: Medicine Lake NWR; Freezout Lake WMA; Benton Lake NWR; Ninepipe NWR.

COMMON NIGHTHAWK

Chordeiles minor

Each June, the male Common Nighthawk flies high above forest clearings and lakeshores, gaining altitude in preparation for the climax of his noisy aerial dance. From a great height, the male dives swiftly, thrusting his wings forward in a final braking action as he strains to pull out of the steep dive. This quick thrust of the wings produces a deep, hollow *vroom* that attracts female nighthawks. • Like other members of the nightjar family, the Common Nighthawk is adapted for catching insects in midair. Its gaping mouth is surrounded by modified feathers that act as a funnel, guiding insects into its mouth. • Nighthawks are generally less nocturnal than other nightjars, but they still spend most daylight hours resting on a tree limb or on the ground. • These birds may spend less time in our state than any other breeding bird, arriving around the first of June and departing by the end of August.

ID: cryptic, mottled plumage; barred underparts. *Male:* white throat. *Female:* buff throat. *In flight:* dark and lanky with pointed wings; bold, white stripes on outer wing; shallowly forked, barred tail; erratic flight.

Size: *L* 8½–10 in; *W* 24 in.

Status: common from June to August.

Habitat: *Breeding:* in forest openings as well as burns, bogs, rocky outcroppings, gravel rooftops and sometimes fields with sparse cover or bare patches; often seen and heard flying above cities and towns, especially in early evening. *In migration:* anywhere large numbers of flying insects are found; usually roosts in trees, often near water.

Nesting: on bare ground; no nest built; female incubates 2 well-camouflaged eggs about 19 days; both adults feed young.

Feeding: primarily at dawn and dusk; catches insects in flight, often high in the air; may fly around streetlights at night to catch prey; eats mosquitoes, blackflies, midges, beetles, moths and other flying insects.

Voice: frequently repeated, nasal *peent;* male also makes deep, hollow *vroom* with wings during courtship flight.

Similar Species: *Common Poorwill:* strictly nocturnal; no white wing stripe; whistled vocalization.

Best Sites: larger towns and cities: Missoula, Billings, Helena, Miles City; Freezout Lake WMA; Blackfeet Indian Reservation.

VAUX'S SWIFT

Chaetura vauxi

Many birders know Vaux's (pronounced "vawks") Swifts as "town birds," but they are regularly found in forested areas as well. Prior to European settlement, these birds nested solely in hollow snags, but they have become adapted in many areas to using chimneys. In late summer and early fall, increasingly large flocks of Vaux's Swifts circle above towns and cities in tight groups before plunging collectively into chimneys.
• When not flying, swifts use their small, strong claws to cling to vertical surfaces, and they never perch, unlike swallows. • John Kirk Townsend named this bird after William Sansom Vaux, an eminent mineralogist. Although Vaux was deserving of the honor, it is rather ironic that one of America's most aerially inclined birds is named for a man whose passion was for earthbound treasures.

ID: cigar-shaped body; brownish gray overall; paler throat and rump; twittery, insect-like vocalization. *In flight:* stiff wings of even breadth nearly to tip; brownish gray upperparts; lighter underparts with pale throat; short, squared-off tail; long wings taper backward.

Size: *L* 5 in; *W* 12 in.

Status: common from mid-April to early September.

Habitat: *Breeding:* cities with chimneys for nesting; coniferous forests, especially near clearings and burns. *Foraging and in migration:* over forest canopy, forest openings, burned-over forests, meadows, rivers and lakes; in migration may also roost in chimneys or crevices in buildings.

Nesting: in natural tree cavity such as woodpecker hole, burned-out hollow or broken-off top; uses chimneys widely; pair uses sticky saliva to glue sticks, twigs and conifer needles to inner wall of cavity; pair

incubates 4–5 white eggs 18–19 days; both adults feed young.

Feeding: long-sustained cruises on the wing, often just above treetops; feeds almost entirely on flying insects, including flies, moths and aphids; often seen feeding high in sky in company of Violet-green Swallows.

Voice: courtship call is clipped, chittering *id-id-id-IS-ziz!*

Similar Species: *Chimney Swift:* nearly identical but found only in cities of eastern Montana plains (no overlap). *Black Swift:* rare near montane waterfalls; black; much larger overall; longer, shallowly forked tail. *White-throated Swift:* near cliffs; light and dark patterning on underparts. *Swallows* (pp. 107–110): wings wider at base; lack twittery calls; often have white or rufous red in plumage.

Best Sites: Missoula; Kalispell; Glacier NP.

CALLIOPE HUMMINGBIRD

Stellula calliope

Glistening in the slanting rays of dawn in a Montana meadow, the iridescent gorget of the male Calliope Hummingbird suggests nectar dripping from the bird's needle-like bill. As it flits about in montane forests and foothills, its dainty colors complement the vivid landscape of summer wildflowers. As females dance and feed among clusters of paintbrushes or columbines, males compete for attention by flashing their seductive haute couture between dazzling high-speed dips and dives.

• This hummingbird is North America's smallest bird. It is also the smallest long-distance migrant: individuals routinely travel up to 5000 miles in a year. Contrary to myth, hummingbirds never hitch rides on the backs of eagles or geese. • Novice birdwatchers often ponder the correct pronunciation of this bird's name, which is "kuh-LYE-o-pee."

ID: miniscule bird; iridescent, green upperparts; at rest, wing tips extend just beyond tail tip. *Male:* narrow, candy red streaks on gorget extend down otherwise white throat from bill; white breast and belly; light green flanks. *Female* and *immature:* lack mature male's pinkish red gorget; white underparts; peach-colored flanks; fine, dark green spots on throat.

Size: *L* 3¼ in; *W* 4¼ in. Female on average larger than male.

Status: fairly common from mid-April to August.

Habitat: mountain meadows, avalanche slopes, streamside thickets, regenerating burned areas and shrubby hillsides among montane and subalpine forests at 4000–9000 ft elevation.

Nesting: saddled on branch under foliage or on overhanging conifer branch; female builds tiny cup nest of plant down, moss, lichen and spiderwebs; often builds over previously used nest; female incubates 2 white eggs up to 16 days.

Feeding: probes flowers for nectar while hovering; also eats small insects and takes sugar water from feeders.

Voice: high-pitched, chattering *tsew* note; territorial male gives quiet, high-pitched *zzing*, especially in April and May.

Similar Species: *Rufous Hummingbird* (p. 82): slightly larger overall; adult male entirely rufous; wing tips fall short of tail tip at rest; longer bill; female has stronger rufous flanks and often has red spotting on throat. *Black-chinned Hummingbird:* larger; male with black and purple gorget; female and immature lack peach-colored flanks; frequently bobs tail in flight.

Best Sites: Missoula; Glacier NP; Bozeman.

RUFOUS HUMMINGBIRD

Selasphorus rufus

The tiny Rufous Hummingbird is a delicate avian jewel, but its beauty hides a mean streak. Sit patiently in a flower-filled meadow or alongside a hummingbird feeder, and you'll soon notice the aggressive territoriality of the males. Although of life-or-death importance to the hummingbirds, to our eyes these miniature conflicts and high-speed chases are cute. • Hummingbirds have to be "power smart." Their metabolic rate is roughly 100 times that of an elephant, and hummingbirds eat up to three times their weight in nectar and insects each day. Males must defend their feeding territories as an insurance policy for their high energy needs. • Male Rufous Hummingbirds abandon females at the onset of nesting and drift to higher elevations as early as mid-May, departing the state by late July. Females and immatures linger in Montana until the end of August, and throughout August they are the most common hummingbirds at lowland feeders.

ID: long, thin, black bill; mostly rufous tail; at rest, wing tips fall short of tail tip. *Male:* orange brown back, tail and flanks; iridescent, orange red throat; green crown; white breast and belly; some adult males have green backs. *Female:* green back; red spots on throat; rufous sides and flanks contrast with white breast. *Immature:* like adult female, but often lacking red spots on throat.

Size: *L* 3¼–3½ in; *W* 4½ in. Female on average larger than male.

Status: common from mid-April to August.

Habitat: *Breeding:* streamside shrubland, montane meadows, open conifer forests, shrubby clear-cuts and burns; spring influx nearly coincident with blooming of early-flowering shrubs. *Postbreeding:* also in higher-elevation meadows, in lowland valleys and at hummingbird feeders.

Nesting: nest saddled on drooping conifer bough; female builds tiny cup nest of plant down and spiderwebs and covers it with lichens; female incubates 2 white eggs up to 14 days.

Feeding: probes mostly red flowers for nectar while hovering; also eats small insects, sap and sugar water.

Voice: call is low *chewp chewp;* also rapid and exuberant confrontation call, *ZEE-chuppity-chup!*

Similar Species: *Calliope Hummingbird* (p. 81): slightly smaller; less rufous in tail; wing tips extend beyond tail tip at rest; female and immature have paler flanks, more peachy rather than bright rufous. *Black-chinned Hummingbird:* larger; male with black and purple gorget; female and immature lack orangy flanks and orange in tail; wags tail in flight.

Best Sites: Glacier NP; Bitterroot Mountains; Beartooth Mountains; any lowland feeder in western Montana in late July and August.

BELTED KINGFISHER

Ceryle alcyon

Many of the lakes, rivers, marshes and beaver ponds of Montana are monitored closely by the boisterous Belted Kingfisher. Never far from water, this bird is often found uttering its distinctive, rattling call while perched on a bare branch that extends over a productive pool. With a precise headfirst dive, the kingfisher can catch fish at depths of up to 23 inches, or snag a frog immersed in a few inches of water. This bird has even been observed diving into water to elude avian predators. • During the breeding season, male and female kingfishers typically take turns excavating their nest burrow. The birds use their bills to chip away at an exposed sandbank and then kick loose material out of the tunnel with their feet. • The female Belted Kingfisher has the usual female reproductive role for birds but is more colorful than her mate—she has a red band across her belly. • In Greek mythology, Alcyon (Halcyone), the daughter of the wind god, grieved so deeply for her drowned husband that the gods transformed them both into kingfishers.

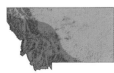

ID: bluish upperparts; shaggy crest; blue gray breast band; white "collar"; long, straight bill; short legs; white underwings; small white patch near eye. *Male:* no "belt." *Female:* rusty "belt" (may be incomplete).
Size: *L* 11–14 in; *W* 20 in.
Status: fairly common from March to November; overwinters where open water is available.
Habitat: rivers, large streams, lakes, marshes and beaver ponds, especially near exposed soil banks, gravel pits or bluffs.

Nesting: in cavity at end of an earth burrow, often up to 6 ft long, dug by the pair with their bills and claws; pair incubates 6–7 white eggs 22–24 days; both adults feed young.
Feeding: dives headfirst into water, either from perch or from hovering flight; eats mostly small fish, aquatic invertebrates and tadpoles.
Voice: loud, fast rattle, a little like a teacup shaking on a saucer.
Similar Species: shaggy crest and huge bill distinctive.
Best Sites: Giant Springs SP; Bitterroot River; Flathead River; Yellowstone River.

LEWIS'S WOODPECKER
Melanerpes lewis

This unique green and pink woodpecker, a summer visitor to Montana, does the vast majority of its feeding on the wing. Among our woodpeckers, only Red-headeds do as much of their feeding in this manner. • In flight, Lewis's Woodpeckers are more likely to be mistaken for crows than for other woodpeckers. They appear all dark and have long, rounded wings, slow, floppy wingbeats and short tails. • The Lewis's Woodpecker frequently perches solitarily in semi-open country on the tops of ponderosa pine trees, poles and snags. It flies off to hawk insects and then returns to its high, exposed perch. Competition with European Starlings and loss of extensive snag habitat through modern wildfire suppression has greatly diminished this woodpecker's numbers. Conservationists now regard it as a Montana species of concern, and they are attempting to find ways to halt its decline. • This large, dark woodpecker was named for Meriwether Lewis, coleader of the western "Expedition of Discovery" in the early 1800s. Lewis's diary details many concise and original observations of natural history.

ID: dark green upperparts; dark red face; pale gray breast and "collar"; pinkish belly; dark undertail coverts; sharp, stout bill. *Immature:* brown head and breast; lacks red face and gray "collar."
Size: *L* 11 in; *W* 21 in.
Status: uncommon to locally common from May to August.
Habitat: open ponderosa pine forest, burned-over pine or fir forest, open riparian woodlands, especially cottonwood; some ranch windbreaks and isolated groves.

Nesting: primarily male excavates cavity in dead or dying tree; pair incubates 6–7 white eggs about 15 days.
Feeding: flycatches for flying insects; probes into cracks and crevices for invertebrates.
Voice: nearly silent away from vicinity of nest; utters harsh series of *chur* notes.
Similar Species: no other woodpecker is dark green; all other woodpeckers fly with pronounced undulations; all others except Red-headed spend less time flycatching.
Best Sites: along Bitterroot and Clark Fork rivers: Kelly Island Fishing Access (Missoula), Lee Metcalf NWR; Polebridge; Long Pines/Ekalaka Hills.

RED-HEADED WOODPECKER
Melanerpes erythrocephalus

Easily identified by its red head, white underparts and black and white upperparts, the adult Red-headed Woodpecker is a favorite visitor to the mature cottonwood stands along eastern Montana's rivers. Spotting one rewards those who are patient and observant. This woodpecker is a quiet, retiring bird that can be overlooked as it works its way furtively between trees. • Like other members of the genus *Melanerpes*, Red-headed Woodpeckers, during the breeding season, will hawk for flying insects and store them, as well as nuts, in cracks and bark crevices. • Red-headed Woodpeckers were once common throughout their range, but their numbers have declined dramatically over the past century. Since the European Starling was introduced, Red-headed Woodpeckers have been largely outcompeted for nesting cavities.

juvenile

ID: bright red head, "chin," throat and "bib" with black border; black back, wings and tail; white breast, belly, rump, lower back and inner wing patches. *Immature:* obvious white lower back and trailing edge of inner wing; brown head, upper back, outer wings and tail; slight brown streaking on white underparts.
Size: *L* 9–9½ in; *W* 17 in.
Status: uncommon from late May to August.
Habitat: open, park-like, mature riparian woodlands (especially cottonwood), river edges and roadsides with groves of scattered trees; occasionally in burns.
Nesting: male excavates nest cavity in dead tree or limb; pair incubates 4–5 white eggs 12–13 days; both adults feed young.
Feeding: flycatches for insects; hammers dead and decaying wood for grubs; eats mostly insects, earthworms, spiders, nuts, berries and seeds; may also eat some young birds and eggs.
Voice: loud series of *kweer* or *kwrring* notes; occasional chattering *kerr-r-ruck*; also drums softly in short bursts.
Similar Species: adult is distinctive; immature has diagnostic white secondaries and lower back but lacks red head.
Best Sites: Yellowstone and Missouri rivers: Pirogue Island SP, Fort Peck area, Charles M. Russell NWR.

RED-NAPED SAPSUCKER

Sphyrapicus nuchalis

The Red-naped Sapsucker has adopted a variation of the typical woodpecker for-aging strategy: it drills lines of parallel "wells" in the bark of living trees and shrubs. The bird is quick to make its rounds once the wells are filled with pools of sap, collecting trapped bugs and oozing fluid from the various sites. • Sapsuckers don't actually suck sap; they lap it up with a long tongue that resembles a frayed paintbrush. This deliberate foraging practice has convinced some people that this bird is capable of planning. • Some people worry that the activities of this sapsucker will kill ornamental trees and shrubs, but most healthy plants can withstand a series of sapsucker wells. • Kinglets, warblers, waxwings and hummingbirds are known to feed from sapsucker wells.

Habitat: *Breeding:* variety of deciduous and mixed forests, especially with aspen, birch or alder; montane riparian stands, clearings, burns. *In migration:* lower-elevation riparian woodlands, orchards, tree groves and shade trees.

Nesting: pair excavates cavity in living or rotting aspen or birch; occasionally uses same tree for 2 years, making a new hole; cavity lined with wood chips; pair incubates 4–5 white eggs 13 days.

Feeding: hammers series of small, square wells in living trees; eats sap and insects from wells; catches flying insects.

Voice: call is cat-like *meow;* tapping is irregular and morse-code-like.

Similar Species: *Downy Woodpecker* (p. 87) and *Hairy Woodpecker* (p. 88): lack red forehead and black "bib." *Williamson's Sapsucker:* male lacks red on crown and nape; female and immature lack white upperwing patch in flight.

Best Sites: Glacier NP; Missoula; Libby; Beartooth Mountains; Madison River.

ID: red fore-head; red patch on nape; black-and-white-striped head; black "bib"; yellow wash on breast; black and white wings and back; white rump; light yellow upper back with fine black streaking. *Male:* red "chin" and throat. *Female:* white "chin"; red throat. *In flight:* obvious white upperwing patch *not* on trailing edge.

Size: *L* 8½ in; *W* 16 in.

Status: uncommon to locally common from mid-April to September.

DOWNY WOODPECKER

Picoides pubescens

A regular patron of backyard suet feeders, the small and widespread Downy Woodpecker is often the first woodpecker a novice birder identifies with confidence. It is generally approachable and tolerant of human activities, and once you become familiar with its dainty appearance, it won't be long before you recognize it by its soft taps and brisk staccato calls. These encounters are not all free of confusion, however, because the closely related Hairy Woodpecker looks remarkably similar. • Like other members of the woodpecker family, the Downy has evolved a number of features to help deal with the repeated shocks of a lifetime of hammering. These characteristics include a strong bill, strong neck muscles, a flexible, reinforced skull and a brain that is tightly packed in its protective cranium. Woodpeckers also have feathered nostrils, which filter out the sawdust birds produce when hammering.

ID: clear white belly and back; black wings have white bars; black "cheek" and crown; short, stubby bill; mostly black tail; black-spotted, white outer tail feathers. *Male:* small, red patch on back of head. *Female:* no red patch.
Size: *L* 6–7 in; *W* 12 in. Male on average larger than female.
Status: common in western Montana year-round; less common in prairie counties of east and north.
Habitat: all wooded environments, especially deciduous and mixed forests and areas with tall, deciduous shrubs.
Nesting: pair excavates cavity in dying or decaying trunk or limb and lines it with wood chips; excavation takes more than 2 weeks; pair incubates 4–5 white eggs 11–13 days; both adults feed young.
Feeding: forages on trunks and branches, often of saplings and shrubs; chips and probes for insect eggs, cocoons, larvae and adults; also eats nuts and seeds; attracted to suet feeders.

Voice: long, unbroken trill; call is sharp *pik* or *ki-ki-ki* or whiny *queek queek;* drums more than Hairy and at higher pitch (usually on smaller trees and dead branches).
Similar Species: *Hairy Woodpecker* (p. 88): nearly identical but noticeably larger; longer bill; no spots on white outer tail feathers. *Red-naped Sapsucker* (p. 86): red on forehead and "chin"; white upperwing patches; irregular drumming pattern.
Best Sites: nearly any wooded area.

HAIRY WOODPECKER

Picoides villosus

A second or third look is often required to confirm the identity of the Hairy Woodpecker, because it is so similar to its smaller cousin, the Downy Woodpecker. One way to learn to distinguish these birds is by watching them at a backyard feeder. It is not uncommon to see these birds vying for food, and the Hairy Woodpecker is larger and more aggressive. • The secret to woodpeckers' feeding success is hidden in their skulls. Most wood-peckers have very long tongues—in some cases more than four times the length of the bill—made possible by twin structures that wrap around the perimeter of the skull. These structures store the tongue in much the same way that a measuring tape is stored in its case. Besides being long and maneuverable, the tongue has a tip that is sticky with saliva and finely barbed to help seize reluctant wood-boring insects. • Rather than singing during courtship, woodpeckers drum rhythmically on trees.

Nesting: pair excavates nest site in live or decaying trunk or limb; excavation takes more than 2 weeks; cavity lined with wood chips; pair incubates 4–5 white eggs 12–14 days; both adults feed young.

Feeding: forages on tree trunks and branches; chips, hammers and probes bark for insects and their eggs, cocoons and larvae; also eats nuts, fruit and seeds; attracted to feeders with suet, especially in winter.

Voice: loud, sharp call, *peek peek;* long, unbroken trill, *keek-ik-ik-ik-ik-ik;* drums less regularly and at lower pitch than Downy Woodpecker, always on tree trunks and large branches.

Similar Species: *Downy Woodpecker* (p. 87): smaller; shorter bill; dark spots on white outer tail feathers. *Red-naped Sapsucker* (p. 86): large, white upperwing patches; red forecrown; lacks clean white back.

Best Sites: almost any wooded area; especially common in burns.

ID: pure white belly and back; white-spotted, black wings; black "cheek" and crown; bill about as long as head (front to back); black tail with unspotted, white outer feathers. *Male:* small, red patch on back of head. *Female:* no red patch.

Size: *L* 8–9½ in; *W* 15 in. Male on average larger than female.

Status: common year-round, especially in western Montana.

Habitat: deciduous and mixed forests of all types; frequents burns.

NORTHERN FLICKER

Colaptes auratus

Unlike most woodpeckers, this species spends much of its time on the ground, feeding mostly on ants. It appears almost robinlike as it hops about on anthills and in grassy meadows and forest clearings. • Flickers are often seen bathing in dusty depressions. The dust particles absorb oils and bacteria. To clean even more thoroughly, flickers squish captured ants and preen with the remains. Ants contain formic acid, which kills small parasites on the flickers' skin and feathers. • Like many woodpeckers, the Northern Flicker has zygodactyl feet—two toes face forward and two backward—that allow the bird to move vertically up and down tree trunks. Stiff tail feathers help prop up woodpeckers' bodies as they scale trees and excavate cavities. • There are two forms of the Northern Flicker in Montana. The Red-shafted Flicker (present statewide) and the Yellow-shafted Flicker (primarily in eastern Montana) are easily identified by the color of their underwings. However, these two forms often interbreed in our area, producing a wide array of "orange-shafted" birds.

red-shafted

yellow-shafted

ID: brown, barred back and wings; spotted, buff to whitish underparts; black "bib"; red or yellow underwings and undertail; white rump; long bill; gray crown. *Red-shafted:* largely gray face; lacks red nape crescent; male has red "mustache"; female lacks "mustache." *Yellow-shafted:* brown face; red on nape; male has black "mustache"; female lacks "mustache."
Size: *L* 12½–13 in; *W* 20 in.
Status: common from March to October; uncommon in winter.
Habitat: open woodlands, forest edges, fields, meadows, beaver ponds and other wetlands.
Nesting: pair excavates cavity in dead or dying deciduous tree; excavation takes

about 2 weeks; may also use nest box; cavity lined with wood chips; pair incubates 5–8 white eggs 11–16 days; both adults feed young.
Feeding: forages on ground for ants and other terrestrial insects; probes bark; also eats berries and nuts; occasionally flycatches.
Voice: loud, laughing, rapid *kick-kick-kick-kick-kick-kick; woika-woika-woika* issued during courtship; very similar to calls of Pileated Woodpecker but doesn't trail off at end of series.
Similar Species: no other woodpecker is light brown and spotted, with dark "bib."
Best Sites: Lee Metcalf NWR; Missoula; Glacier NP; Charles M. Russell NWR; Ekalaka; Billings.

PILEATED WOODPECKER

Dryocopus pileatus

With its flaming red crest, swooping wingbeats and maniacal call, this impressive deep-forest dweller can stop hikers in their tracks. Unfortunately, because they require large home territories, these magnificent birds are not encountered with much frequency. A pair of breeding Pileated Woodpeckers generally needs more than 100 acres of mature forest to call home. • Using its powerful, dagger-shaped bill, the Pileated Woodpecker chisels out uniquely shaped rectangular cavities in its search for grubs and ants. These cavities are often the first indication that a breeding pair resides in an area. • As a primary cavity nester, this woodpecker plays an important role in forest ecosystems. Ducks, small falcons, owls and even flying squirrels are frequent nesters in abandoned Pileated Woodpecker cavities. • Not surprisingly, a woodpecker's bill becomes shorter as the bird ages. In his historic painting of the Pileated Woodpecker, John Audubon correctly depicted the bills of juveniles as slightly longer than those of adults. • There is no real consensus on whether this bird's name is pronounced "pie-lee-ated" or "pill-ee-ated"—it's a matter of preference and good-natured debate.

ID: predominantly black; white wing linings; flaming red crest; yellow eyes; stout, dark bill; white stripe runs from bill to shoulder; white "chin." *Male:* red "mustache"; red extends from bill to nape. *Female:* no red "mustache"; gray brown forehead.
Size: *L* 16–19 in; *W* 29 in. Male on average larger than female.
Status: uncommon year-round.
Habitat: extensive tracts of mature forest west of the Continental Divide; occurs in open riparian woodlands or woodlots in suburban areas.

Nesting: pair excavates cavity in dead or dying tree trunk; excavation takes 3–6 weeks; cavity lined with wood chips; pair incubates 4 white eggs 15–18 days; both adults feed young.
Feeding: often hammers base of rotting trees, creating fist-sized or larger rectangular holes; eats carpenter ants, wood-boring beetle larvae, berries and nuts.
Voice: loud, fast, laughing, rolling *kuk-kuk-kuk-kuk-kuk*, trailing off at end; loud, resonant drumming.
Similar Species: *Other woodpeckers* (pp. 84–89): much smaller; lack crest. *American Crow* (p. 104) and *Common Raven* (p. 105): lack white underwings and flaming red crest.
Best Sites: Lee Metcalf NWR; Missoula; Kalispell; Glacier NP.

WESTERN WOOD-PEWEE

Contopus sordidulus

This bird's burry, down-slurred call will usually lead you to a forest edge or clearing, where the songster makes itself heard throughout the hot hours of a summer afternoon. Aspiring birders will quickly come to recognize the call of the Western Wood-Pewee as one of the most common summertime noises in Montana woodlands. • Wood-Pewees launch themselves into aerobatic, looping foraging ventures in search of flying insects, often returning immediately to the same perch. • The nest of the Western Wood-Pewee is well camouflaged by both its shape and color—the completed structure resembles a mere bump on a horizontal limb. When cryptic concealment doesn't provide enough protection against predators, this flycatcher will vigorously defend its nest by chasing hawks, jays and chipmunks. • The scientific descriptor *sordidulus* refers to the Western Wood-Pewee's dusky, "dirty" color.

Nesting: on horizontal limb in tree; female builds small cup nest of plant fibers bound with spider silk; female incubates 3 brown-spotted, whitish eggs 12–13 days.

Feeding: flycatches for insects, often from perch high in mature tree.

Voice: plaintive whistle, *purREER*, that drops off at end; song is *oom-VLIVVIT... purREER*.

Similar Species: *Olive-sided Flycatcher:* found mainly in high-elevation burns and forest clearings; larger; 2 white rump tufts; obvious dark flanks contrasting with white center of belly. Empidonax *flycatchers—Least* (p. 92), *Willow, Dusky, Hammond's* and *Cordilleran:* smaller; shorter wing tips; white eye rings (except in Willow); different calls.

Best Sites: any river with large cottonwoods: Missouri, Yellowstone, Bitterroot, Clark Fork.

ID: dark olive brown upperparts; light underparts with a blurrily dark-vested look; 2 faint white wing bars; no eye ring; pale throat; slightly peaked hindcrown; dark lower mandible; light undertail coverts.

Size: *L* 5–6 in; *W* 10½ in.

Status: common from mid-May to mid-September.

Habitat: most semi-open forest habitats including cottonwood riparian, ponderosa pine and montane conifer or mixed woodlands.

LEAST FLYCATCHER

Empidonax minimus

Empidonax flycatchers are infamously difficult to identify. Montanans have to deal with no fewer than six species of these look-alike birds during the breeding season. Fortunately, however, a trained ear and a basic knowledge of habitat preferences is often all that's needed to name these birds. • During the nesting season, the Least Flycatcher's noisy *che-bek* call is conspicuous in wet, wooded areas. Intense song battles normally replace physical aggression between rival males, but feathers do fly in occasional territorial and courtship fights. • These birds often fall victim to nest parasitism by the Brown-headed Cowbird, whose hatched young can smother the much smaller Least Flycatcher nestlings. • *Empidonax* flycatchers are aptly named: the literal translation is "mosquito king" and refers to their insect-hunting prowess.

ID: best identified by voice and habitat; olive brown upperparts; 2 white wing bars; bold, white eye ring; fairly long, narrow tail; mostly dark bill has yellow orange lower base; white throat; gray breast; grayish white to yellowish belly and undertail coverts.
Size: L 4½–6 in; W 7½ in.
Status: fairly common from late May through August.
Habitat: open deciduous or mixed woodlands, especially near water; shrubby forest openings and edges; open, park-like cottonwood stands.
Nesting: in fork of small tree or shrub, often against trunk; female builds small cup nest of plant fibers and bark and lines it with fine grass, plant down and feathers; female incubates 4 creamy white eggs 13–15 days; both adults feed young.
Feeding: flycatches insects; gleans trees and shrubs for insects while hovering; may also eat some fruit and seeds.

Voice: male song is constantly repeated, dry *che-bek*.
Similar Species: *Western Wood-Pewee* (p. 91): larger; lacks eye ring; longer wing tips; plaintive song. *Alder Flycatcher:* Pine Butte Swamp Preserve only; song is *fee-bee-o;* faint eye ring. *Willow Flycatcher:* brushy habitats near water; song is explosive *fitz-bew;* lacks eye ring. *Hammond's Flycatcher:* tall conifers; voice a series of low-pitched phrases. *Dusky Flycatcher:* dry shrubby hillsides; voice like Hammond's but with some higher clear whistles. *Cordilleran Flycatcher:* shaded forests near streams and often cliffs; high-pitched, up-slurred whistle, *per-wee.* *Ruby-crowned Kinglet* (p. 118): gleans insects from foliage; broken eye ring; daintier bill; shorter tail.
Best Sites: Bowdoin NWR; Giant Springs SP; Westby; Lee Metcalf NWR.

SAY'S PHOEBE

Sayornis saya

Unlike its close relative, the Black Phoebe of the American Southwest, this flycatcher is partial to dry environments. Say's Phoebes thrive in sun-parched grassy valleys and hot, dry canyons. They are particularly common where abandoned or little-used farm buildings provide safe, sheltered nesting sites that can be reused every year and where livestock conveniently stir up insects. The phoebe hawks these insects from a fence post or other low perch. • The Say's Phoebe is Montana's hardiest flycatcher, arriving as early as late March, fully two months ahead of the first Willow and Cordilleran flycatchers. • This is the only bird whose genus and species names both honor the same person, Thomas Say. A versatile naturalist, his primary contributions were in the field of entomology. • The name "phoebe" comes from the call of a close relative, the Eastern Phoebe.

ID: apricot buff belly and under-tail coverts; dark tail; brown gray breast and upperparts; dark head; no eye ring; very faint wing bars; constantly bobs tail.

Size: *L* 7½ in; *W* 13 in.

Status: uncommon from late March to September.

Habitat: hot, dry canyons, ravines, rimrocks, valleys and gullies dominated by grasses and shrubs; also uses abandoned farmyards, agricultural areas and scrublands.

Nesting: in niche on cliff face, or beneath eave or bridge; nest of grass, moss and fur; female incubates 4–5 white eggs up to 17 days.

Feeding: flycatches for aerial insects; also gleans buildings, vegetation, streamsides and ground for insects; sometimes runs short distances in pursuit of prey.

Voice: song is *pitseedar;* call is softly whistled *pee-ur.*

Similar Species: *Other flycatchers* (pp. 91–95): all lack apricot belly.

Best Sites: Billings; Great Falls; Decker; Miles City.

WESTERN KINGBIRD

Tyrannus verticalis

Although the Western Kingbird is a common sight across much of the Treasure State, the species is actually less common than the Eastern Kingbird. Still, Western Kingbirds are often observed surveying for prey from fence posts, power lines or utility poles. When a kingbird spots an insect, it may chase it for up to 50 feet before a capture is made. • Once you have witnessed a kingbird's brave attacks against much larger birds, such as crows and hawks, you'll understand why this hard-headed rabble-rouser was awarded its regal common name. The scientific descriptor *verticalis* refers to the bird's hidden orange crown patch, which is flared during courtship displays and in combat with rivals. This orange patch, however, is not a good identification mark because it is only rarely visible. • The tumbling aerial courtship display of the Western Kingbird is a good indication that this bird might be breeding. The male twists and turns as he rises to heights of 65 feet above the ground, then stalls as he tumbles and flips his way back to earth. • On several occasions, Western Kingbirds have hybridized with Eastern Kingbirds.

ID: gray head and breast; yellow belly and undertail coverts; black tail; white edges on outer tail feathers; white "chin"; black bill; ashy gray upperparts; faint, dark gray "mask"; thin, orange crown (rarely seen).
Size: *L* 8–9 in; *W* 15½ in.
Status: fairly common from May to September.
Habitat: open, dry country; grassy areas with scattered brush or hedgerows; edges of open fields; riparian woodlands.
Nesting: in deciduous tree near trunk; also uses utility poles; bulky cup nest of grass, weeds and twigs lined with fur, plant down and feathers; female incubates 3–5 whitish, heavily blotched eggs 18–19 days.
Feeding: flycatches aerial insects, including bees, wasps, butterflies, moths, grasshoppers and flies; occasionally eats berries.
Voice: chatty, twittering *whit-ker-whit;* also a short *kit* or extended *kit-kit-keetle-dot.*
Similar Species: *Eastern Kingbird* (p. 95): black upperparts; white underparts; white-tipped tail.
Best Sites: National Bison Range; Charles M. Russell NWR; Ekalaka.

EASTERN KINGBIRD

Tyrannus tyrannus

When you think of a tyrant, you are more likely to envision an oppressive dictator or a large carnivorous dinosaur than a little bird. Yet no one familiar with the pugnacious Eastern Kingbird is likely to refute its scientific name. This bird is a brawler, and it will fearlessly attack crows, hawks and even humans that pass through its territory. Intruders are often vigorously pursued, pecked and plucked for some distance until the kingbird is satisfied there is no further threat. In contrast, its butterfly-like courtship flight, characterized by short, quivering wingbeats, reveals a gentler side of this bird. • Eastern Kingbirds are common and widespread, so during a drive in the country you are likely to spot at least one sitting on a fenceline or utility wire. • Eastern Kingbirds rarely walk or hop on the ground—they prefer to fly, even for very short distances.

ID: dark gray to black upperparts; white underparts; white-tipped tail; black bill; small head crest; thin orange crown (rarely seen); no eye ring; black legs.
Size: *L* 8½ in; *W* 15 in.
Status: very common from mid-May to September.
Habitat: fields with scattered trees or hedgerows; clearings in fragmented forests; open roadsides; burned areas and near human settlements.
Nesting: on horizontal tree or shrub branch; also on standing stump or upturned tree root; pair builds cup nest of weeds, twigs and grass and lines it with root fibers, fine grass and fur; female incubates 3–4 darkly blotched, white to pinkish white eggs 14–18 days.
Feeding: flycatches aerial insects; infrequently eats berries.
Voice: call is quick, loud, chattering *kit-kit-kitter-kitter;* also buzzy *dzee-dzee-dzee.*
Similar Species: tail "dipped in white paint" distinctive. *Western Kingbird* (p. 94): yellow underparts; tail has white sides, lacks white tip. *Olive-sided Flycatcher:* high-elevation burns and forest clearings; 2 white tufts border rump; lacks white-tipped tail and all-white underparts. *Western Wood-Pewee* (p. 91): smaller; bicolored bill; lacks white-tipped tail and all-white underparts.
Best Sites: Blackfeet Indian Reservation; Charles M. Russell NWR; Medicine Lake NWR; Billings; Bozeman.

LOGGERHEAD SHRIKE

Lanius ludovicianus

The words predatory and songbird sound oxymoronic, but both apply to the Loggerhead Shrike. This miniature raptor catches its small prey in fast, direct flight or a swooping dive. Males display their hunting prowess by impaling prey on thorns or barbed wire. This behavior may also serve to store excess food during times of plenty. In spring, you may see a variety of skewered creatures baking in the sun. • Loggerhead Shrike populations have severely declined in many areas, and the species is now listed as endangered in Canada. Habitat destruction and pesticide use are thought to explain much of the decline. Another problem is collisions with motor vehicles: while wintering in the southern U.S., shrikes often become traffic fatalities when they prey on insects attracted to warm pavement. • During the winter this species is replaced statewide by the similar Northern Shrike.

ID: black tail and wings; gray crown and back; white underparts; black "mask" extends above hooked bill onto forehead. *Juvenile:* brownish gray, barred upperparts. *In flight:* white wing patches; white-edged tail.

Size: *L* 9 in; *W* 12 in.

Status: uncommon from May to September.

Habitat: variety of open habitats with scattered thorny shrubs for nesting and often barbed wire fencing for impaling prey; mixed- or short-grass prairie, riparian areas, shrub-steppe and grazed or abandoned farmland.

Nesting: low in crotch of shrub or small tree; thorny shrubs often preferred; pair builds bulky cup nest of twigs and grass lined with animal hair, feathers, plant down and rootlets; female incubates 5–6 pale buff to grayish white eggs, darkly spotted mainly at larger end, 15–17 days.

Feeding: swoops down on prey from perch or attacks in pursuit; takes mostly large insects; regularly eats small birds and rodents; also eats carrion, small snakes and amphibians.

Voice: high-pitched, hiccupy *bird-ee bird-ee* in summer; infrequently a harsh *shack-shack* year-round.

Similar Species: *Northern Shrike:* winter visitor; larger; bill more strongly hooked; fine barring on sides and breast; thinner black "mask"; immature has brownish upperparts and strongly but finely barred underparts.

Best Sites: Billings; Miles City; Bannack.

WARBLING VIREO
Vireo gilvus

The charming Warbling Vireo is a common summer resident of Montana. By late May, its wondrous voice fills many local parks and backyards. Because this vireo often settles close to urban areas, its bubbly, warbling song should be familiar to most people, though they may not be able to name its source. • The Warbling Vireo lacks splashy field marks and is readily observed only when it moves from one leaf-hidden perch to another. Searching treetops for this generally inconspicuous vireo may literally be a pain in the neck, but visually confirming its identity is exceptionally rewarding. • When courting, the male spreads his wings and tail and struts around the female, warbling his appeal. Like other vireos, male Warbling Vireos often sing from the nest while incubating. • The hanging nests of vireos are usually even harder to find than the birds themselves. In winter, though, the nests are revealed as they swing precariously from bare deciduous branches.

fall adult

ID: dark partial eye line borders white "eyebrow"; no wing bars; olive gray upperparts; greenish flanks; white to pale gray underparts; gray crown; bluish gray legs.
Size: *L* 5–5½ in; *W* 8½ in.
Status: common from late May to September.
Habitat: variety of shrubby, early successional habitats: open deciduous woodlands, riparian areas, woodland edges; also parks and gardens with deciduous trees.

Nesting: in horizontal fork of deciduous tree or shrub; pair builds hanging, basket-like cup nest of grass, roots, plant down, spider silk and a few feathers; pair incubates 4 darkly speckled, white eggs 12–14 days.
Feeding: gleans foliage for insects; occasionally hovers to glean.
Voice: long, musical warble of slurred whistles; call note similar to that of Red-eyed Vireo, but with slight upward inflection.
Similar Species: *Red-eyed Vireo* (p. 98): black eye line extends to bill; blue gray crown; red eyes. *Orange-crowned Warbler:* yellower overall; slimmer, unhooked bill.
Best Sites: Missoula; Glacier NP; Westby; Two Moon Park (Billings).

RED-EYED VIREO

Vireo olivaceus

The Red-eyed Vireo is the undisputed champion of vocal endurance in our region. In spring and early summer, males sing continuously through the day. They carry on long after most songbirds have curtailed their courtship melodies, which is about five or six hours after sunrise. One particularly vigorous Red-eyed Vireo male holds the record for most songs delivered in a single day: over 22,000! • This vireo is among the most common and widespread of all songbirds in North America, but in Montana it is limited primarily to riparian corridors of tall cottonwoods and aspens. The species is sensitive to habitat loss and nest parasitism by Brown-headed Cowbirds. • Red-eyed Vireos sound a lot like American Robins, and beginning birders are often delighted to discover these nifty birds hiding behind a familiar song.

breeding

ID: dark eye line; white "eyebrow"; black-bordered, blue gray crown; olive "cheek"; olive green upperparts; white to pale gray underparts; may have yellow wash on sides, flanks and undertail coverts, especially in fall; no wing bars; red eyes (seen only at close range).

Size: *L* 6 in; *W* 10 in.

Status: locally fairly common from May to September.

Habitat: deciduous riparian woodlands with tall canopy and shrubby understory; park-like cottonwood or aspen stands; occasionally suburban shade trees.

Nesting: in horizontal fork of deciduous tree or shrub; female builds hanging, basket-like cup nest of grass, roots, spider silk and cocoons; female incubates 4 white eggs, darkly spotted at the larger end, 11–14 days.

Feeding: gleans foliage for insects, especially caterpillars; often hovers; also eats berries.

Voice: call is short, scolding *neeah*. *Male:* song is continuous, variable, robinlike run of quick, short phrases with distinct pauses in between: *Look-up, way-up, tree-top, see-me, here-I-am!*

Similar Species: *Warbling Vireo* (p. 97): dusky eye line does not extend to bill; lacks black border on gray "cap."

Best Sites: Missoula; Billings; Miles City; Lewistown; Westby (in migration).

GRAY JAY
Perisoreus canadensis

Few birds in Montana rival the Gray Jay for boldness. Small family groups glide through mountain conifer forests, attracted by the slightest commotion or movement. These sociable creatures quickly endear themselves to passersby. • Gray Jays lay their eggs and begin incubation as early as March. Their nests are well insulated to conserve heat, and nesting early means the adults will be feeding their quickly growing nestlings when the forests are full of fresh spring food. • In preparation for tough times, Gray Jays often store food. To preserve their cache, they coat the food with a sticky mucus from specialized salivary glands. • Gray Jays are widely distributed throughout the Rocky Mountains, the Pacific Northwest, Canada and Alaska. In other parts of their range they may be known as "Camp Robbers," "Canada Jays" or "Whiskey Jacks."

ID: fluffy, pale gray plumage; long tail; light forehead and "cheek"; darker crown and nape; dark gray upperparts; light gray underparts; dark, stubby bill. *Immature:* dark sooty gray overall, with pale lateral throat stripe. *In flight:* slow flight; much gliding; deliberate, rowing wingbeats.
Size: *L* 11½ in; *W* 18 in.
Status: uncommon to locally common year-round.
Habitat: high conifer forests.
Nesting: in fork of conifer; pair builds bulky, well-insulated nest of plant fibers, roots, moss, twigs, feathers and fur; female incubates 3–4 spotted, light gray eggs 17 days.
Feeding: searches ground and vegetation for insects, fruit, songbird eggs and nestlings, carrion and berries; stores food items; carries off unguarded human food.
Voice: complex vocal repertoire; soft, whistled *quee-oo;* chuckled *cla-cla-cla;* also imitates other birds, especially the Northern Pygmy-Owl.
Similar Species: *Clark's Nutcracker* (p. 102): larger, heavy black bill; black and white wings and tail. *Loggerhead Shrike* (p. 96) and *Northern Shrike:* open country only; black mask; black and white wings and tail.
Best Sites: Lost Trail Pass; Glacier NP; Rogers Pass; Bridger Range; Beartooth Mountains.

STELLER'S JAY

Cyanocitta stelleri

The stunning Steller's Jay is a resident jewel, uncommon in the montane forests of western Montana. This crested bird generally presents itself as noisy and pugnacious, but in the vicinity of its nest, it suddenly becomes silent, cautious and cleverly elusive. This jay gets used to humans at campgrounds, and like other corvids will not hesitate to steal food scraps from inattentive picnickers. In winter it often descends upon feeders in search of peanuts and sunflower seeds. • Like other jays, the Steller's Jay has a varied diet of small vertebrates, insects, seeds, berries and nuts. It takes eggs and nestlings of small birds, and it has even been observed attacking and eating adult birds. In turn, this jay falls victim to accipiters. • The Steller's Jay has an extensive range, from Alaska along the coast to central California, and through the Rocky Mountains south to Central America. • George Wilhelm Steller, the first European naturalist to visit Alaska, collected the type specimen (first formally described individual) of this species.

ID: glossy, deep blue plumage; black head, nape and back; large, black crest; bluish forehead streaks; barred wings and tail.
Size: *L* 11½ in; *W* 19 in.
Status: uncommon year-round.
Habitat: coniferous and mixed montane woodlands; occasionally seen at lower elevations in winter.
Nesting: in fork of conifer; pair builds bulky stick and twig nest lined with mud, grass and conifer needles; female incubates 4 brown-spotted, blue green eggs 16 days.
Feeding: searches ground and vegetation for insects, small vertebrates and other food items; forages in treetops for nuts, berries and other birds' eggs; visits feeders in winter.
Voice: harsh, far-carrying *shack-shack-shack;* grating *kresh, kresh;* under-breath spring song.
Similar Species: *Pinyon Jay* (p. 101): lacks crest, barring on tail and wings, and black head, nape and back. *Blue Jay:* gray underparts; dark "necklace"; blue crest.
Best Sites: Bitterroot Mountains; Lolo Pass; Glacier NP; Bigfork.

PINYON JAY

Gymnorhinus cyanocephalus

Pinyon Jays are loud, highly gregarious birds that behave much like American Crows. When not breeding, these jays wander in sometimes enormous flocks that consist of many smaller family groups. While foraging, the birds adhere to an orderly social structure—some take turns acting as lookouts, while others concentrate on feeding. • In the Great Basin, this bird's namesake tree provides the habitat and food of choice, but in Montana, where pinyon pine is absent, Pinyon Jays are found primarily in ponderosa pine, limber pine and juniper. Cached seeds and nuts help supplement freshly harvested foods when it comes time to feed growing young. • Nesting takes place in late winter with loose colonies of up to 150 birds. Pinyon Jays might nest again in late summer, depending on pine seed crops. When these crops fail, the jays become nomadic and disperse widely in search of other food.

ID: gray blue plumage; light streaks on throat; long, dark, pointed bill; short tail.

Size: *L* 9–11½ in; *W* 19 in.

Status: locally common year-round.

Habitat: *Breeding:* dry, open ponderosa pine, limber pine and juniper forest from about 3000 to 6000 ft. *Foraging:* sagebrush flats, forests of pine and tall sagebrush.

Nesting: in loose colonies in pines, junipers and shrubs; pair builds large, bulky nest of sticks, twigs and fibers;

female incubates 4–5 brown-marked, blue green eggs up to 17 days.

Feeding: searches ground and vegetation for pine nuts, seeds and insects; also eats berries and other birds' eggs and nestlings.

Voice: flight call is high, piercing *mew* or laughing, repeated *hah-hah;* warning call is low *krawk-krawk-krawk.*

Similar Species: *Steller's Jay* (p. 100): never in large flocks; large black crest; dark head, nape and back; barred wings and tail.

Best Sites: Livingston; Billings; Bear Canyon (Pryor Mountains).

CLARK'S NUTCRACKER

Nucifraga columbiana

Raucous and extroverted, Clark's Nutcrackers break the profound hush of mid-afternoon at timberline with conversational rasps. They are often encountered in campgrounds and picnic areas, looking to scavenge a meal. • In fall, these birds spend much of their time using their long, sturdy bills to pry apart the cones of whitebark pine and other conifers. A special pouch at the base of the tongue allows mass transport of the seeds to carefully selected storage spots. These caches might be eight miles or more apart, and together may contain more than 30,000 seeds. Over winter and throughout the nesting cycle, nutcrackers use their phenomenal memory to relocate cache sites, which are often hidden under deep snow. • The whitebark pine is entirely dependent on Clark's Nutcracker for dispersal of its seeds, and the nutcracker is equally dependent on the pine's energy-rich seeds for successfully raising its young—an extraordinary relationship termed a symbiosis. • When Captain William Clark of the Lewis and Clark expedition first sighted this bird, its large, straight bill misled him into believing it was a woodpecker. The Clark's Nutcracker was originally placed in the genus *Picicorvus*, which meant "woodpecker-crow."

ID: light gray head, back and underparts; large, black bill; black wings with flashy white secondaries. *In flight:* black central tail feathers; white outer tail feathers; stoops and tumbles unerringly along upper slopes of tall peaks.

Size: *L* 12–13 in; *W* 24 in.
Status: fairly common year-round.
Habitat: *Breeding:* upper-elevation forest of whitebark pine, Douglas-fir, spruces or other conifers; may use lower-elevation limber pine forest. *Nonbreeding:* may move to lower elevations.
Nesting: on horizontal conifer limb; pair builds twig and stick platform nest lined with grass and strips of bark; pair incubates 2–4 dark-marked, greenish eggs 16–22 days.
Feeding: forages on ground and in treetops for pine seeds; hammers cones and nuts with bill; also eats insects and some carrion; stores food for winter.
Voice: loud, unpleasant, grating *kra-a-a-a,* delivered mostly from perch.
Similar Species: *Gray Jay* (p. 99): smaller; gray wings and tail; shorter bill.
Best Sites: Glacier NP; Red Rock Lakes NWR; Rogers Pass; Bitterroot Mountains.

BLACK-BILLED MAGPIE
Pica hudsonia

The saying "familiarity breeds contempt" is well illustrated by this species. Magpies are very common and well known in Montana to birders and non-birders alike. Truly among North America's most beautiful birds, they are too often discredited as trash birds because of their raucous, aggressive demeanor and proclivity for scavenging. • The Black-billed Magpie is one of the most exceptional architects among our birds. Its elaborate domed nest can be found in a spruce or deciduous tree or on an iron bridge or utility pole. Constructed of sticks, and held together with mud, the large domed compartment conceals and protects the eggs and young from harsh weather and predators. The nests are so well constructed that they remain in trees for years after they are abandoned, often serving as nest sites for nonbuilders, such as Long-eared Owls. Although the nest may take a pair 40 days to build, one study showed that the effort uses only 1 percent of the birds' daily energy budget. By contrast, laying eggs consumes 23 percent of the female's energy budget.

ID: long, black tail; black head, breast and back; rounded, black and white wings; iridescent highlights on wings and tail; black undertail coverts; black bill; white belly.
Size: *L* 19 in; *W* 25 in. Male on average longer than female.
Status: common year-round.
Habitat: open areas, especially those with shrubs or scattered trees: agricultural areas, riparian thickets, townsites and campgrounds.

Nesting: in tree or tall shrub; pair builds domed stick and twig nest, often held together with mud; female incubates 5–8 brown-spotted, greenish eggs up to 24 days.
Feeding: forages mostly on ground for insects, carrion and garbage; picks insects and ticks off large ungulates; takes small numbers of eggs and nestlings.
Voice: loud, nasal, frequently repeated *ueh-ueh-ueh;* many other vocalizations.
Similar Species: none.
Best Sites: hard to miss: cities, towns, parks, farmlands.

103

AMERICAN CROW

Corvus brachyrhynchos

American Crows are wary and intelligent birds that have flourished despite considerable human effort, over many generations, to reduce their numbers. These birds are ecological generalists, and much of their strength lies in their ability to adapt to a variety of habitats. • The American Crow is a common bird throughout Montana. In fall, crows group together in flocks numbering in the hundreds or thousands. In some places, many thousands of crows may roost together on any winter night. An aggregation of crows is inexplicably known as a "murder." • In western Montana, where crows and ravens both occur, observers will note that only crows spend much of their time within city limits. Ravens tend to be wilder and warier, and prefer to remain on the outskirts of towns. • Crows are impressive mimics, able to whine like a dog, cry like a child, squawk like a hen and laugh like a human. Some crows in captivity are able to repeat simple spoken words. • The American Crow's cumbersome scientific name, *Corvus brachyrhynchos*, is Latin for "raven with the small nose."

ID: black body; black bill and legs; slim, sleek head and throat; fan-shaped tail.

Size: *L* 17–21 in; *W* 3 ft.

Status: common year-round.

Habitat: urban areas, agricultural fields and other open areas with scattered woodlands; also clearings, marshes, lakes and rivers in densely forested areas.

Nesting: in coniferous or deciduous tree or on utility pole; pair, occasionally assisted by others, builds large stick nest lined with fur and soft plant materials; female incubates 4–6 gray green to blue green eggs, blotched with brown and gray, for about 18 days.

Feeding: very opportunistic; feeds on carrion, small vertebrates, other birds' eggs and nestlings, berries, seeds, invertebrates and human food waste; also visits bird feeders.

Voice: distinctive, far-carrying, repetitive *caw-caw-caw*.

Similar Species: *Common Raven* (p. 105): larger; wedge-shaped tail; deeper and more variable calls; shaggy throat; heavier bill.

Best Sites: cities: Missoula, Helena, Billings, Kalispell.

COMMON RAVEN

Corvus corax

The Common Raven earns its reputation as a clever, daring bird, whether harassing a Golden Eagle, stealing food from a flock of gulls or executing tumbling aerobatic feats. Glorified in many cultures as a magical being, the raven does not act by instinct alone. This species has an immense vocal repertoire, and individuals are able to communicate complex information to each other using specific sounds. Whether "talking" to each other or playfully sliding down a snowbank on their backs, ravens exhibit behaviors that many people think of as exclusively human. • Common Ravens thrive in a variety of habitats, living on coastlines, in deserts, on mountains and in the bitter winter cold and darkness of the arctic tundra. It is a common resident throughout western Montana but is absent on the eastern plains. • Breeding ravens maintain lifelong pair bonds and endure together, for better or worse, everything from raising young to harsh weather and food scarcity.

ID: all-black plumage; heavy, black bill; shaggy throat; blunt-pointed wings; wedge-shaped tail; soars often.

Size: *L* 24 in; *W* 50 in. Male on average larger than female.

Status: common year-round.

Habitat: variety of habitats, from alpine tundra to forests to suburban garbage dumps; often in mountainous terrain; tends to avoid habitats occupied by crows, such as urban parks, farmyards and orchards; forages in some towns and cities, mainly on outskirts.

Nesting: on steep cliffs, ledges, bluffs, power poles and tall conifers; pair builds large stick nest lined with fur and soft plant materials; female incubates 4–6 brown-spotted, greenish eggs 18–21 days.

Feeding: opportunistic omnivore; feeds on carrion, small vertebrates, other birds' eggs and nestlings, berries, invertebrates and human food waste.

Voice: deep, far-carrying, croaking *crawwcraww* or *quork quork;* many other vocalizations; dependent juveniles contact adults with falsetto caricature of adult's croak (very familiar forest sound from mid-June to August).

Similar Species: *American Crow* (p. 104): smaller; fan-shaped tail; slim throat; slimmer bill; call is higher-pitched *caw;* never soars.

Best Sites: Mission Valley; Missoula (dump); Polson; Glacier NP; Helena.

HORNED LARK
Eremophila alpestris

The tinkling sound of Horned Larks flying over pastures and fields is a sure sign that another spring has arrived. The male performs an elaborate song-flight courtship display. Flying and gliding in circles as high as 800 feet, the male issues his sweet, tinkling song before closing his wings and plummeting in a dramatic, high-speed dive. He aborts the dive at the last second to avoid hitting the ground. • These open-country inhabitants are common year-round as they congregate in flocks on farm fields, beaches and airfields, often in the company of longspurs and Snow Buntings. Horned Larks are commonly found along the shoulders of gravel roads, where they search for seeds. These birds are easy to see but often tough to identify because they fly off into adjacent fields at the approach of any vehicle.

ID: *Male:* small black "horns" (rarely raised); black line under eye extends from bill to "cheek"; light yellow to white face; dull brown upperparts; black breast band; dark tail with white outer tail feathers; pale throat. *Female:* less distinctively patterned; duller plumage overall.

Size: *L* 7 in; *W* 12 in.

Status: common year-round.

Habitat: *Breeding:* open areas, including prairie, pastures, croplands, sparsely vegetated fields, weedy meadows and airfields. *In migration* and *winter:* croplands, fields and roadside ditches.

Nesting: on ground; female chooses nest site and lines shallow scrape with grass, plant fibers and roots; female incubates 3–4 pale gray to greenish white eggs, blotched and spotted with brown, for 10–12 days.

Feeding: gleans ground for seeds; feeds insects to young during breeding season.

Voice: call is tinkling *tsee-titi* or *zoot;* flight song is long series of tinkling, twittered whistles.

Similar Species: *Sparrows* (pp. 136–147): all lack distinctive facial pattern, "horns" and solid black breast band.

Best Sites: Freezout Lake WMA; Eureka; Blackfeet Indian Reservation; Benton Lake NWR; Bozeman; Bowdoin NWR.

TREE SWALLOW

Tachycineta bicolor

Tree Swallows are often seen perched beside nest boxes on fence posts. When conditions are favorable, these busy birds may return to their young 10 to 20 times each hour, providing observers with many opportunities to watch and photograph them in action. These swallows prefer to nest in natural tree hollows or woodpecker cavities in standing dead trees, but where cavities are scarce, nest boxes may be used as temporary sites. Increasingly, landowners, park managers and forestry companies are realizing the value of dead trees as homes for wildlife and are choosing to leave them standing. • The arrival of Tree Swallows in western Montana is one of the first signs of spring. These hardy birds usually begin to arrive in late March, when snow and ice are still present. • Unlike other North American swallows, female Tree Swallows do not acquire their full adult plumage until their second or third year.

ID: iridescent, dark blue or green head and upperparts; white underparts; no white behind eye; dark rump; small bill; long, pointed wings; shallowly forked tail. *Female:* slightly duller. *Immature:* brown above; white below.
Size: *L* 5½ in; *W* 14½ in.
Status: common from April to August.
Habitat: wide variety of lowland open areas, such as beaver ponds, marshes, lakeshores, field fencelines, townsites and open woodlands.
Nesting: mainly female lines tree cavity or nest box with weeds, grass and feathers; female incubates 4–6 white eggs up to 19 days.

Feeding: catches flies, midges, mosquitoes, beetles and flying ants on the wing; also takes stoneflies, mayflies and caddisflies over water; may eat some berries and seeds.
Voice: alarm call is metallic, buzzy *klweet*. *Male:* song is liquid, chattering twitter.
Similar Species: *Violet-green Swallow* (p. 108): white of face extends above eye; white on both sides of rump nearly meets in middle. *Bank Swallow* and *Northern Rough-winged Swallow:* brown upperparts with sharply demarcated breast band (Bank) or buffy throat (Northern Rough-winged). *Barn Swallow* (p. 110): obviously forked tail; buff orange to reddish brown throat. *Cliff Swallow* (p. 109): dark throat; pale forehead; pale rump.
Best Sites: Lee Metcalf NWR; Kalispell; Benton Lake NWR; Charles M. Russell NWR.

VIOLET-GREEN SWALLOW
Tachycineta thalassina

Their affinity for cliffs, open areas, natural tree cavities and nest boxes allows Violet-green Swallows to inhabit most of western Montana's diverse habitats. They often occupy cliffs that also support White-throated Swifts, and mixed foraging flocks of the two species are a common sight. • Swallows are swift and graceful fliers, routinely traveling at speeds of 30 miles per hour. Violet-greens are often distinguished by their habit of foraging at 1000 to 2000 feet, far higher than other swallows. • Swallows sometimes eat mineral-rich soil, eggshells and exposed shellfish fragments, possibly to recoup minerals lost during egg formation. In this way, nonliving minerals and ancient clam beds are slowly being recycled and incorporated into the living tissues of these birds. • The scientific descriptor *thalassina* is Latin for "sea green," in reference to this bird's body color.

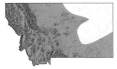

ID: two-toned, iridescent body plumage: greenish (back) and purplish (head); white on "cheek" extends behind and above eye; white patches on sides of rump; long, pointed wings; shallowly forked tail; small feet. *Female:* duller and more bronze than male; brownish face.
Size: L 5¼ in; W 13½ in.
Status: uncommon to locally common from April to September.
Habitat: wide variety of open areas with available cliffs, buildings, snags or boxes for nesting, including open forest, burns, wetlands, lakes, meadows, canyons, agricultural lands, mowed lawns and suburban parks; range up to elevations beyond timberline.

Nesting: semicolonial; mainly female builds nest of weeds, grass and feathers in tree cavity, cliff crevice, nest box or crack in building; female incubates 4–6 white eggs up to 15 days.
Feeding: catches flying insects, such as flies, flying ants and wasps; drinks on the wing by skimming water's surface; may forage overhead at limit of human vision.
Voice: exuberant, irregular chatter, *ch-ch-ch-ch-chairTEE, chairTEE-ch-ch;* call note sounds like telephone wire during high winds.
Similar Species: *Tree Swallow* (p. 107): lacks white above eye and on sides of rump; glossiness of upperparts uniform. *Bank Swallow* and *Northern Rough-winged Swallow:* brown upperparts; lack white behind eye. *Cliff Swallow* (p. 109): brown and blue upperparts; pale buffy rump; dark throat. *Barn Swallow* (p. 110): deeply forked tail; rusty throat. *Swifts* (p. 80): very thin, backswept wings.
Best Sites: Missoula; Kalispell; Glacier NP; Billings.

CLIFF SWALLOW

Petrochelidon pyrrhonota

Should the Cliff Swallow be renamed today, it would probably be called "Bridge Swallow," because so many bridges over North American rivers are home to a colony of these birds. If you stop to inspect the underside of a bridge, you may see hundreds of gourd-shaped mud nests stuck to the pillars and structural beams. Clouds of Cliff Swallows will often swirl up along either side of the roadway, dazzling passersby with their acrobatics and sheer numbers. • Cliff Swallows roll mud into balls with their bills and press the pellets together to form their characteristic nests. A brooding parent peers out of the circular neck of the nest, the bird's whitish "headlight" warning intruders that somebody is home. • Cliff Swallows are brood parasites—females often lay one or more eggs in the temporarily vacant nests of their neighbors. The Cliff Swallows who own the parasitized nests accept the foreign eggs and care for them as if they were their own. • These intelligent birds observe the feeding habits of their neighbors to find the best spots for foraging.

ID: sharply defined, whitish forehead patch; blue gray "cap," throat and wings; rusty "cheek"; buff breast and rump; white belly; spotted undertail coverts; nearly square tail.

Size: L 5½ in; W 13½ in.

Status: common from late April to August.

Habitat: bridges, steep banks, cliffs and buildings, often near watercourses.

Nesting: colonial; under bridge or on cliff or building; often under eaves of barn; pair builds gourd-shaped mud nest with small opening near base; pair incubates 4–5 brown-spotted, white to pinkish eggs 14–16 days.

Feeding: forages over water, fields and marshes; catches flying insects on the wing; occasionally eats berries; drinks on the wing by skimming water's surface.

Voice: twittering chatter, *churrr-churrr;* also an alarm call, *nyew.*

Similar Species: *Barn Swallow* (p. 110): deeply forked tail; dark rump; usually has rust-colored underparts and forehead. *Other swallows* (pp. 107–108): lack pale forehead and buff rump.

Best Sites: any bridge, especially over larger rivers.

BARN SWALLOW
Hirundo rustica

Although Barn Swallows do not occur in mass colonies, they are familiar birds because they usually build their nests on human-made structures. Barn Swallows once nested on cliffs and in entrances to caves, but their cup-shaped mud nests are now found under house eaves, in barns and boathouses, under bridges or on almost any other structure that provides shelter. • Not everyone appreciates nesting Barn Swallows—the waste around the nest can be very messy—and people often illegally scrape the nests off buildings just as the breeding season begins. However, these graceful birds are natural pest controllers, and their close association with urban areas and tolerance for human activity affords us a wonderful opportunity to observe the normally hidden reproductive cycle of birds. • "Swallow tail" has become used to describe something that is deeply forked. • *Hirundo* is Latin for "swallow," while *rustica* refers to this bird's preference for rural habitats.

ID: long, deeply forked tail; rufous throat and forehead; blue black upperparts; rust- to buff-colored underparts; long, pointed wings.
Size: *L* 7 in; *W* 15 in.
Status: fairly common from late April to August.
Habitat: open rural and urban areas where bridges, culverts or buildings are found near rivers, lakes, marshes or ponds.

Nesting: singly or in small, loose colonies; on vertical or horizontal building structure under suitable overhang, on bridge or in culvert; pair builds half or full cup nest of mud and grass or straw; pair incubates 4–7 brown-spotted, white eggs 13–17 days.
Feeding: catches flying insects on the wing.
Voice: continuous, twittering chatter, *zip-zip-zip;* also *kvick-kvick.*
Similar Species: *Cliff Swallow* (p. 109): squared tail; buff rump; pale forehead and underparts. *Tree Swallow* (p. 107): clean white underparts; notched tail.
Best Sites: Great Falls; Glacier NP; Medicine Lake NWR.

BLACK-CAPPED CHICKADEE

Poecile atricapillus

When cold weather comes, and most birds retreat into a slower mode of living or escape to warmer climes, the spunky Black-capped Chickadee reminds us that winter can never keep a good bird down. Flocks of energetic chickadees can be seen flitting from tree to tree, scouring branches and shriveled leaves for insects and sometimes hanging upside down to catch the fleeing bugs. • During migration and winter, many other species of birds join groups of chickadees to form mixed foraging flocks. Each chickadee in a winter flock knows its exact place in the complex hierarchy, a remarkable level of social sophistication. • Most songbirds, including the Black-capped Chickadee, have both songs and calls. The chickadee's *swee-tee* song is heard primarily during spring courtship, and its *chick-a-dee-dee-dee* call keeps flocks together and maintains contact among flock members year-round. • Black-capped Chickadees cache seeds and other food items, and the birds can remember where they've hidden thousands of these caches. • The scientific descriptor *atricapillus* is Latin for "black crown."

ID: black "cap" and "bib"; white "cheek"; gray back and wings; white underparts; light buff sides and flanks; dark legs; white edging on wing feathers.
Size: *L* 5–6 in; *W* 8 in.
Status: common to very common year-round.
Habitat: deciduous and mixed forests; riparian woodlands; wooded urban parks and backyards with bird feeders.
Nesting: pair excavates cavity in soft, rotting stump or tree and lines it with fur, feathers, moss, grass and cocoons; often uses birdhouse; female incubates 6–8 white eggs, finely dotted with reddish brown, for 12–13 days.
Feeding: gleans vegetation, branches and ground for small insects and spiders; visits backyard feeders; also eats conifer seeds and invertebrate eggs.
Voice: call is chipper, whistled *chick-a-dee-dee-dee;* song is slow, whistled *swee-tee* or *fee-bee.*
Similar Species: *Mountain Chickadee* (p. 112): similar but with white stripe above eye, smaller "bib" and much less buff in flanks.
Best Sites: nearly any wooded habitat; backyard feeders.

MOUNTAIN CHICKADEE
Poecile gambeli

This year-round resident of high-elevation forests spends much of its time feeding on seeds and insects high in a canopy of conifers. During winter, harsh weather can cause Mountain Chickadees to freeze or starve, and many move to lower elevations in search of higher temperatures and more abundant food. Townsites in the mountains offer excellent viewing opportunities in winter, especially at feeders—scan the flocks of chickadees and you will often find Mountain and Black-capped chickadees foraging together. These closely related species also occasionally interbreed, and some apparently pure Black-cappeds occasionally show a very faint "eyebrow." • The Mountain Chickadee breeds at higher elevations than most other chickadees. It routinely nests in subalpine conifers between 6000 and 8500 feet and is often seen foraging up to the treeline. • The scientific descriptor *gambeli* honors William Gambel, a 19th-century ornithologist who died of typhoid fever in the Sierra Nevada at the age of 28.

ID: white "eyebrow" through the black "cap"; white "cheek"; black "bib"; gray upperparts and tail; light gray underparts.

Size: *L* 5¼ in; *W* 8½ in.

Status: fairly common year-round.

Habitat: montane coniferous forests and lower portions of subalpine forests; irregular downslope flights to lowlands and foothills.

Nesting: in natural cavity or abandoned woodpecker nest; can excavate cavity in soft, rotting wood; lines nest with fur, feathers, moss and grass; incubates 5–9 usually unspotted, white eggs up to 14 days.

Feeding: gleans vegetation, branches and ground for small insects and spiders; visits backyard feeders for seeds; also eats conifer seeds and invertebrate eggs.

Voice: song is sweet, clear, whistled *fee-bee-bay* or *fee-bay;* call is drawling *chick a-day, day, day.*

Similar Species: *Black-capped Chickadee* (p. 111): lacks white "eyebrow"; buffy sides; faster, higher-pitched *chick-a-dee-dee* call.

Best Sites: Glacier NP; Red Lodge; Bitterroot Mountains; Bridger Range.

RED-BREASTED NUTHATCH

Sitta canadensis

The Red-breasted Nuthatch looks like a miniature red rocket as it streaks toward a bird feeder from the cover of a conifer. The nuthatch ejects empty shells left behind by other birds and then selects its own meal before speeding off, never lingering longer than the moment it takes to pick up a seed. • Red-breasted Nuthatches frequently join bird waves—groups of warblers, chickadees, kinglets and small woodpeckers that forage together through woodlands in winter or during migration. Nuthatches stand out from other songbirds because of their unusual body form and their habit of moving headfirst down tree trunks. Unlike woodpeckers and creepers, they do not hold their tails against the trunk. Also distinctive are their loud, nasal *yank-yank-yank* calls, frequently heard year-round. • This bird smears pine or spruce pitch at the entrance to its nesting cavity. This sticky doormat may prevent ants and other animals from entering the nest chamber. • *Sitta* means "nuthatch" in Greek, while *canadensis* refers to this bird's partially Canadian distribution.

ID: rusty underparts; gray blue upperparts; white "eyebrow"; black eye line; dark "cap"; straight bill; short tail; white "cheek." *Male:* deep rust on breast; black crown. *Female:* light red wash on breast; dark gray crown.

Size: *L* 4½ in; *W* 8½ in.

Status: common year-round.

Habitat: *Breeding:* spruce–fir and pine forests; mixed forests. *In migration* and *winter:* wide variety of woodlands, often near bird feeders.

Nesting: mainly female excavates cavity or uses abandoned woodpecker nest; usually smears entrance with pitch; nest lined with bark shreds, grass and fur; female incubates 5–6 white eggs, spotted with reddish brown, for about 12 days.

Feeding: moves down trees while probing under loose bark for larval and adult invertebrates; eats pine and spruce seeds in winter; often seen at feeders.

Voice: call is slow, continually repeated, nasal *eenk eenk eenk*, higher than the White-breasted Nuthatch's; also a short *tsip*.

Similar Species: *White-breasted Nuthatch:* larger; lacks black eye line and red underparts. *Black-capped Chickadee* (p. 111): black "bib"; short, stubby bill; lacks red breast.

Best Sites: hard to miss in any conifer forest in western Montana.

BROWN CREEPER

Certhia americana

The cryptic Brown Creeper is never easy to find. Inhabiting old-growth forests for much of the year, it often goes unnoticed until a flake of bark suddenly takes the shape of a bird. If a creeper is frightened, it will freeze and flatten itself against a tree trunk, becoming even more difficult to see. • The Brown Creeper feeds by slowly spiraling up a tree trunk, searching for hidden invertebrates. Its long, stiff tail feathers prop it up against the trunk as it hitches its way skyward. When it reaches the upper branches, the creeper floats down to the base of a neighboring tree to begin another foraging ascent. This behavior is unique to creepers and can be used as an aid to identification. • Like the call of the Golden-crowned Kinglet, the thin, whistled call note of the Brown Creeper is so high-pitched that many birders fail to hear it—and those who do often cannot locate it. To increase the confusion, the creeper often sings with a boisterous, warbling quality, rather like a wood-warbler. • There are many species of creepers in Europe and Asia, but the Brown Creeper is the only member of its family in North America.

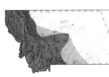

ID: brown back with buffy white streaks; white "eyebrow"; white underparts; downcurved bill; long, pointed tail feathers; rusty rump.

Size: *L* 5–5½ in; *W* 7½ in.

Status: uncommon year-round.

Habitat: old-growth coniferous and mixed forests, especially in moist cedar–hemlock forests of northwestern Montana. *In migration* and *winter:* also in lowland deciduous and mixed woodlands.

Nesting: under loose bark; mainly female builds nest of grass and conifer needles, woven together with spider silk; female incubates 5–6 whitish eggs, dotted with reddish brown, for 14–17 days.

Feeding: hops up tree trunks and large limbs, probing loose bark for adult and larval invertebrates; takes some nuts and seeds.

Voice: song is faint, high-pitched *trees-trees-trees see the trees;* call is high *tseee.*

Similar Species: behavior and brownish plumage unique.

Best Sites: Glacier NP (especially west of Continental Divide); Bigfork; Seeley Lake.

HOUSE WREN

Troglodytes aedon

The House Wren's bubbly song and energetic demeanor make it a welcome addition to any neighborhood. A small cavity in a standing dead tree or a custom-made nest box is usually all it takes to attract this joyful bird. Sometimes even an empty flowerpot or a vacant drainpipe is deemed a suitable nest site, provided there is a local abundance of insect prey. Occasionally, you may find that your nest site offering is packed full of twigs and left abandoned without any nesting birds in sight. Male wrens often build numerous nests, some of which later serve as decoys or "dummy" nests. • House Wrens puncture and remove eggs from many species' nests within their territories. Cavity nesters, including chickadees, Mountain Bluebirds and Tree Swallows, are vulnerable to these attacks. • House Wrens are Montana's least hardy wrens, generally leaving our state before the onset of cold weather.

ID: brown upperparts; fine, dark barring on upper wings and lower back; faint, pale "eyebrow" and eye ring; short, upraised tail finely barred with black; whitish throat; whitish to buff underparts; faintly barred flanks.
Size: *L* 4½–5 in; *W* 6 in.
Status: common from May to September.
Habitat: thickets and shrubby openings in or at edge of deciduous or mixed woodlands; often in shrubs and thickets near buildings.
Nesting: in natural cavity or abandoned woodpecker nest; also in nest box; pair builds nest of sticks and grass lined with feathers, fur and other soft materials; female incubates 6–8 white eggs, heavily dotted with reddish brown, for 12–15 days.
Feeding: gleans ground and vegetation for insects, especially beetles, caterpillars, grasshoppers and spiders.
Voice: song is smooth, running, bubbly warble, *tsi-tsi-tsi-tsi oodle-oodle-oodle-oodle*, lasting about 2–3 seconds.
Similar Species: *Winter Wren:* smaller; darker overall; shorter, stubby tail; prominent, dark barring on flanks. *Marsh Wren* (p. 116): marsh habitat only; prominent white "eyebrow"; black and white on back.
Best Sites: Missoula; Youngs Creek; Billings; Bozeman.

115

MARSH WREN
Cistothorus palustris

Fueled by newly emerged aquatic insects, the Marsh Wren zips about in short bursts through tall stands of cattails and bulrushes. This expert hunter catches flying insects with lightning speed, but don't expect to see it in action. The reclusive Marsh Wren prefers to remain hidden deep within its dense marshland habitat. A patient observer might be rewarded with a brief glimpse of the bird, but it is more likely that the distinctive song, reminiscent of an old-fashioned treadle sewing machine, will inform you of its presence. • The Marsh Wren occasionally destroys the nests and eggs of other Marsh Wrens and of other marsh-nesting songbirds such as the Red-winged Blackbird. Retribution is difficult for the other birds; the Marsh Wren's globe nest keeps the eggs well hidden, and several decoy nests help to divert predators from the real nest. • The scientific descriptor *palustris* is Latin for "marsh." This bird was formerly known as "Long-billed Marsh Wren."

ID: white "chin" and belly; upperparts mainly rufous except for white-streaked black triangle on upper back; bold, white "eyebrow"; unstreaked brown crown; long, thin, downcurved bill.
Size: *L* 5 in; *W* 6 in.
Status: common from April to October; some overwinter.
Habitat: large cattail and bulrush marshes; occasionally in tall grass and sedge marshes, especially in northeastern Montana.
Nesting: in marsh among cattails or other tall emergent vegetation; mainly male weaves globelike nest from cattails, bulrushes and grass and lines it with cattail down; female incubates 4–6 white to pale brown eggs, heavily dotted with dark brown, for 12–16 days.
Feeding: gleans vegetation for adult aquatic invertebrates; also eats contents of other birds' eggs.
Voice: call is harsh *chek. Male:* rapid, rattling, staccato warble sounds like an old-fashioned treadle sewing machine.
Similar Species: *House Wren* (p. 115): not in marshes; much fainter "eyebrow"; brown back.
Best Sites: Lee Metcalf NWR; Bowdoin NWR; Benton Lake NWR; Ninepipe NWR.

AMERICAN DIPPER
Cinclus mexicanus

The American Dipper is among the world's most unusual songbirds: it is aquatic. Along fast-flowing mountain waters, it stands on an exposed boulder, performing deep knee bends to the gurgle and roar of the raging torrent. Suddenly it plunges into the frigid water. Using its wings to "fly" underwater, it makes its way along the streambed of rocks and gravel in search of hidden aquatic insect larvae. Fitted with scaly nose plugs, strong claws, dense plumage, inner eyelids to protect against water spray, and an oil gland to waterproof its feathers, the American Dipper survives a lifetime of these ice-cold forays. • Naturalist John Muir wrote of the American Dipper (once called "Water Ouzel"): "Find a fall, or cascade, or rushing rapid…and there you will find the complementary Ouzel, flitting about in the spray, diving in foaming eddies, whirling like a leaf among beaten foam-bells; ever vigorous and enthusiastic, yet self-contained, and neither seeking nor shunning your company."

ID: slate gray plumage; head and neck darker than body; short tail; pinkish legs; straight, black bill; stout body; flashes whitish nictitating membrane (3rd eyelid). *Immature:* paler bill; paler underparts.
Size: *L* 7½ in; *W* 11 in. Male slightly larger than female.
Status: uncommon year-round.
Habitat: *Breeding:* swift, clear, cold permanent mountain streams with boulders and often waterfalls; subalpine tarns. *Winter:* also in larger, slower-flowing rivers and lowland lakes.

Nesting: built into rock ledge, overhang, uprooted tree or commonly underside of human-made bridge; female builds bulky globe nest of moss and grass; nest entrance faces water; female incubates 4–5 white eggs up to 17 days.
Feeding: wades or "flies" through water or plunges below surface for larval aquatic insects, fish fry and eggs.
Voice: vocal throughout year; warbled song is clear and melodious; alarm call is harsh *tzeet.*
Similar Species: none.
Best Sites: Sula Creek (especially in winter); Lolo Creek; Glacier NP; Kootenai Falls; Beartooth Mountains.

RUBY-CROWNED KINGLET
Regulus calendula

The loud, rolling song of the Ruby-crowned Kinglet is a familiar summertime melody that echoes through the coniferous montane forests of western Montana. The male kinglet erects his brilliant red crown and sings to impress prospective mates during courtship. Throughout most of the year, though, his crown remains hidden among dull gray feathers on his head and is impossible to see even through binoculars. • While in migration, Ruby-crowned Kinglets are regularly seen flitting among lowland trees and shrubs, intermingling with a colorful assortment of warblers and vireos, and emitting their characteristic scratchy *chh-chh* call. This bird might be mistaken for an *Empidonax* flycatcher, but the kinglet's constant action and foliage-gleaning behavior quickly set it apart from look-alikes. The wing-flicking typical of this species is thought to startle insects into movement, allowing the kinglet to spot them and pounce.

ID: bold, broken eye ring; 2 bold, white wing bars; olive green upperparts; dark wings and tail; whitish to yellowish underparts; short tail; flicks wings. *Male:* small, red crown (usually hidden). *Female:* lacks red crown.

Size: *L* 4 in; *W* 7½ in.

Status: common from April to September.

Habitat: mixed woodlands and pure coniferous forests, especially those dominated by spruce; often found near wet forest openings and edges.

Nesting: usually in spruce or hemlock; female builds hanging nest of moss, lichen, twigs and leaves and lines it with feathers, fur and plant down; female incubates 7–8 brown-spotted, whitish to pale buff eggs 13–14 days.

Feeding: gleans and hovers for insects and spiders; also eats seeds and berries.

Voice: *Male:* breeding song is accelerating and rising *tea-tea-tea-tew-tew-tew look-at-Me, look-at-Me, look-at-Me. Fall migration:* diagnostic soft, quick, double-noted *chh-chh.*

Similar Species: *Golden-crowned Kinglet:* year-round in conifers; dark "cheek"; black border around crown; male has orange and yellow crown; female has yellow crown. *Orange-crowned Warbler:* no eye ring or wing bars. Empidonax *flycatchers* (p. 92): do not foliage glean; complete eye ring or no eye ring at all; larger bill; longer tail; all lack red crown.

Best Sites: Glacier NP; Bigfork; Bozeman; Helena; Beartooth Mountains. *In migration:* Giant Springs SP.

MOUNTAIN BLUEBIRD

Sialia currucoides

The male Mountain Bluebird is like a piece of spring sky come to life. Few birds rival it for good looks, cheerful disposition and boldness, so it is not surprising that bluebirds are viewed as the "birds of happiness." For bluebirds, both good and bad have come from close association with humans. They have profited from forest clearing, ranching and erection of nest boxes, but have clearly suffered from fire suppression, manicuring of overgrown pastures and the introduction of aggressive European Starlings and House Sparrows, which usurp natural cavities for nesting. • The spring and fall migrations of the Mountain Bluebird generally consist of small groups of birds, but on occasion they migrate in flocks numbering more than 100.

ID: black eyes, bill and legs. *Male:* sky blue body; upperparts darker than underparts. *Female:* sky blue wings, tail and rump; blue gray back and head; gray underparts; generally lacks obvious rusty tones to underparts.

Size: *L* 7 in; *W* 14 in.

Status: locally common from March to September.

Habitat: open forests, forest edges, grasslands, agricultural areas and burned forests.

Nesting: in abandoned woodpecker cavity, other natural cavity or nest box; nest built of plant stems, grass, conifer needles and twigs and frequently lined with a few feathers; female incubates 5–6 pale blue eggs 13 days.

Feeding: swoops from perch, such as roadside fence or snag, to take flying and terrestrial insects; also forages on ground for variety of invertebrates, such as beetles and ants.

Voice: call is low *turr turr*. *Male:* song is short warble of *chur* notes.

Similar Species: *Western Bluebird:* male has rusty belly; female usually has rusty tones to underparts. *Eastern Bluebird:* male and female both have obvious rusty breast and flanks. *Townsend's Solitaire* (p. 120): longer and slimmer; not blue; peachy patches on wings and tail; white outer tail feathers.

Best Sites: Hot Springs; Choteau; East Front of Rockies; Red Rock Lakes NWR.

TOWNSEND'S SOLITAIRE
Myadestes townsendi

Few birds characterize the mountain forests of the West better than the Townsend's Solitaire. Slim and graceful, this bird makes up for its plain plumage with remarkable bursts of sustained song. It is an inconspicuous bird, perching for minutes at a time at the top of a tall tree or snag, or on the upturned roots of a fallen tree. From its perch, it flutters out to catch insects in midair or follows them to the ground and grasps them with a soft pounce reminiscent of a bluebird. Solitaires also have the unusual habit of picking fruit off trees while in flight. • During the winter months, Townsend's Solitaires cluster around berry-laden junipers and other fruit-bearing trees, especially in the foothills. Each bird fiercely defends its own territory on these feeding grounds. During the summer months, these birds are true to their name and are rarely seen in groups.

ID: gray body; darker wings and tail; peach-colored wing patches (very evident in flight); white eye ring; white outer tail feathers; long tail. *Immature:* brown body heavily spotted with buff; pale eye ring.
Size: *L* 8½ in; *W* 14½ in.
Status: fairly common year-round.
Habitat: wide variety of woodland habitats. *Breeding:* montane coniferous or mixed forest, often in burns or clearings. *In migration* and *winter:* lowland juniper, aspen or other woodlands, especially with fruit-bearing shrubs and trees.
Nesting: on ground, in bank or among upturned tree roots; cup nest built with twigs and grasses and well lined with conifer needles; 4 pale blue eggs, patterned with brown, are incubated up to 13 days.
Feeding: flycatches and gleans vegetation and ground for invertebrates and berries; plucks berries from branches while in flight.
Voice: call is loud, whistled *piink. Male:* song is long, bubbly warble.
Similar Species: *Gray Catbird* (p. 123): secretive habits; black "cap"; red undertail coverts. *Mountain Bluebird* (p. 119): female has faint rusty breast, pale blue wings with no peach stripe, and shorter, blue tail.
Best Sites: Beavertail Hill SP; Rogers Pass; Bozeman; Glacier NP. *Winter:* Mission Mountain foothills.

SWAINSON'S THRUSH

Catharus ustulatus

The upward spiral of this thrush's song lifts the soul of a listener with each rising note. The Swainson's Thrush is an integral part of the morning chorus, and its inspiring song is also heard at dusk. In fact, this bird is often the last of the forest singers to be silenced by nightfall. • Most thrushes feed on the ground, but the Swainson's Thrush is also adept at gleaning food from the airy heights of trees, sometimes briefly hover-gleaning like a warbler or vireo. • On its breeding grounds, the Swainson's Thrush is most often seen perched high in a treetop, cast in silhouette against the sky. In migration, this bird skulks low on the ground under shrubs and tangles, often finding itself in backyards and neighborhood parks it would never breed in. A wary bird, this thrush does not allow many viewing opportunities, and it often gives a sharp warning call from some distance. • William Swainson was an English zoologist and illustrator in the early 19th century. He is also the namesake for the Swainson's Hawk.

ID: gray brown upperparts; noticeable buff eye ring; buff wash on "cheek" and upper breast; spots arranged in streaks on throat and breast; tail same color as back; brownish gray flanks.
Size: *L* 7 in; *W* 12 in.
Status: common from mid-May to September.
Habitat: edges and openings of coniferous and mixed boreal forests; prefers moist areas with spruce and fir. *In migration:* variety of forested and open shrubby areas, parks and backyards.
Nesting: usually in shrub or small tree; female builds small cup nest of grass, moss, leaves, roots and lichen and lines it with fur and soft fibers; female incubates 3–4 pale blue eggs, with brown spots toward the larger end, for 12–14 days.
Feeding: gleans vegetation and forages on ground for invertebrates; also eats berries.
Voice: song is slow, rolling, rising spiral, *Oh, Aurelia, will-ya, will-ya will-yeee;* call is sharp *wick.*
Similar Species: *Hermit Thrush:* higher elevations when breeding; song spirals downward; reddish tail and rump contrast with brown back; lacks buff coloration to eye ring and breast. *Veery:* upperparts, including tail, are brighter reddish; very faint breast spotting.
Best Sites: Bigfork; Rattlesnake NRA; Glacier NP. *In migration:* Giant Springs SP; Westby.

AMERICAN ROBIN

Turdus migratorius

American Robins are widely recognized harbingers of spring, often arriving in numbers in early March. However, in certain years many hundreds of these hardy thrushes will overwinter, feasting upon mountain-ash berries and waiting out the intense Montana winter. Robins are probably the most ubiquitous birds in our state, found in an incredible diversity of habitats ranging from manicured lawns to alpine meadows. They are believed to be the most numerous of all North American birds. • A hunting robin may appear to be listening for prey, but it is actually looking for movements in the soil—it tilts its head because its eyes are on the sides of its head. • The American Robin was named by English colonists after the Robin *(Erithacus rubecula)* of their native land. The two species look and behave similarly, even though they are only distantly related. The American Robin's closest European relative is, in fact, the Blackbird *(T. merula)*, which is identical in all aspects except plumage.

ID: gray brown back; dark head; white throat streaked with black; white undertail coverts; incomplete white eye ring; black-tipped yellow bill. *Male:* deep brick red breast; black head. *Female:* dark gray head; light red orange breast. *Juvenile:* heavily spotted breast.

Size: *L* 10 in; *W* 17 in.

Status: abundant from March to October; large numbers overwinter in some years.

Habitat: generalist; residential lawns and gardens, pastures, urban parks, broken forests, riparian zones, alpine and sub-alpine meadows.

Nesting: in tree or shrub; mainly female builds sturdy cup nest of grass, moss and loose bark cemented with mud; female incubates 4 light blue eggs 11–16 days; may raise up to 3 broods each year in some areas.

Feeding: forages on ground and among vegetation for larval and adult insects, earthworms, other invertebrates and berries.

Voice: song is evenly spaced warble, *cheerily cheer-up cheerio*; call is rapid *tut-tut-tut*.

Similar Species: *Varied Thrush:* found in dense coniferous forest; black breast band; 2 orange wing bars.

Best Sites: difficult to miss almost anywhere.

GRAY CATBIRD

Dumetella carolinensis

True to its name, the Gray Catbird has a call that sounds like a mewing cat—but it spoils the effect by adding phrases that sound like a rusty gate hinge and by mimicking other birds. This bird is often far easier to hear than to see, because it prefers to remain in the underbrush and in dense riparian shrubs. • The Gray Catbird's courtship activities involve an unusual "mooning" display in which the male raises his long, slender tail to show off his red undertail coverts. As if proud of his red posterior, the male sometimes looks back over his shoulder during the performance. • Gray Catbirds vigorously defend their nesting territories. They are so thorough in chasing away intruders that the nesting success of neighboring warblers and sparrows increases as a result of their vigilance. Even if a cowbird sneaks past a watchful female catbird, the foreign egg is immediately recognized and ejected. • *Dumetella* is Latin for "small thicket"; it is an appropriate genus name for a bird that inhabits dense tangles.

ID: dark gray overall; black "cap" and tail; red undertail coverts; black eyes, bill and legs; long tail.

Size: *L* 8½ in; *W* 11 in.

Status: fairly common from mid-May to September.

Habitat: dense thickets and shrublands, riparian shrubs.

Nesting: in dense shrub or thicket; bulky cup nest loosely built with twigs, leaves and grass and lined with fine materials; female incubates 4 blue eggs up to 15 days.

Feeding: forages on ground and in vegetation for wide variety of ants, beetles, grasshoppers, caterpillars, moths and spiders; also eats berries and visits feeders.

Voice: call is cat-like *meoow;* song is of variable warbles, usually in pairs, often interspersed with mimicry of other species.

Similar Species: *Gray Jay* (p. 99): in high-elevation conifers only; lacks black "cap" and red undertail coverts.

Best Sites: Youngs Creek; Miles City; Bozeman; Pine Butte Swamp Preserve.

BROWN THRASHER
Toxostoma rufum

Amid the chirps and warbles that rise from eastern Montana's hedgerows in spring and early summer, the song of the male Brown Thrasher stands alone. Its lengthy, complex chorus of twice-repeated phrases is truly unique. This thrasher has the most extensive vocal repertoire of any North American bird, with as many as 3000 distinctive combinations of phrases. • Despite its relatively large size, the Brown Thrasher generally goes unnoticed in its shrubby domain. A typical sighting consists of a flash of rufous as it zips from one tangle to another. • Because the Brown Thrasher nests on or close to the ground, its eggs and nestlings are vulnerable to predation by snakes, weasels, skunks and other animals. Even though the birds are aggressive and vigilant nest defenders, their spirited attacks, sometimes to the point of drawing blood, are not always enough to protect their progeny. • Unlike other notable singers, such as the shrub-dwelling Gray Catbird, the Brown Thrasher prefers to live well away from urban areas.

ID: reddish brown upperparts; pale underparts with heavy brown streaking; long, slender, downcurved bill; yellow orange eyes; long, rufous tail; yellow legs; 2 white wing bars.

Size: *L* 11½ in; *W* 13 in.

Status: locally common from May to September.

Habitat: dense shrubs and thickets, overgrown pastures (especially with hawthorns), woodland edges and rural villages.

Nesting: usually in low shrub; often on the ground; pair builds cup nest of grass, twigs and leaves and lines it with fine vegetation; pair incubates 4 bluish white to pale blue eggs, dotted with reddish brown, for 11–14 days.

Feeding: gleans ground and vegetation for larval and adult invertebrates; occasionally tosses leaves aside with bill; also eats seeds and berries.

Voice: sings large variety of phrases, with each phrase usually repeated twice: *dig-it dig-it, hoe-it hoe-it, pull-it-up pull-it-up;* calls include loud crackling note, harsh *shuck*, soft *churr* and whistled, 3-note *pit-cher-ee*.

Similar Species: Catharus *thrushes—Hermit Thrush, Swainson's Thrush* (p. 121), *Veery:* much shorter tail; gray brown back and crown; dark brown eyes; much shorter bill; lack wing bars. *Sage Thrasher:* sagebrush habitat; gray brown upperparts.

Best Sites: Havre; Westby; Medicine Lake NWR; Bowdoin NWR; Miles City.

EUROPEAN STARLING

Sturnus vulgaris

The European Starling was introduced to North America in 1890 and 1891. About 100 birds were released into New York's Central Park as part of the local Shakespeare society's plan to introduce all the birds mentioned in their favorite author's writings. The European Starling quickly established itself in the New York landscape, then spread rapidly across the continent, often at the expense of native cavity nesters, such as Tree Swallows and bluebirds. Despite concerted efforts to control or even eradicate this species in its nonnative landscape, the European Starling has conquered our continent and is found from Alaska to Baja California to Florida, and everywhere between. The more than 200 million individuals present in North America today are believed to have sprung from those first 100 birds. • Courting European Starlings are infamous for their ability to reproduce the sounds of other birds, such as Killdeers, Red-tailed Hawks, Soras and Western Meadowlarks.

breeding

ID: only all-black bird with yellow bill; short, squared tail; dark eyes. *Breeding:* blackish, iridescent plumage; yellow bill. *Nonbreeding:* blackish wings; feather tips heavily spotted with white and buff. *Immature:* gray brown plumage; brown bill. *In flight:* pointed, triangular wings.
Size: *L* 8½ in; *W* 16 in.
Status: common to abundant year-round.
Habitat: agricultural areas, townsites, woodland and forest edges, landfills and roadsides.
Nesting: in cavity, such as old woodpecker cavity or nest box; pair builds nest of grass, twigs and straw; mostly female incubates 4–6 bluish to greenish white eggs 12–14 days.
Feeding: forages mostly on ground; diverse diet includes many invertebrates, berries, seeds and human food waste.
Voice: variety of whistles, squeaks and gurgles; imitates other birds.
Similar Species: *Brewer's Blackbird* (p. 152): longer tail; black bill; lacks spotting; male has yellow eyes; female is brown overall. *Brown-headed Cowbird* (p. 154): dark and much shorter bill; lacks spotting; adult male has brown head; juvenile has streaked underparts. *Red-winged Blackbird* (p. 149): lacks yellow bill; female and immature have white-streaked underparts.
Best Sites: most cities.

CEDAR WAXWING
Bombycilla cedrorum

Flocks of handsome Cedar Waxwings gorge on berries during late summer and fall. Waxwings can digest a remarkable variety of berries, some of which are inedible or even poisonous to humans. If the fruits have fermented, these birds show definite signs of tipsiness. • Native berry-producing trees and shrubs planted in your backyard can attract Cedar Waxwings and will often encourage them to nest in your area. Cedar Waxwings are late nesters, which ensures that berries will be ripe when nestlings are ready to be fed. • Cedar Waxwing pairs perform a wonderful courtship ritual. The male first lands slightly away from the female, then tentatively hops toward her and offers her a berry. The female accepts the berry and hops away from the male, then stops, hops back and offers him the berry. This gentle exchange can last for several minutes. • The Cedar Waxwing is the waxwing of summer in Montana, but in winter the Bohemian Waxwing, a similar species from the north, dominates. Practiced observers learn to recognize the Cedar Waxwing by its high-pitched, lispy calls and white undertail coverts.

ID: "smooth" appearance to plumage; cinnamon crest; brown upper-parts; black "mask"; yellow wash on belly; gray rump; yellow-tipped tail; white undertail coverts; small red "drops" on wings. *Juvenile:* no "mask"; streaked underparts; gray brown body.
Size: *L* 7 in; *W* 12 in.
Status: fairly common from April to October; variable numbers overwinter.
Habitat: wooded parks and gardens, over-grown fields, forest edges, second-growth, riparian and open woodlands.
Nesting: in tree or shrub; pair builds cup nest of twigs, grass, moss and lichen and lines it with fine grass; female incubates

3–5 pale gray to bluish gray eggs, with fine dark spotting, for 12–16 days.
Feeding: catches flying insects on the wing or gleans vegetation; also eats large amounts of wild fruit, especially in fall and winter.
Voice: faint, high-pitched, trilled whistle, *tseee-tseee-tseee;* has no song.
Similar Species: *Bohemian Waxwing:* winter only; larger; chestnut undertail coverts; yellow markings on wing, in addition to red and white; rattling quality to call.
Best Sites: Red Rock Lakes NWR; Missoula; Madison River.

YELLOW WARBLER

Dendroica petechia

Yellow Warblers usually arrive in mid-May in search of invertebrates. Flitting from branch to branch, these inquisitive birds seem to be in perpetual motion. • Yellow Warblers are frequent targets of attempted nest parasitism by Brown-headed Cowbirds. Unlike many birds, these warblers recognize the foreign eggs and many pairs either abandon their nest or build another nest overtop the old eggs. Some persistent Yellow Warblers build over and over, creating bizarre, multilayered, high-rise nests. • Before departing our state in September, adults molt nearly all their feathers on the breeding grounds. Some individuals lose so many flight feathers at once that they become nearly flightless, requiring them to retreat into dense thickets where they are rarely noticed. • Because of their bright yellow plumage, Yellow Warblers are often mistakenly called "Wild Canaries."

♀

breeding ♂

ID: thin, insect-eating bill; bright yellow body; yellowish legs; black bill and eyes; bright yellow highlights on dark yellowish olive tail and wings. *Breeding male:* red breast streaks. *Breeding female:* faint, or no, red breast streaks. *Juvenile:* plain yellowish overall; wing coverts and tail feathers have yellow edgings.
Size: *L* 5 in; *W* 8 in.
Status: common from mid-May to September.
Habitat: *Breeding:* riparian thickets, cattail marshes. *In migration:* moist, open woodlands with dense, low scrub; also shrubby meadows, willow tangles, shrubby fencerows and riparian woodlands.
Nesting: in fork in deciduous tree or small shrub; female builds compact cup nest of grass, weeds and shredded bark and lines it

with plant down and fur; female incubates 4–5 speckled or spotted, greenish white eggs 11–12 days.
Feeding: gleans foliage and vegetation for invertebrates, especially caterpillars, inch-worms, beetles, aphids and cankerworms; occasionally hover-gleans.
Voice: calls include bright, sharp *chip* and high, thin, buzzy *zeep*. *Male:* song is fast, frequently repeated *sweet-sweet-sweet summer sweet.*
Similar Species: *Orange-crowned Warbler:* darker olive plumage overall; lacks reddish breast streaks. *American Goldfinch* (p. 162): thick, seed-eating bill; black wings and tail; male often has black forehead. *Wilson's Warbler* (p. 134): shorter, darker tail; male has black "cap"; female and immature lack yellow-edged wing coverts and tail feathers. *Common Yellowthroat* (p. 133): under-parts not entirely yellow; female and immature lack yellow edgings to wing coverts and tail feathers.
Best Sites: nearly any shrubby, riparian habitat.

YELLOW-RUMPED WARBLER
Dendroica coronata

The common and widespread Yellow-rumped Warbler is often affectionately called "Butterbutt." During the breeding season, it is found mainly in montane coniferous forests of western Montana, but during migration large numbers are found throughout the state in diverse habitats. This species is the dominant migrant warbler across Montana from August to October. • Two races of the Yellow-rumped Warbler were once considered separate species—the yellow-throated western race, formerly called "Audubon's Warbler," and the white-throated eastern race, formerly called "Myrtle Warbler." Only Audubon's Warblers breed in Montana; Myrtle Warblers are migrants mainly in eastern parts of the state.

♀

"Audubon's" breeding

♂

ID: yellow foreshoulder patches and rump; white underparts; faint white wing bars; thin "eyebrow." *Male:* yellow crown; blue gray upperparts with black streaking; black breast and streaking along sides and flanks. *Female:* gray brown upperparts with dark streaking; dark streaking on breast, sides and flanks. *Audubon's:* yellow throat. *Myrtle:* white throat and sharply defined blackish "cheek."
Size: *L* 5–6 in; *W* 9 in.
Status: *Audubon's:* common from mid-April to October; rarer eastward. *Myrtle:* uncommon to rare from April to May and September to November; rarer westward; generally earlier in spring and later in fall than Audubon's.
Habitat: *Breeding:* montane coniferous and mixed forests; rarely in pure deciduous woodlands. *In migration:* wide variety of woodlands and shrubby areas at lower elevations.
Nesting: in conifer; female builds compact cup nest of grass, bark strips, moss, lichen

and spider silk and lines it with feathers and fur; female incubates 4–5 creamy white eggs, marked with brown and gray, about 12 days.
Feeding: hawks and hovers for insects; gleans vegetation; sometimes eats berries.
Voice: call is sharp *chip* or *check,* noticeably "puckier" in Myrtle. *Male:* song is tinkling trill, often in variable 2-note phrases that rise or fall at end.
Similar Species: obvious yellow rump unique. *Townsend's Warbler* (p. 129): much yellower in face; obvious white wingbars. *Common Yellowthroat* (p. 133): low, skulking habits; lacks yellow rump and dark streaking on breast.
Best Sites: *Breeding:* Glacier NP; Beartooth Mountains; Missoula; Helena; Bozeman. *In migration:* Giant Springs SP; Lee Metcalf NWR; Westby.

TOWNSEND'S WARBLER

Dendroica townsendi

The combination of rich yellows and greens against a black and white backdrop distinguishes the Townsend's Warbler from Montana's other songbirds. Catching a sight of this stunning beauty is something not soon forgotten by anybody lucky enough to see one up close. • Conifer crowns are preferred foraging sites for Townsend's Warblers, making watching the birds a neck-straining experience. These often "underlooked" birds are much more easily located by their distinctive song: a variable series of soft, wheezy notes. • This species is quite common in old-growth montane conifer forests, especially in wet forests with a cedar component. Townsend's Warblers prefer unbroken, mature forest and may decrease in response to logging. • Sometimes a female Townsend's Warbler begins to build a nest in one tree, then changes her mind and moves all materials to another tree, where she finishes the nest. • This bird bears the name of one of the West's pioneer ornithologists, John Kirk Townsend.

breeding

♂

♀

ID: yellow breast and sides streaked with black; white lower belly and undertail coverts; yellow face with distinct dark ear patch behind eye; olive greenish upperparts; 2 white wing bars. *Male:* black "chin," throat and crown. *Female:* yellow "chin" and throat; white upper belly; dusky crown and ear patch.
Size: *L* 5 in; *W* 8 in.
Status: common from May to September.
Habitat: *Breeding:* montane conifer or mixed forest, especially in moist settings with western redcedar or hemlock; also uses fir and pine, occasionally in drier settings. *In migration:* wide variety of lowland woodlands and tangles.
Nesting: in crotch or on horizontal limb in conifer; pair builds compact cup nest of grass, moss, lichen and spider silk; female incubates 4–5 brown-marked, white eggs 12 days.
Feeding: gleans vegetation and flycatches for insects.
Voice: male's song, heard in May and June, is wheezy, ascending and variable; call is incisive, electronic *tzp*.
Similar Species: yellow face with blackish ear patch distinctive.
Best Sites: Glacier NP; Missoula; Bigfork; Troy.

129

AMERICAN REDSTART

Setophaga ruticilla

The American Redstart is a consistent favorite among birders. This super-charged bird flits from branch to branch in dizzying pursuit of prey. Even when it perches, its tail sways rhythmically back and forth. Few birds can rival a mature male redstart for appeal, with his contrasting black and orange plumage and amusing behavior. • A common foraging technique used by the American Redstart is to flash its wings and tail patches to flush prey. If a concealed insect tries to flee, the redstart will give chase. The American Redstart behaves much the same way on its Central American wintering grounds, where it is known locally as *candelita*, meaning "little candle." • Although redstarts are common on the northern Great Plains, their beautiful, trilly songs are so variable that identifying the bird by sound is a challenge even for experienced birders. A good rule of thumb is that when an unfamiliar warbler song trips you up, it will usually turn out to be a redstart's.

ID: *Male:* black overall; red orange foreshoulder and wing and tail patches; white belly and undertail coverts. *Female:* olive brown upperparts; gray green head; yellow foreshoulder and wing and tail patches; clean white underparts.
Size: *L* 5 in; *W* 8 in.
Status: fairly common from May to early September.
Habitat: second-growth riparian corridors, shrubby woodland edges, open and semi-open deciduous and mixed forests with regenerating deciduous understory of shrubs and saplings; often near water.
Nesting: in fork of shrub or sapling, usually 3–23 ft above ground; female builds open cup nest of plant down, bark shreds, grass and rootlets and lines it with feathers; female incubates 4 whitish eggs, marked with brown or gray, for 11–12 days.
Feeding: hawks for insects and gleans for insects and spiders on leaves, buds and branches; often hover-gleans.
Voice: male's song is highly variable series of *tseet* or *zee* notes, often given at different pitches; call is sharp, sweet *chip*.
Similar Species: none.
Best Sites: Bitterroot River; Swan River; Glacier NP; Two Moon Park (Billings).

OVENBIRD

Seiurus aurocapilla

The Ovenbird's loud and joyous "ode to teachers" is a distinctive sound that echoes through deciduous forests in spring: *tea-cher! tea-cher! tea-CHER! tea-CHER!* What may sound like one long-winded Ovenbird may actually be two neighboring males responding on the heels of each other's songs. Unfortunately, pinpointing the exact location of the resonating call is not always easy. An Ovenbird rarely exposes itself, and even when it does, active, patient searching is necessary to get a good look at it. • Though very common in the eastern United States, Ovenbirds are uncommon in Montana, where they are rather patchily distributed east of the Rockies. • The name "Ovenbird" refers to this bird's unusual, dome-shaped ground nest. • Robert Frost was so moved by the Ovenbird's spring songs, he dedicated a poem to them fittingly entitled "Ovenbird."

ID: olive brown upperparts; white eye ring; heavy, dark streaking on white breast, sides and flanks; rufous crown has black border; pink legs; white undertail coverts; no wing bars.
Size: *L* 6 in; *W* 9½ in.
Status: uncommon from May to September.
Habitat: *Breeding:* cottonwood gallery forest, aspen stands, mixed and coniferous forests with closed canopy and substantial leaf litter; often in ravines and riparian areas. *In migration:* city parks, dense riparian shrubbery and various woodlands.
Nesting: on ground; female builds oven-shaped, domed nest of grass, weeds, bark, twigs and dead leaves and lines it with animal hair; female incubates 4–5 white eggs, spotted with gray and brown, for 11–13 days.
Feeding: gleans ground for worms, snails, insects and occasionally seeds.
Voice: loud, distinctive *tea-cher tea-cher tea-CHER tea-CHER*, increasing in speed and volume; night song is elaborate series of bubbly, warbled notes, often ending in *teacher-teacher;* call is brisk *chip, cheep* or *chock.*
Similar Species: *Northern Waterthrush* (p. 132): bold, yellowish or white "eyebrow"; darker upperparts; lacks rufous crown. *Catharus thrushes* (p. 121): all larger and lack rufous crown outlined in black; much less spotting on belly.
Best Sites: *Breeding:* Charles M. Russell NWR; Alzada; Miles City. *In migration:* Westby.

NORTHERN WATERTHRUSH

Seiurus noveboracensis

Although this bird's long body looks thrushlike, the Northern Waterthrush is actually a wood-warbler. • Birders who are not satisfied with simply hearing a Northern Waterthrush in its nesting territory must get their feet wet if they hope to see one. This bird skulks along the shores of deciduous swamps or coniferous watercourses, where fallen logs, shrubby tangles and soggy ground discourage many human visitors. During the relatively bug-free months in spring and fall, migrating Northern Waterthrushes appear in drier, upland forests or along lofty park trails and boardwalks. Backyards featuring small garden ponds may also attract migrating waterthrushes. • The voice of the Northern Waterthrush is loud and raucous for such a small bird. It seems fitting, therefore, that this bird was once known as "New York Warbler," in reference to a city so well known for its decibels. The scientific descriptor *noveboracensis* means "of New York."

ID: pale yellowish to white "eyebrow"; pale yellowish to white underparts with dark streaking; finely spotted throat; olive brown upperparts; pinkish legs; frequently bobs tail.

Size: *L* 5–6 in; *W* 9½ in.

Status: uncommon from May to early September.

Habitat: wooded edges of swamps, lakes, beaver ponds and rivers; also in moist, wooded ravines and riparian thickets.

Nesting: on ground, usually near water; female builds cup nest of moss, leaves, bark shreds, twigs and pine needles and lines it with moss, hair and rootlets; female incubates 4–5 whitish eggs, spotted and blotched with brown and purplish gray, for about 13 days.

Feeding: gleans foliage and ground for invertebrates, frequently tossing aside ground litter with bill; may also take aquatic invertebrates and small fish from shallow water.

Voice: song is loud, emphatic 3-part *sweet sweet sweet, swee wee wee, chew chew chew chew;* call is brisk *chip* or *chuck.*

Similar Species: *Ovenbird* (p. 131): rufous crown bordered by black stripes; white eye ring; unspotted throat; lacks pale "eyebrow."

Best Sites: Red Lodge; Glacier NP; Madison River south of Ennis.

COMMON YELLOWTHROAT

Geothlypis trichas

This energetic songster of our wetlands is a favorite among birders. It is one of our most common warblers, even though its nests are commonly parasitized by Brown-headed Cowbirds. • The Common Yellowthroat favors shrubby marshes and wet, overgrown meadows, shunning the forest habitat preferred by most of its wood-warbler relatives. In May and June, the male yellowthroat issues his distinctive *wichity-witchity-witchity* songs while perched atop tall cattails or shrubs. Observing a male in action will reveal the location of his favorite singing perches, which he visits in rotation. These strategic outposts mark the boundary of his territory, which is fiercely guarded from intrusion by other males.

ID: yellow throat, breast and undertail coverts; dingy white belly; olive green to olive brown upperparts; orangy legs. *Breeding male:* broad, black "mask" with white upper border. *Female:* no "mask"; yellow throat contrasts with dusky face.
Size: *L* 5 in; *W* 6½ in.
Status: common from mid-May to September.
Habitat: cattail marshes, riparian willow and alder clumps, sedge wetlands, beaver ponds and wet overgrown meadows; sometimes dry, abandoned fields, especially during migration.
Nesting: on or near ground, often in small shrub or among emergent aquatic vegetation; female builds bulky, open cup nest of weeds, grass, sedges and other materials and lines it with hair and soft plant fibers; female incubates 3–5 creamy white eggs, spotted with brown and black, for 12 days.
Feeding: gleans vegetation and hovers for adult and larval insects and spiders; occasionally eats seeds.

Voice: song is clear, oscillating *witchity witchity witchity-witch;* call is sharp *tcheck* or *tchet.*
Similar Species: male's black "mask" is distinctive. *Yellow Warbler* (p. 127): female and immature are brighter yellow overall; yellow edgings on wing coverts and tail feathers; entirely yellow underparts. *Wilson's Warbler* (p. 134): female and immature lack sharp demarcation of yellow throat and dusky "cheek"; forehead, "eyebrow" and "cheek" are as bright as yellow underparts; may show dark "cap." *Orange-crowned Warbler:* dull yellow olive overall; faint breast streaks. *Nashville Warbler:* bold, complete eye ring; blue gray crown.
Best Sites: Lee Metcalf NWR; Ninepipe NWR; Pine Butte Swamp Preserve; Benton Lake NWR; Red Rock Lakes NWR; Bowdoin NWR.

WILSON'S WARBLER

Wilsonia pusilla

One of Montana's commoner warbler migrants, the petite Wilson's Warbler darts energetically through the undergrowth in its tireless search for insects. Fueled by its energy-rich prey, this indefatigable bird seems to behave as if a motionless moment would break some unwritten law of warblerdom. • Breeding occurs solely in higher-elevation riparian thickets of western Montana, so birders on the plains are forced to go without this beauty during the breeding season. Shrubs still laden with heavy spring snow often greet Wilson's Warblers arriving in their sub-alpine breeding grounds at the beginning of May. • This bird is appropriately named, epitomizing the energetic devotion that ornithologist Alexander Wilson exhibited in his pioneering studies of North American birds.

ID: yellow underparts; yellowish green upperparts; large, beady eyes; thin, black bill; frail orange legs. *Breeding male:* black "cap." *Female:* "cap" is faint, partial or absent.

Size: *L* 4½–5 in; *W* 7 in.

Status: common from May to September.

Habitat: cool, moist riparian habitat with dense deciduous shrub cover, especially streamside thickets of willow and alder; also uses wet mountain meadows and edges of small lakes and springs.

Nesting: sunken into soft ground, or in low shrub or thicket; female builds neat cup nest of moss, grass and leaves, occasionally lined with fine grass; female incubates 4–6 brown-spotted, whitish eggs 10–13 days.

Feeding: gleans vegetation; hovers and catches insects on the wing; eats mostly adult and larval invertebrates.

Voice: song is loud, staccato chatter that accelerates toward end: *chi chi chi chi chi chi chet chet;* call is soft, brittle *chet.*

Similar Species: male's black "cap" is distinctive. *Yellow Warbler* (p. 127): crown and back as bright as underparts; wing coverts and tail feathers edged in yellow; male has red breast streaks. *Common Yellowthroat* (p. 133): female has dark face and broken white eye ring; lacks bright yellow belly and sides. *Orange-crowned Warbler:* faint breast streaks; darker face; not as intensely yellow below.

Best Sites: National Bison Range; Glacier NP; Therriault Lakes; Beartooth Mountains.

WESTERN TANAGER

Piranga ludoviciana

Few Montana birds match the splendor of a gold, black and red male Western Tanager. These birds are tropical denizens for most of the year; they fly to Montana for only a few short months to raise a new generation on the seasonal explosion of food in our forests. Their exotic colors remind us of the ecological ties between Montana's coniferous forests and Latin American rainforests. • The somewhat robinlike song of the male tanager can be difficult to learn. The tanager's phrases tend to be hoarser, however, as if the bird has a sore throat, and the song ends with a distinctive, hiccuplike *tick-a-tuck*, which can also be given alone. • Late in summer, the young of the year migrate to higher elevations. There they molt their body feathers amidst a late-season burst of insect life. Most adults, on the other hand, migrate to the American Southwest for their molt, and are rarely seen after early August. • "Tanager" comes from *tangara*, the Tupi name for this group of birds in the Amazon basin.

breeding

ID: *Breeding male:* yellow underparts and rump; one yellow and one white wing bar; black back, wings and tail; often has red on forehead or entire head (variable); pale bill. *Breeding female:* olive green overall, with lighter underparts and darker upperparts; obvious yellow wing bars.
Size: *L* 7 in; *W* 11½ in.
Status: common from May to early September.
Habitat: *Breeding:* variety of foothill and mountain forests and woodlands; generally tall conifers (especially Douglas-fir). *In migration:* almost any stand of trees, no matter how small or isolated.

Nesting: in fork or on horizontal branch of conifer, placed well out from trunk; cup nest is loosely built of twigs, grass and other plant materials and lined with fine vegetation; female incubates 4 bluish, brown-spotted eggs 13–14 days.
Feeding: gleans vegetation for insects and catches flying insects on the wing; also eats fruit; drinks from ground.
Voice: song sounds like American Robin with sore throat: hoarse, rapid series of dry 2- or 3-note phrases; call is distinctive, quick *tick-a-tuck*.
Similar Species: male distinctive. *Bullock's Oriole* (p. 155): female has thinner, sharper, all-dark bill and lacks all-yellow underparts.
Best Sites: Glacier NP; Bigfork; Missoula; Beartooth Mountains.

GREEN-TAILED TOWHEE

Pipilo chlorurus

Green-tailed Towhees are birds of arid scrub habitats in southcentral parts of our state. Green-tails can be common summer birds of hillsides and foothills, while remaining entirely unknown in the nearby valleys. The birds spend most of their lives concealed in shrubby undergrowth, industriously scratching away debris with both feet in their search for insects and hidden seeds. If a threat is presented, they will unwillingly flush or run from cover, giving an annoyed mewing call. • The male Green-tailed Towhee normally emerges only in spring, when he sings clear, whistled notes and raspy trills from an exposed woody perch. • Green-tailed Towhees often join up with White-crowned Sparrows during their fall migration to Mexican wintering grounds. • *Pipilo* is derived from a Latin word meaning "to twitter"; *chlorurus* means "green tail."

ID: orange rufous crown; green upperparts, most intense on tail; white throat bordered by dark stripe and white stripe; sooty gray face and breast; gray legs; conical, gray bill. *Immature:* brownish overall; streaked upperparts and underparts; pale throat bordered by dark stripe and white stripe.

Size: *L* 6½–7 in; *W* 9¾ in.

Status: uncommon from late May to September.

Habitat: arid, shrubby hillsides featuring sagebrush, juniper or other well-spaced trees and shrubs; also found in dense, low thickets.

Nesting: on ground or very low in bush; deep, bulky, thick-walled cup nest of twigs, grass and bark shreds is lined with fine materials; female incubates 3–4 darkly spotted, white eggs 11 days; female will run from nest in advance of human intrusion.

Feeding: scratches ground for insects, seeds and berries; drinks morning dew from leaves.

Voice: song is clear, whistled notes followed by squealing, raspy trills: *swee-too weet chur cheee-churr;* call is distinctive, nasal *mew.*

Similar Species: green wings and rusty "cap" distinctive.

Best Sites: Bear Canyon (Pryor Mountains); Mt. Helena; Red Lodge.

SPOTTED TOWHEE

Pipilo maculatus

Where dried leaves form a crunchy carpet beneath a thicket, you might encounter the Spotted Towhee. Like the Green-tailed Towhee, this large sparrow is a noisy forager that scratches at loose leaf litter by kicking with both feet. In fact, this bird is sometimes so noisy that you might expect an animal of sasquatch proportions to be the source of the ruckus. • Spotted Towhees rarely leave their subarboreal world, except to perform their simple courtship song or to furtively eye a threat to their territory. These shy birds can often be enticed into view by "squeaking" or "pishing," noises that draw curious birds to the intrusion. Discerning birders, however, prefer not to disturb these busy birds, and instead enjoy simply listening to their clamorous exploits. • Until recently, the Spotted Towhee was grouped together with the Eastern Towhee (a "spotless" eastern bird) as one species, known as "Rufous-sided Towhee."

ID: *Male:* red eyes; black "hood," back, wings and tail; rufous flanks; dark, conical bill; bold white spotting on wings; white tail "corners"; white belly and undertail. *Female:* somewhat drabber and paler. *Juvenile:* seen briefly in July and August; brown overall, heavily streaked on upperparts and underparts; white tail "corners." **Size:** L 7–8½ in; W 9¾ in.
Status: common from April to September; rare in winter at feeders.
Habitat: riparian thickets, brushy ravines and hillsides, scrubby patches among open woodlands; shady canyons; thick undergrowth in suburban parks and gardens.
Nesting: low in bush, on ground under cover or in brushy pile; female builds cup nest of leaves, grass and bark shreds and lines it with fine materials; primarily female incubates 3–4 brown-spotted, off-white eggs 12–13 days.

Feeding: scratches ground vigorously for seeds and insects; visits feeding stations periodically; seldom feeds in trees.
Voice: song is 0 to several introductory notes followed by trill: *here here here PLEASE* or just *PLEASE;* call is low-pitched, whining *chee* or *chwaay,* usually up-slurred.
Similar Species: *Black-headed Grosbeak:* often in trees; stockier; much heavier bill; lacks red eyes; rufous wraps around back of male's neck; female has white in face. *Dark-eyed Junco* (p. 145): smaller; "Oregon" race has pale rufous on back and sides; yellow bill; dark eyes.
Best Sites: Missoula; Bozeman; Helena; Youngs Creek; Billings.

CHIPPING SPARROW
Spizella passerina

The Chipping Sparrow and Dark-eyed Junco do not share the same tailor, but they must attend the same voice lessons. Their songs are so similar, some ornithologists think the two species may actually defend territories against each other. The rapid trill of the Chipping Sparrow tends to be slightly faster, drier and less musical than the junco's, but even experienced birders can have difficulty telling them apart. • Chipping Sparrows commonly nest at eye level, so you can easily watch their breeding and nest-building rituals. They prefer conifers for nesting and often use hair to line the nest. By planting conifers in your backyard and offering samples of your pet's hair—or even your own— in backyard baskets in spring, you may attract nesting Chipping Sparrows to your area and contribute to their nesting success. • "Chipping" describes this small, fairly tame sparrow's call.

breeding

ID: *Breeding:* prominent rufous "cap"; white "eyebrow"; black eye line; light gray, unstreaked underparts. *Nonbreeding:* paler crown with dark streaks; dark lores; brown "eyebrow," "cheek" and "mustache"; pale lower mandible.
Size: *L* 5–6 in; *W* 8½ in.
Status: very common from May to September.
Habitat: wide variety of dry woodlands; open mature conifers or mixed woodland edges, usually with shrub component; burns; yards and gardens with tree and shrub borders.
Nesting: usually at midlevel in coniferous tree; female builds compact cup nest of woven grass and rootlets, often lined with hair; female incubates 4 pale blue eggs 11–12 days.

Feeding: gleans seeds from ground and from outer branches of trees or shrubs; prefers seeds of grass, dandelions and clovers; also eats adult and larval invertebrates; occasionally visits feeders.
Voice: song is rapid, dry trill of *chip* notes; call is high-pitched *chip.*
Similar Species: *Clay-colored Sparrow* (p. 139): resembles nonbreeding Chipping but has pale lores, more contrasting, colorful face pattern and obvious pale central crown stripe. *Brewer's Sparrow:* sagebrush only; very similar to nonbreeding Chipping but with pale lores, less obvious "mustache" stripe. *American Tree Sparrow:* winter only; dark central breast spot. *Field Sparrow:* eastern Montana only; lacks dark striping on face; rufous stripe extends behind eye; orangy pink bill; lacks bold white "eyebrow."
Best Sites: Missoula; Bozeman; Pryor Mountains; Glacier NP.

CLAY-COLORED SPARROW

Spizella pallida

For the most part, Clay-colored Sparrows go completely unnoticed, thanks to their cryptic plumage and voice. Even when males are singing at the top of their lungs, they are usually mistaken for buzzing insects, actually a valuable field mark. • Although subtle in plumage, the Clay-colored Sparrow still possesses an unassuming beauty. Birders looking closely at this sparrow to confirm its identity can easily appreciate its delicate shading, texture and form—features so often overlooked in birds with more colorful plumage. • Often found in shrubby grassland or sagebrush, Clay-colored Sparrows will tag along with migrant and wintering Chipping Sparrows and show up in a variety of open-ground habitats. The very similar Brewer's Sparrow, restricted to sagebrush, is found with the Clay-colored Sparrow in some parts of the state, and the two species are known to hybridize.

breeding

ID: unstreaked, white underparts; buff breast wash; gray nape; light brown "cheek," edged with darker brown; brown crown with dark streaks and pale central stripe; white "eyebrow"; white jaw stripe is bordered with brown; white throat; mostly pale bill. *Juvenile:* pale lores; dark streaks on buff breast, sides and flanks.
Size: *L* 5–6 in; *W* 7½ in.
Status: common from May to September.
Habitat: brushy open areas, sagebrush, lightly grazed fields, regenerating burn sites, riparian thickets.

Nesting: in grassy tuft or small shrub; female builds open cup nest of twigs, grass, weeds and rootlets and lines it with rootlets, fine grass and fur; mostly female incubates 4 brown-speckled, bluish green eggs 10–12 days.
Feeding: forages for seeds and insects on ground and in low vegetation.
Voice: song is series of 2–5 slow, low-pitched, insectlike buzzes; call is soft *chip*.
Similar Species: *Brewer's Sparrow:* extremely similar in all plumages; crown lacks obvious white central stripe; less contrasting facial markings; varied song. *Chipping Sparrow* (p. 138): nonbreeding birds very similar to Clay-colored, but with dark lores and weaker dark "mustache" stripe below eye.
Best Sites: Freezout Lake WMA; Pine Butte Swamp Preserve; Medicine Lake NWR; Blackfeet Indian Reservation.

VESPER SPARROW

Pooecetes gramineus

For birders who live near grassy fields with multitudes of confusing little brown sparrows, the Vesper Sparrow offers welcome relief. White outer tail feathers and a chestnut shoulder patch announce its identity, especially when the bird is in flight. The Vesper Sparrow is also known for its bold and easily distinguished song, which begins with one or two sets of unforgettable double notes: *here-here! there-there!* • The Vesper Sparrow is a common sight along Montana's roadsides, where it is often seen perched on fencelines and telephone wires. • "Vesper" is Latin for "evening," a time when this bird often sings. *Pooecetes* is Greek for "grass dweller"; the Vesper Sparrow often nests in a grassy hollow.

ID: chestnut shoulder patch (often not visible at rest); white outer tail feathers; complete white eye ring; breast streaking that often coalesces into obvious central spot; pale pink legs and bill.
Size: *L* 6 in; *W* 10 in.
Status: common from late April to September.
Habitat: open fields bordered or interspersed with shrubs; sagebrush; also in agricultural areas and on roadsides.
Nesting: in scrape on ground, often under canopy of grass or at base of shrub; loosely woven cup nest of grass is lined with rootlets, fine grass and hair; mostly female incubates 3–5 whitish to greenish white eggs, blotched with brown and gray, for 11–13 days.

Feeding: walks and runs along ground, picking up grasshoppers, beetles, cutworms, other invertebrates and seeds.
Voice: song begins with 1–2 pairs of distinctive introductory notes: *here-here there-there*, followed by a bubbly trill.
Similar Species: *Savannah Sparrow* (p. 142), *Song Sparrow* (p. 143) and female *Lark Bunting* (p. 141): share streaks or central spot on breast but lack combination of white outer tail feathers and chestnut shoulder patch. *Lark Sparrow:* white tail "corners," not sides; unstreaked breast with central spot; harlequin face pattern; lacks chestnut wing patch. *American Pipit:* thinner bill; grayer upperparts without brown streaking; lacks chestnut shoulder patch. *Lapland Longspur:* blackish or buff wash on upper breast; nonbreeders have broad, pale "eyebrow" and reddish edging on wing feathers.
Best Sites: Freezout Lake WMA; National Bison Range; Pine Butte Swamp Preserve.

LARK BUNTING

Calamospiza melanocorys

Wherever there are grasslands or hayfields within the Lark Bunting's range, you will have a good chance of seeing the male's spectacular courtship flight. As he rises into the air, he flutters about in circles above the prairie, beating his wings slowly and deeply. His bell-like, tinkling song spreads over the landscape until he folds his wings and floats to the ground like a falling leaf. Because the Lark Bunting's courtship behavior evolved before the arrival of fence posts and power poles on which to perch, the bird delivers its song on the wing. • Lark Buntings vary greatly in number from year to year, apparently in response to moisture levels and prevailing habitat conditions. In drought years, it breeds farther north than usual and becomes one of the most conspicuous and abundant birds on the Great Plains. It breeds in native short- and mixed-grass prairies and hayfields, as well as in roadside ditches, and in certain areas it is a common sight along roads. • Despite its name, the Lark Bunting is actually a sparrow. It bears no close relation with the other species sharing its surname.

♂

breeding

ID: dark, conical bill; white patch at tip of tail. *Breeding male:* black plumage; bright white wing patch. *Female:* mottled brown upperparts; very bold lateral throat stripe; heavily streaked underparts; pale "eyebrow"; obvious white-edged inner wing in flight. **Size:** *L* 7 in; *W* 10½ in.
Status: variably uncommon to common from year to year, from May to early September.
Habitat: short-grass and mixed-grass prairie, sagebrush, hayfields, grassy ditches, lightly grazed pastures.

Nesting: on ground, sheltered by canopy of grass or by small bush; cup nest loosely built with grass, roots and other plant material and lined with plant down and fur; mostly female incubates 4–5 pale blue eggs 11–12 days.
Feeding: walks or hops along ground collecting insects, seeds and waste grain.
Voice: rich and warbling, with clear notes.
Similar Species: *Savannah Sparrow* (p. 142), *Song Sparrow* (p. 143), *Lark Sparrow:* distinguished from female Lark Bunting by lack of white wing patch and lack of very contrasty lateral throat stripe. *Bobolink:* male has creamy nape, white rump and back patches.
Best Sites: Bowdoin NWR; Charles M. Russell NWR; Molt; Medicine Lake NWR.

SAVANNAH SPARROW

Passerculus sandwichensis

The Savannah Sparrow is one of the most common open-country birds. Most people have probably seen or heard one, although they may not have been aware of it. With its streaky, dull brown and white plumage, this bird resembles so many other grassland sparrows that it is easily overlooked. • From early spring to early summer, male Savannah Sparrows belt out their distinctive buzzy tunes while perched atop prominent shrubs, tall weeds or strategic fence posts. A useful mnemonic for their oft-heard, ethereal song is *I'm a spaaaaaar-ow*. Later in summer and throughout early fall, these birds are most often seen darting across roads and open fields in search of food. However, except when singing, Savannahs generally stay out of sight. When danger appears, they take flight only as a last resort, preferring to run swiftly and inconspicuously through the grass, almost like feathered voles. • The common and scientific names of this bird reflect its broad North American distribution: "Savannah" refers to the city in Georgia, while *sandwichensis* refers to Sandwich Bay in the Aleutian Islands.

Nesting: on ground in shallow scrape well concealed by grass or shrub; female builds open cup nest woven from and lined with grass; female incubates 3–6 brown-marked, whitish to greenish or pale tan eggs 10–13 days.

Feeding: gleans insects and seeds while walking or running along ground; occasionally scratches.

Voice: song is high-pitched, buzzy *tea tea teeeeea*, or *I'm a spaaaaaarow;* call is high, thin *tsit*.

ID: the quintessential "little brown job": mottled brown upperparts; heavily streaked breast with dark central spot; heavily streaked sides and flanks; yellowish lores and "eyebrow."

Size: *L* 5–6 in; *W* 6½ in.

Status: very common from mid-April to early October.

Habitat: agricultural fields (especially hay and alfalfa), short- and mixed-grass prairie, moist grassy meadows, pastures.

Similar Species: *Vesper Sparrow* (p. 140): white outer tail feathers; chestnut shoulder patch. *Grasshopper Sparrow:* unstreaked breast. *Song Sparrow* (p. 143): frequents denser habitats including some forests and swamps; lacks yellow lores; more rufous on wing coverts.

Best Sites: Freezout Lake WMA; Pine Butte Swamp Preserve; Bowdoin NWR; Red Rock Lakes NWR; Bozeman.

SONG SPARROW

Melospiza melodia

The Song Sparrow's low-key plumage doesn't prepare you for its symphonic song. This well-named sparrow is known for the complexity, rhythm and emotion of its springtime rhapsodies, and for being one of our earliest songbirds to begin singing each spring. • Young Song Sparrows and many other songbirds learn to sing by eavesdropping on their fathers or on rival males. By the time a young male is a few months old, he will have formed the basis for his own courtship tune. • Most songbirds are lucky if they are able to produce one brood per year. Song Sparrows, by contrast, successfully raise two broods in our region in most years. • Some 31 different subspecies of the Song Sparrow range from pale desert birds to larger, darker Alaskan forms.

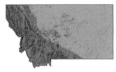

ID: whitish underparts with heavy brown streaking that converges into central breast spot; grayish face, especially the "eyebrow"; dark line behind eye; white jaw stripe is bordered by dark "mustache" stripe and lateral throat stripe; dark crown with pale central stripe; mottled brown upperparts; rounded tail tip.
Size: *L* 5½–7 in; *W* 8½ in.
Status: very common from March to October; some overwinter.
Habitat: shrubby areas, often near water: willow shrublands, riparian thickets, forest openings, streamsides, marshes and wet pastures.
Nesting: usually on ground or low in shrub or small tree; female builds open cup nest of grass, weeds, leaves and bark shreds and lines it with rootlets, fine grass and hair; female incubates 3–5 greenish white eggs, heavily spotted with reddish brown, for 12–14 days; may raise 2–3 broods each summer.
Feeding: gleans ground, shrubs and trees for invertebrates and seeds; also eats wild fruit and visits feeders.
Voice: song is 1–4 bright, distinctive introductory notes, such as *sweet, sweet, sweet*, followed by variable sequence of buzzy notes and trills; calls include short *tsip* and nasal *tchep*.
Similar Species: *Fox Sparrow:* heavier breast spotting and streaking; lacks pale, central crown stripe and dark "mustache"; reddish rather than dark brownish streaking and upperparts. *Lincoln's Sparrow:* thinner streaks on breast and flanks; buff wash to breast and side of throat. *Savannah Sparrow* (p. 142): lightly streaked breast; yellow lores; notched tail; lacks grayish face and dark, triangular "mustache."
Best Sites: Lee Metcalf NWR; Ninepipe NWR; Pine Butte Swamp Preserve; Red Rock Lakes NWR; Bozeman; Helena.

WHITE-CROWNED SPARROW
Zonotrichia leucophrys

Large, bold and smartly patterned, White-crowned Sparrows brighten many high-elevation brushy expanses and wet meadows in summer with varied songs. During migration, these birds become different creatures altogether, favoring backyard feeders and hedgerows. Large flocks of these sprites can be found flitting between shrubs, picking seeds from leaf litter and sounding their surprisingly loud, high-pitched *seep* notes. • Several White-crowned Sparrow races have been identified, at least three of which occur in Montana. Research on this species has given us tremendous insight into bird physiology, molting, homing behavior and the geographic variability of song dialects. • The word *Zonotrichia* is Greek for "band" and "hair," a reference to the White-crowned Sparrow's head pattern.

ID: bold black and white head stripes; orange pink bill; gray face; gray unstreaked underparts; streaked brown back. *Immature:* head stripes are brown and gray, not black and white.
Size: *L* 5½–7 in; *W* 9½ in.
Status: common from mid-April to early October; very rare in winter.
Habitat: *Breeding:* usually above 4000 ft; wet shrubby meadows, stunted montane forest, thickets. *In migration:* lower-elevation woodlots, parkland edges, brushy tangles and riparian thickets; may be in open, weedy fields, lawns and roadsides with juncos and other sparrows.

Nesting: usually in shrub, in small coniferous tree or on ground; female weaves neat cup nest of twigs, grass, leaves and bark shreds and lines it with fine materials; female incubates 3–5 darkly marked, blue green eggs 11–14 days.
Feeding: scratches ground to expose insects and seeds; also eats berries, buds and moss caps; visits bird feeders.
Voice: song is highly variable mix of bright whistles, slurs and churring trills (many regional dialects are recognized by ornithologists); call is hard *pink* or high *seep*.
Similar Species: *White-throated Sparrow:* yellow in front of and above eye; never shows black and white head stripes without yellow.
Best Sites: *Breeding:* Logan Pass (Glacier NP); Red Rock Lakes NWR; Beartooth Mountains; Pine Butte Swamp Preserve. *In migration:* backyard feeders.

DARK-EYED JUNCO

Junco hyemalis

In winter, juncos often congregate in backyards with bird feeders and sheltering conifers. But in the summer, these familiar little birds forsake the comfort of feeder handouts for montane conifer forests. • Juncos spend most of their time on the ground, and they are readily flushed from wooded trails and backyard feeders. Their distinctive white outer tail feathers flash in alarm as they seek cover in a nearby tree or shrub. • Juncos rarely perch at feeders, preferring to snatch up seeds that are knocked to the ground by other visitors, such as chickadees, sparrows, nuthatches and jays. • In 1973, the American Ornithologists' Union grouped five junco species into a single species, the Dark-eyed Junco. No fewer than four recognizable forms of the species occur in Montana (Oregon, Pink-sided, Slate-colored and White-winged). It is not uncommon to see three types at your winter feeder simultaneously.

"Oregon Junco"

"Slate-colored Junco"

ID: white outer tail feathers; pale bill. *Male:* dark slate gray overall, except for white lower breast, belly and undertail coverts; certain forms have orange or buff in flanks and back. *Female:* brown rather than gray.
Size: *L* 5½–7 in; *W* 9½ in.
Status: common year-round.
Habitat: *Breeding:* coniferous and mixed forests and edges, young pine stands, burned areas and shrubby regenerating clearings. *In migration* and *winter:* shrubby woodland borders; also backyard feeders.
Nesting: usually on ground, often with overhanging canopy, or low in shrub or small tree; mainly female weaves deep cup nest of grass, bark strips and roots and lines it with fine materials and fur; female incubates 3–5 dark-spotted, whitish eggs 12–13 days.
Feeding: scratches ground for invertebrates; also eats berries and seeds.
Voice: song is long, dry trill, very similar to that of Chipping Sparrow, but usually slower and more musical; call is smacking *chip* note, often given in series.
Similar Species: *Spotted Towhee* (p. 137): larger; white-spotted wings; rufous sides; red eyes; grayish bill; white tail corners, not sides.
Best Sites: Glacier NP; Missoula; Butte; Bigfork; Ekalaka (White-winged form).

CHESTNUT-COLLARED LONGSPUR

Calcarius ornatus

When spring comes, in areas where the dry smell of stale prairie dust hangs in the breeze, cock your ear for the tinkling song of the Chestnut-collared Longspur. The colorful males can be seen in flight or atop boulders, shrubs or fence posts that rise out of the dancing waves of grass. The male Chestnut-collared Longspur is the most colorful of the grassland sparrows—it is gaudily marked compared with the dull plumage typical of its neighbors. • The Chestnut-collared Longspur was one of the most abundant birds on the Great Plains before the plow arrived and altered the landscape. Now it is found mainly in areas that have escaped cultivation, or where natural grassland has regenerated. • Longspurs are so named because they have an extremely long hind claw.

breeding

ID: *Breeding male:* chestnut nape; black underparts; yellow throat; black "cap"; white "eyebrow"; mottled brown upperparts; white outer tail feathers; black central tail feathers; white undertail coverts. *Breeding female:* might show chestnut nape; mottled brown overall; light breast streaks.
Size: *L* 6 in; *W* 10½ in.
Status: locally common from April to September.
Habitat: mixed-grass prairie, lightly grazed pastures, reclaimed cultivated fields; short-grass prairie not usually tolerated; also avoids overly shrubby areas.
Nesting: well concealed by grass in depression or scrape; small cup nest woven of grass and lined with feathers and fur; female incubates 3–5 brown-spotted, white eggs 10–13 days.

Feeding: gleans ground for plant seeds and invertebrates.
Voice: song is musical warble rather reminiscent of Western Meadowlark's, given mainly by male in display flight; call notes include hiccuped *deedle,* staccato rattle and quick, down-slurred whistle, *phew.*
Similar Species: breeding male is distinctive; female and immature much drabber, but all have white on sides of tail, obvious in flight. *McCown's Longspur:* short-grass prairie habitat; more white in tail outlines black, inverted "T" on upper surface of tail; male has gray face and rufous wing patch; female has hint of chestnut in wing. *Vesper Sparrow* (p. 140): much less white in tail, thin strip on outer 2 feathers only; chestnut wing patch; more white in face. *Savannah Sparrow* (p. 142): lacks white outer tail feathers.
Best Sites: Benton Lake NWR; Chester; Medicine Lake NWR; Westby.

SNOW BUNTING

Plectrophenax nivalis

When flocks of Snow Buntings descend on Montana in late fall, their startling black and white plumage flashes in contrast to the snowy backdrop. It may seem strange that Snow Buntings are whiter in summer than in winter, but the darker winter plumage may help these birds absorb heat on clear, cold days. Birders may also be surprised to learn that the crisp summer plumage is actually just the dark winter plumage in an abraded state, not a new set of feathers. • Snow Buntings venture farther north than any other songbird in the world. A single individual, likely lost, was recorded not far from the North Pole in May 1987. • In winter, Snow Buntings prefer expansive areas, including grainfields and pastures, where they scratch and peck at exposed seeds and grains. They also ingest small grains of sand or gravel from roadsides as a source of minerals and to help digestion. • Snow Buntings are definitely cold-weather songbirds, often bathing in snow in early spring, and burrowing into it during bitter cold snaps to stay warm.

nonbreeding

Status: uncommon to locally common from October to March.

Habitat: manured fields, feedlots, pastures, grassy meadows, lakeshores, roadsides and railroads.

Nesting: does not nest in Montana.

Feeding: gleans ground and snow for seeds and waste grain; also takes insects when available.

Voice: fast, short, musical rattle; calls include whistled *tew* and dry, raspy *bjjjj*.

Similar Species: *Lapland Longspur:* brown, sparrow-like; white outer tail feathers; lacks black and white wing pattern.

Best Sites: Eureka; Benton Lake NWR; Fort Peck.

ID: black and white wings and tail; white underparts. *Nonbreeding male:* yellowish bill; golden brown crown, "cheek," side of breast and rump; dark-streaked, golden brown back. *Nonbreeding female:* similar to nonbreeding male but with blackish forecrown, less white on wings in flight.

Size: *L* 6–7½ in; *W* 14 in.

LAZULI BUNTING

Passerina amoena

Lazuli Buntings nest in open shrubby country throughout Montana, but they are most abundant in western parts of the state. Males set up territorial districts in which neighboring males copy and learn their songs from one another, producing "song territories." Each male within a song territory sings with slight differences in the syllables, producing his own acoustic fingerprint. • Ornithologists have only recently discovered that, before leaving our state in late summer, Lazuli Buntings undergo an incomplete molt of certain body feathers. They then fly to the American Southwest and northwestern Mexico to complete their change of wardrobe during the short-lived "Mexican monsoon" of late summer. • This bird is named after the colorful gemstone lapis lazuli. The generally accepted pronunciation of the name is "LAZZ-you-lie," but personal variations are plentiful. The scientific descriptor *amoena* is from the Latin for "charming," "delightful" or "dressy," all of which this bird certainly is.

and lines it with finer grass and hair; female incubates 3–5 bluish white eggs 12 days.

Feeding: gleans ground and low shrubs for grasshoppers, beetles, other insects and native seeds; visits feeders.

ID: stout, conical bill. *Male:* turquoise blue hood and rump; chestnut breast; white belly; dark wings and tail; 2 white wing bars. *Female:* soft brown overall; hints of blue on rump.

Size: *L* 5½; *W* 8¾ in.

Status: common from May to August.

Habitat: open brushy areas, forest edges, riparian thickets, young burns, hedges and willow and alder shrublands.

Nesting: in upright crotch low in shrubby tangle; female weaves small cup of grass

Voice: song a variable series of wiry, piercing notes, *swip-swip-swip zu zu ee, see see sip see see;* call a strong, dry *chip*.

Similar Species: *Western Bluebird:* male is larger, has slimmer bill and lacks wing bars. *Clay-colored Sparrow* (p. 139), *Chipping Sparrow* (p. 138), *Brewer's Sparrow, American Tree Sparrow:* all lack body streaking and so are easily confused with drab female bunting, but note bunting's unpatterned face and blue-tinged rump and tail.

Best Sites: Mt. Sentinel (Missoula); Bozeman; Miles City.

RED-WINGED BLACKBIRD
Agelaius phoeniceus

For many birders, the definitive sound of spring is that of Red-winged Blackbirds staking out territory at a nearby wetland. The small flocks that may last through the winter break apart as individuals strive to claim the best corner of the marsh. • The male's bright red epaulets and short, raspy song are key tools in the often intricate strategy he employs to defend his territory. A flashy, richly voiced male who has established a large and productive territory can attract several mates to his cattail kingdom. In field experiments, males whose red shoulders were painted black soon lost their territories to rivals they had previously defeated. • After the male has wooed the female, she starts the busy work of weaving a nest amid the cattails. Cryptic coloration allows the female to sit inconspicuously upon her nest. • *Agelaius* is a Greek word meaning "flocking," accurately describing the winter flocks these birds form. The descriptor *phoeniceus* is a reference to the color red; a red dye was introduced to the Greeks by the ancient Phoenicians.

ID: *Male:* all black, except for large red shoulder patch edged in yellow (occasionally concealed). *Female:* heavily streaked underparts; mottled brown upperparts; faint red shoulder patch; light "eyebrow."
Size: *L* 7–9½ in; *W* 13 in. Male on average larger than female.
Status: common to abundant from March to November. Small flocks overwinter, usually near wetlands or agricultural fields.
Habitat: cattail marshes, wet meadows and ditches, croplands and shoreline shrubs; sometimes uses dry shrubby fields.
Nesting: colonial; in cattails or shoreline bushes; female weaves an open cup nest of dried cattail leaves and grass and lines it with fine grass; female incubates 3–4 darkly marked, pale blue green eggs 10–12 days.

Feeding: gleans ground for seeds, waste grain and invertebrates; also gleans vegetation for seeds, insects and berries; occasionally flycatches; may visit feeders.
Voice: song a loud, raspy *konk-a-ree* or *ogle-reeeee;* calls include a harsh *check* and a high *tseert;* female may give a loud *che-che-che chee chee chee.*
Similar Species: male is distinctive when shoulder patch shows. *Brewer's Blackbird* (p. 152): female lacks streaked underparts. *Brown-headed Cowbird* (p. 154): juvenile is smaller and paler brown and has stubbier, conical bill.
Best Sites: almost any cattail wetland.

WESTERN MEADOWLARK

Sturnella neglecta

The brightly colored Western Meadowlark is one of the most abundant and widely distributed birds in the western United States. It is also one of the most popular—the Western Meadowlark is the state bird in Montana and five other states. • Birders are encouraged to exercise extreme caution when walking through meadowlark nesting habitat. The grassy, domed nests are difficult to locate and are so well concealed that they are often accidentally crushed before they are seen. • The Western Meadowlark bears a striking resemblance to the Yellow-throated Longclaw of Africa, a completely unrelated species that lives in similar habitats. Scientists refer to this situation as convergent evolution, and many a biology student has been introduced to the concept by way of these species. • The Western Meadowlark was overlooked by members of the Lewis and Clark expedition, who mistakenly thought it was the same species as the Eastern Meadowlark, found east of Montana. This oversight is represented in the scientific descriptor *neglecta*.

breeding

ID: yellow underparts; broad, black breast band; mottled brown upperparts; short, wide tail with white outer tail feathers; long, pinkish legs; yellow lores; brown crown stripes and eye line bordering pale "eyebrow" and median crown stripe; dark streaking on white sides and flanks; long, sharp bill; yellow on throat extends onto lower "cheek."
Size: *L* 9–9½ in; *W* 14½ in. Male on average larger than female.
Status: common from April to early October; small numbers overwinter.
Habitat: grassy meadows and pastures, sagebrush, mixed-grass prairie; also some croplands, weedy fields and roadsides.

Nesting: in depression or scrape on ground, concealed by dense grass or rarely low shrubs; female weaves domed grass nest into surrounding vegetation; nest has side entrance; female incubates 3–7 white eggs, heavily spotted with brown and purple, for 13–15 days.
Feeding: gleans grasshoppers, crickets, other insects and spiders from ground and vegetation; extracts grubs and worms by probing bill into soil; also eats seeds.
Voice: commonly heard song a startlingly loud, rich, melodic series of bubbly, flute-like notes; calls include low, loud *chuck* or *chup*, rattling flight call or a few clear, whistled notes.
Similar Species: none.
Best Sites: easily found in shrubby grasslands, often on roadside fences.

YELLOW-HEADED BLACKBIRD

Xanthocephalus xanthocephalus

You might expect the handsome Yellow-headed Blackbird to have a song as splendid as its gold and black plumage. Unfortunately, a trip to an inhabited wetland will quickly reveal the shocking truth: when the male arches his golden head backward, he produces only a painful, pathetic grinding noise. Although the "song" of the Yellow-headed Blackbird might be the worst in North America, it soon becomes a familiar and appreciated aspect of this bird's marshy home. • A large cattail marsh is often highlighted by the presence of male Yellow-headed Blackbirds perched high atop the plants like candle flames. Where Yellow-headed Blackbirds occur together with Red-winged Blackbirds, the larger Yellow-heads dominate, commandeering the center of the wetland and pushing their red-winged competitors to the less desirable periphery. Yellow-heads often nest in small colonies of about 30 pairs.

ID: large blackbird. *Male:* yellow head and breast; black body; white wing patches; black lores; long tail; black bill. *Female:* dusky brown overall; yellow breast, throat and "eyebrow"; hints of yellow on face.
Size: *L* 8–11 in; *W* 15 in. Male larger than female.
Status: common from mid-April to early October; rare in winter in Red-winged Blackbird flocks.
Habitat: deep, permanent marshes, sloughs, lakeshores and river impoundments where cattails dominate.
Nesting: loosely colonial; female builds bulky, deep basket of emergent aquatic plants and lines it with dry grass and other vegetation; nest is woven into emergent vegetation over water; female incubates 4 pale green to pale gray eggs, marked with gray or brown, for 11–13 days.
Feeding: gleans for seeds, beetles, snails, aquatic invertebrates and dragonflies; also probes into cattail heads for larval invertebrates.
Voice: song is strained, metallic grating note followed by descending buzz; call is deep *krrt* or *ktuk;* low quacks and liquidy clucks may be given when breeding.
Similar Species: male is distinctive. *Brewer's Blackbird* (p. 152): female lacks yellow throat and face.
Best Sites: Lee Metcalf NWR; Red Rock Lakes NWR; Bowdoin NWR; Medicine Lake NWR; Benton Lake NWR.

151

BREWER'S BLACKBIRD
Euphagus cyanocephalus

The glossy Brewer's Blackbird can be seen even in residential areas, strutting its stuff to impress dowdy females. Modern development has helped these blackbirds, with agriculture and ranching providing foraging sites, and landscaped trees and shrubs affording sheltered nest locations. Roads provide a bounty of car-struck insects for Brewer's Blackbirds, which exploit the "roadkill resource niche" better than any other songbird. • Brewer's Blackbirds tend to nest in colonies, which often include up to 14 pairs. As fall approaches, the colonies join with other family groups to form large, migrating flocks. • The iridescent feathers of this blackbird reflect rainbows of sunlight. As it walks, the bird jerks its head back and forth like a chicken, enhancing the glossy effect and distinguishing it from other blackbirds.

ID: *Male:* iridescent, blue green body and purplish head often look black; yellow eyes; some nonbreeding males may show faint, rusty feather edgings. *Female:* flat brown plumage; dark eyes.
Size: *L* 8–10 in; *W* 15½ in. Male on average larger than female.
Status: common from mid-April through October; some overwinter, sometimes in small flocks.
Habitat: *Breeding:* moist, grassy meadows, riparian woodlands and agricultural lands. *In migration:* parks, lawns, roadsides with nearby wetlands and patches of trees and shrubs.
Nesting: in small colonies; on ground or in shrub or small tree, often near water; female builds bulky, open cup nest of twigs, grass and plant fibers and lines it with rootlets, fine grass and hair; female incubates 4–6 brown-spotted, pale gray to greenish gray eggs for 12–14 days.
Feeding: gleans invertebrates and seeds while walking along shorelines and open areas.
Voice: song is creaking, 2-noted *k-shee;* call a metallic *chick* or *check.*
Similar Species: *Common Grackle* (p. 153): much longer, keeled tail; larger body and bill; glossy bronze color on body. *Brown-headed Cowbird* (p. 154): shorter tail; stubbier, thicker bill; male has dark eyes and brown head; female has paler, streaked underparts and very pale throat. *Red-winged Blackbird* (p. 149): shorter tail; male has red shoulder patch and dark eyes; female has obvious white streaking on underparts. *European Starling* (p. 125): speckled appearance; dark eyes; yellow bill in summer.
Best Sites: Red Rock Lakes NWR; Charles M. Russell NWR.

COMMON GRACKLE

Quiscalus quiscula

The Common Grackle is a poor but spirited singer. A male grackle slowly takes a deep breath to inflate his breast, causing his feathers to spike outward, then closes his eyes and gives a loud, strained *tssh-schleek*. Despite his lack of musical talent, the male remains smug and proud, posing with bill held high. • The Common Grackle is fairly common east of the Continental Divide and rare west of it. In fall, flocks of grackles are common in open fields, where they forage for waste grain. Smaller bands occasionally venture into urban neighborhoods and assert their dominance at backyard bird feeders—much to the dismay of homeowners and other birds. • At night, grackles commonly roost with groups of European Starlings, Redwinged Blackbirds and even Brown-headed Cowbirds.

ID: *Male:* iridescent plumage (purple blue head and breast, bronze back and sides), often looks blackish; long, keeled tail; yellow eyes; long, heavy bill. *Female:* smaller, duller and browner. *Immature:* dull brown overall; dark eyes.

Size: *L* 11–13½ in; *W* 17 in. Male on average larger than female.

Status: fairly common from late April to September.

Habitat: wetlands, hedgerows, fields, wet meadows, riparian woodlands and edges of coniferous forests and woodlands; also shrubby urban and suburban parks and gardens.

Nesting: singly or in small colonies; in dense tree or shrub branches or emergent vegetation, often near water; female builds bulky, open cup nest of twigs, grass, plant fibers and mud and lines it with fine grass or feathers; female incubates 4–5 brown-blotched, pale blue eggs 12–14 days.

Feeding: slowly struts along ground, gleaning, snatching and probing for insects, earthworms, seeds, waste grain and fruit; also catches insects in flight and eats small vertebrates; may take some bird eggs.

Voice: song is series of harsh, strained notes ending with metallic squeak: *tssh-schleek* or *gri-de-leeek;* call is quick, loud *swaaaack* or *chaack*.

Similar Species: *Brewer's Blackbird* (p. 152): smaller overall; lacks long, heavy bill and long, keeled tail; lacks bronze sheen to body. *Red-winged Blackbird* (p. 149): shorter tail; male has red shoulder patch and dark eyes. *European Starling* (p. 125): very short tail; long, thin bill (yellow in summer); speckled appearance; dark eyes; triangular, pointy wings.

Best Sites: Westby; Red Lodge; Billings; Charles M. Russell NWR.

BROWN-HEADED COWBIRD
Molothrus ater

Brown-headed Cowbirds once followed bison herds across the Great Plains, feeding on insects kicked up by the animals (they now follow cattle). As nomads, the birds were unable to build and tend nests. Instead, cowbirds learned to engage in brood parasitism, laying their eggs in nests of other songbirds. Many of the parasitized songbirds do not recognize the eggs as foreign, so they incubate them and raise the cowbird young as their own. Cowbird chicks typically hatch first and develop more quickly than their nestmates, which are pushed out of the nest or outcompeted for food. • The expansion of livestock farming, the extirpation of bison and the extensive network of roadways in Montana have significantly increased the cowbird's range and habitats. It now parasitizes more than 220 species of birds on the continent, including species that had no contact with it before widespread human settlement.

ID: thick, conical bill; short, squared tail; dark eyes. *Male:* iridescent, green blue body plumage usually looks glossy black; dark brown head. *Female:* brown plumage overall; faint streaking on light brown underparts; pale throat.
Size: *L* 6–8 in; *W* 12 in. Male on average larger than female.
Status: common to abundant from May to August; very rare in winter.
Habitat: stockyards; open agricultural and residential areas, including fields, ranches, woodland edges, riparian corridors, utility cutlines, roadsides, landfills and campgrounds; enters woodlands to parasitize songbird nests.

Nesting: does not build nest; each female may lay up to 40 eggs per year in nests of other birds, usually 1 egg per nest (multiple eggs, up to 8 in one nest, are probably from several cowbirds); whitish eggs, marked with gray and brown, hatch after 10–13 days.
Feeding: gleans ground for seeds, waste grain and invertebrates.
Voice: song is high, liquidy gurgle, *glug-ahl-whee* or *bubbloozeee;* call is squeaky, high-pitched *seep, psee* or *wee-tse-tse*, often given in flight; also fast, chipping *ch-ch-ch-ch-ch-ch.*
Similar Species: *Brewer's Blackbird* (p. 152): slimmer, longer bill; longer tail; male lacks brown head and has yellow eyes; female darker brown, lacks white throat and streaking on breast. *Common Grackle* (p. 153): much larger; longer, heavier bill; longer, keeled tail.
Best Sites: stockyards; agricultural fields; roadsides.

BULLOCK'S ORIOLE

Icterus bullockii

Although Bullock's Orioles are common and widespread in much of Montana, most residents are unaware of them. The male's colorful plumage blends remarkably well with the dappled light of the bird's upper-canopy summer home. Finding the drab olive, gray and white female is even more difficult. The orioles' elaborate hanging nests, however, become easily visible when the cottonwoods lose their leaves in fall. • The Bullock's Oriole well exemplifies the vagaries of avian nomenclature. It and the Baltimore Oriole of eastern North America were considered separate species for more than a century until they were lumped, as "Northern Oriole," because of hybridization in areas of overlap. Then scientists changed their minds and separated them once again. Eastern Montana sits squarely in the hybrid region, often confounding identification.

ID: *Male:* bright orange "eyebrow," "cheek," underparts, rump and outer tail feathers; black throat, eye line, "cap," back and central tail feathers; large white wing patch. *Female:* dusky yellow face, throat, upper breast and usually undertail coverts; gray belly; olive gray upperparts and tail; white wing bars.

Size: *L* 7–9 in; *W* 12 in.

Status: common from mid-May to August.

Habitat: cottonwood gallery forests, willow shrublands and urban areas.

Nesting: high in deciduous tree, suspended from branch; mainly female weaves hanging pouch nest of fine plant fibers, hair, string and fishing line and lines it with plant down, fur and moss; female incubates 4–5 dark-spotted, grayish eggs 12–14 days.

Feeding: gleans canopy vegetation and shrubs for invertebrates; eats fruit and nectar; may visit hummingbird feeders and feeders offering orange halves.

Voice: accented series of 6–8 whistled, rich and guttural notes; common call a series of *chhh* notes.

Similar Species: *Baltimore Oriole:* eastern Montana only; male lacks orange "cheek" and large white wing patch; female has more uniformly orange underparts. *Black-headed Grosbeak:* skulking habits; very heavy, conical bill; darker underparts; male has black "cheek"; female has obvious white stripes on face. *Western Tanager* (p. 135): yellow body plumage; thicker, yellow bill; lacks black "cap" and throat.

Best Sites: Clark Fork River (Missoula); Billings; National Bison Range; Great Falls; Miles City.

155

GRAY-CROWNED ROSY-FINCH
Leucosticte tephrocotis

Rosy-Finches are remarkable birds, spending summer and fall on high mountain slopes that support permanent snowfields or glaciers. During the nesting season, Rosy-Finches rely heavily on chilled or weakened insects, which are fed to the young. In fall, family groups assemble into larger flocks, which remain in and around the alpine zone until driven into the lowlands by the first big storms of winter. • In addition to the Gray-crowned Rosy-Finch, which breeds from Glacier National Park south to the Little Belt Mountains, Montana also hosts the Black Rosy-Finch, mainly in the southwestern ranges such as the Bitterroots, Big Belts and Beartooths. The Black Rosy-Finch is best recognized by its darker body in all plumages, especially on the back, breast and belly. Both species can be seen in mixed winter flocks down to about 4000 feet, making welcome additions to anyone's backyard bird list.

breeding

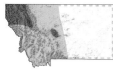

ID: yellow, conical bill (dark during breeding season); black forehead and forecrown; conspicuous gray hindcrown; rosy shoulder, rump and belly; brown "cheek," back, "chin," throat and breast; short black legs; dark tail and flight feathers.
Size: *L* 5½–6½ in; *W* 13 in.
Status: locally common year-round.
Habitat: *Breeding:* generally close to snowfields, frequenting alpine tundra, talus slopes, glacial cirques and edges of streams and tarns above timberline (9000–11,000 ft). *Winter:* shrubby lower-elevation slopes, arid valleys, roadsides and townsites from about 4000 to 7000 ft; known to roost at night in caves, tunnels, abandoned buildings, mine shafts and disused Cliff Swallow nests.

Nesting: on ground, among rocks or in rock crevices; rarely in abandoned buildings; female builds bulky nest of moss, grass, fur and feathers; female incubates 4–5 white eggs 12–14 days.
Feeding: walks and hops on ground, on snow, or at edge of snow or water, gleaning small seeds and invertebrates; occasionally visits feeders in winter.
Voice: song is long, goldfinchlike warble; calls are high, chirping notes and constant chattering.
Similar Species: *Black Rosy-Finch:* very similar except brown of body plumage largely replaced by black. *Red Crossbill* (p. 159) and *Pine Grosbeak* (p. 157): tree-loving; males brighter red overall; lack gray and black crown. *Cassin's Finch* and *House Finch* (p. 158): lack gray and black crown; have reddish throat and breast; not found around summits or alpine snows.
Best Sites: Logan Pass (Glacier NP).

PINE GROSBEAK

Pinicola enucleator

It is a great moment in a typical western Montana winter when Pine Grosbeaks emerge from the wilds to settle on your backyard feeder or mountain-ash. During the summer these birds migrate uphill to montane conifer forests for nesting, when they rarely visit feeders. • When birders are out "pining" for grosbeaks, the prize is the sight of a mature male. Search the tops of spruce and pine trees—the spires are favorite perching sites for this grosbeak. The male's splendid red plumage strikes a vivid contrast against the snow and spruce boughs. • Chilled pedestrians can be warmed somewhat by the soft warbles these birds sing during the coldest days. Many a mistaken Montana birder has seen the red breast, heard the lovely song and announced, "The robins have come back early this year!" • *Pinicola* means "pine dweller"; *enucleator* means "one who takes off shells."

ID: large finch; stout, conical, dark bill; white wing bars; black wings and tail. *Male:* rosy red head, underparts and back. *Female* and *immature:* rusty crown, face and rump; ashy gray back and underparts.
Size: *L* 8–10 in; *W* 14½ in.
Status: uncommon to locally common year-round.
Habitat: spruce–fir forests; lower-elevation conifers in winter; occasionally in cities, especially on mountain-ash or other fruit-bearing trees.
Nesting: in conifer; bulky cup nest loosely constructed of twigs, grasses and lichens and lined with rootlets, grass, moss or hair; female incubates 4–5 dark-spotted, blue green eggs 13–15 days.

Feeding: gleans buds, berries and seeds from trees; also forages on ground; in summer regularly eats insects; in winter may visit seed feeders.
Voice: song is short, musical warble; flight call is loud and distinctive, a descending *tew tew tew.*
Similar Species: *Red Crossbill* (p. 159): much smaller; lacks white wing bars; has crossed mandible tips. *Evening Grosbeak* (p. 163): yellow, black and white; smaller and shorter-tailed; female has stout, pale bill, dark lateral throat stripe and broad, white wing patches. *Cassin's Finch* and *House Finch* (p. 158): much smaller; lack obvious gray flanks and belly; brown body plumage; females heavily streaked.
Best Sites: Georgetown Lake; Glacier NP; Swan Lake.

HOUSE FINCH

Carpodacus mexicanus

Native to western North America, including western Montana, the House Finch was brought to eastern parts of the continent as an illegally captured cage bird known as the "Hollywood Finch." In the early 1940s, New York pet shop owners released their birds to avoid prosecution, and the descendants of those birds are thought to have colonized the entire eastern U.S. and Great Plains—all the way to eastern Montana. • Like the House Sparrow, this finch has prospered in urban environments. Both species often build their messy nests in eaves, rafters, chimneys and other human-fashioned habitats, and both thrive on seeds. In the west, the House Finch is often found in natural settings as well as urban centers; in the east it is seldom found outside urban and suburban settings. • The male House Finch's plumage varies in color from light yellow to bright red, but females choose the reddest males with which to breed.

♂ ♀

ID: streaked undertail coverts; brown-streaked back; square tail. *Male:* brown "cap"; bright red "eyebrow," forecrown, throat and breast; heavily streaked flanks. *Female:* indistinct facial patterning; heavily streaked underparts.
Size: *L* 5–6 in; *W* 9½ in.
Status: common year-round.
Habitat: cities, towns and agricultural areas.
Nesting: in cavity, building, dense foliage or abandoned bird nest; especially in evergreens and ornamental shrubs near buildings; mostly female builds open cup nest of grass, twigs, leaves, hair and feathers, often adding string and other debris; female incubates 4–5 pale blue eggs, dotted with lavender and black, for 12–14 days.
Feeding: gleans vegetation and ground for seeds; also takes berries, buds and some flower parts; often visits feeders.
Voice: song is bright, disjointed warble lasting about 3 seconds, often ending with harsh *jeeer* or *wheer;* flight call is sweet *cheer,* given singly or in series.
Similar Species: *Cassin's Finch:* in higher-elevation conifers; notched tail; male has red "cap," nearly lacks flank streaking; female has distinct "cheek" patch. *Red Crossbill* (p. 159): bill has crossed mandibles; male has more red overall and darker wings. *Pine Grosbeak* (p. 157): much larger; male brighter red overall, with gray flanks and belly; female unstreaked.
Best Sites: feeders in Missoula, Helena, Great Falls, Billings and other cities.

RED CROSSBILL

Loxia curvirostra

Red Crossbills are the gypsies of our bird community, wandering through forests in search of pine seeds. They may breed at any time of year if they discover a bumper crop—it's not unusual to hear them singing and see them building nests in midwinter. Their nomadic ways can make them difficult birds to find, but in years of plenty they seem to be everywhere, their distinctive *jip-jip* calls emanating from the skies as they pass overhead. • The crossbill's oddly shaped bill is an adaptation for prying open conifer cones. While holding the cone with one foot, the crossbill inserts its closed bill between the cone and scales and pries them apart by opening its bill. Once a cone is cracked, a crossbill uses its nimble tongue to extract the soft, energy-rich seeds hidden within. • The scientific descriptor *curvirostra* is Latin for "curve billed."

ID: bill has crossed tips (hard to see from distance). *Male:* dull orange red to brick red plumage; dark wings and tail. *Female:* olive gray to dusky yellow plumage; plain, dark wings.
Size: *L* 5–6½ in; *W* 11 in.
Status: variably uncommon to common year-round.
Habitat: coniferous forests and plantations; favors ponderosa pine, but also found in higher-elevation Douglas-fir and spruce–subalpine fir forests.
Nesting: high on outer branch of conifer; female builds open cup nest of twigs, grass, bark shreds and rootlets and lines it with moss, lichen, rootlets, feathers and hair; female incubates 3–4 pale bluish white to greenish white eggs, dotted with black and purple, for 12–18 days.
Feeding: eats primarily conifer seeds (especially pine); also eats buds, deciduous tree seeds and occasionally insects; often eats grit and road salt; rarely visits feeders.
Voice: song is varied series of warbles, trills and chips (similar to other finches); call note distinctive *jip-jip*, often given in flight.
Similar Species: *White-winged Crossbill:* rare in high Rockies; 2 broad, white wing bars. *Pine Grosbeak* (p. 157): stubby, conical bill; white wing bars. *House Finch* (p. 158): conical bill; less red overall; lighter brownish wings; lacks red on lower belly.
Best Sites: Bigfork; Lolo Pass; Missoula; Libby; Kalispell; Glacier NP; Bozeman.

COMMON REDPOLL

Carduelis flammea

A predictably unpredictable winter visitor, the Common Redpoll is seen in varying numbers—it might appear in flocks in the hundreds one year and be totally absent the next. • Redpolls can endure colder temperatures than other small songbirds. These birds will sit with their highly insulating feathers fluffed out, trapping layers of warm air around their bodies. Still, because redpolls are so small, they have only a small internal volume to produce and retain heat and a relatively large surface area from which heat can be lost. As a result, they face the danger in winter of running out of fuel and dying of hypothermia. The birds must eat almost constantly, and redpolls are seen continually gleaning waste grain from bare fields or stocking up on seed at winter feeders. • In particularly good winters, it is worthwhile to scan redpoll flocks for the rare Hoary Redpoll, a whiter version of the Common from farther north.

nonbreeding

ID: red fore-crown; black "chin"; yellowish bill; streaked upperparts, including rump; lightly streaked sides, flanks and undertail coverts; notched tail. *Male:* pinkish red breast (brightest in breeding plumage). *Female:* whitish to pale gray breast.
Size: *L* 5 in; *W* 9 in.
Status: unpredictable from November to March: very common some years, completely absent others.
Habitat: open fields, meadows, roadsides, power lines, railroads, forest edges and backyards with feeders.
Nesting: does not nest in Montana.

Feeding: gleans ground, snow and vegetation in large flocks for seeds in winter; fond of common tansy where available; often visits feeders.
Voice: call is soft *chit-chit-chit-chit* or faint *swe-eet,* very similar to that of the Pine Siskin; indistinguishable from Hoary Redpoll's songs and calls.
Similar Species: *Hoary Redpoll:* extremely similar, but with unstreaked or partly streaked rump and little or no streaking on sides, flanks and undertail coverts; generally paler and plumper overall; smaller, more "pinched-in" bill. *Pine Siskin* (p. 161): heavily streaked overall; yellow highlights on wings and tail.
Best Sites: Eureka; Missoula; Kalispell; Fort Peck; Medicine Lake NWR.

PINE SISKIN
Carduelis pinus

Pine Siskins travel widely in Montana because their favored foods, seeds, are unpredictable and vary from year to year. Perhaps the best way to meet these birds is to set up a finch feeder filled with black niger seed and wait for them to appear. If the feeder is in the right location, you can expect your backyard to be visited by siskins sooner or later. • Tight flocks of these gregarious birds are frequently heard before they are seen. Once you recognize their characteristic rising *zzzreeeee* calls and boisterous chatter, you can confirm the presence of these finches simply by listening. • Aside from occasional flashes of yellow, the Pine Siskin's wardrobe is drab and sparrowlike. But for those who get to know this bird, its behavior radiates the gentle playfulness and enthusiasm of a goldfinch.

ID: small, pointy bill; upperparts darker than underparts, heavily streaked everywhere; yellow highlights at base of tail feathers and on wings (easily seen in flight); dull wing bars; slightly forked tail; indistinct facial pattern.
Size: *L* 4½–5½ in; *W* 9 in.
Status: year-round resident; very common some years, rare in others.
Habitat: *Breeding:* coniferous and mixed forests; urban and rural ornamental and shade trees. *Winter:* coniferous and mixed forests, forest edges, meadows, roadsides, agricultural fields and backyards with feeders.
Nesting: loosely colonial; typically midway up conifer on outer branch; female builds loose cup nest of twigs, grass and rootlets and lines it with feathers, hair and fine plant fibers; female incubates 3–5 darkly dotted, pale blue eggs 13 days.
Feeding: gleans ground and vegetation for seeds (especially thistle seeds), buds and some insects; attracted to road salts, mineral licks and ashes; regularly visits feeders.
Voice: song is variable, bubbly mix of squeaky, raspy, metallic notes, sometimes resembling a jerky laugh; call is buzzy, rising *zzzreeeee.*
Similar Species: *Common Redpoll* (p. 160) and *Hoary Redpoll:* red forecrown; lack yellow on wings and tail. *Cassin's Finch* and *House Finch* (p. 158): females have thicker bills and no yellow on wings or tail; less streaked. *Savannah Sparrow* (p. 142), *Vesper Sparrow* (p. 140), *Song Sparrow* (p. 143), female *Lark Bunting* (p. 141): ground-loving habits, and all lack yellow on wings and tail.
Best Sites: Glacier NP; Missoula; Bozeman; Lewistown; Red Lodge.

AMERICAN GOLDFINCH
Carduelis tristis

Amerian Goldfinches in breeding plumage are bright, cheery songbirds that are commonly seen among backyard shrubs throughout summer and fall. The drab winter plumage fools some birders into thinking they're seeing a different species. • Goldfinches often perch upon thistle and spotted knapweed heads in late summer as they search for seeds to feed their offspring. It's hard to miss their jubilant *po-ta-to-chip* calls as they pass by in a distinctive, undulating flight. • Young goldfinches leave the nest as late as mid-September. The young of these late broods tend to hatch asynchronously, probably because the female begins to incubate well before laying her entire clutch. • The scientific descriptor *tristis*, "sad," refers to the goldfinch's voice, but seems rather inapt for such a pleasing and playful bird.

breeding

Nesting: in late summer and early fall; in fork in deciduous shrub or tree, often hawthorn, serviceberry or sapling maple; female builds compact cup nest of plant fibers, grass and spider silk and lines it with plant down and hair; female incubates 4–6 pale bluish white eggs, occasionally spotted with light brown, for about 12–14 days.
Feeding: gleans vegetation for seeds, primarily thistle, birch and alder, as well as for insects and berries; commonly visits feeders.
Voice: song is long, varied series of trills, twitters, warbles and hissing notes; calls include *po-ta-to-chip* or *per-chic-or-ee* (often delivered in flight) and a whistled *dear-me, see-me.*
Similar Species: *Evening Grosbeak* (p. 163): much larger; massive, pale bill; lacks black forehead. *Wilson's Warbler* (p. 134): favors low thickets; constantly flits about in search of insects; much thinner bill; olive upperparts; olive wings without wing bars; thin, dark bill; black "cap" does not extend onto forehead.

ID: *Breeding male:* black "cap" that extends onto forehead; black wings and tail; bright yellow body; white wing bars, undertail coverts and tail base; orange bill and legs. *Nonbreeding male:* olive brown back; yellow-tinged head; gray underparts. *Female:* yellowish green upperparts and belly; yellow throat and breast.
Size: *L* 4½–5½ in; *W* 9 in.
Status: common from May to September; some overwinter, especially in intermountain valleys.
Habitat: weedy fields, woodland edges, meadows, riparian areas, parks and gardens.

Best Sites: Lee Metcalf NWR; Great Falls; Billings; Fort Peck; Miles City.

EVENING GROSBEAK
Coccothraustes vespertinus

One chilly winter day, a flock of Evening Grosbeaks descends upon your backyard feeder filled with sunflower seeds. You watch the stunning gold and black birds with delight, but soon realize that they are both an aesthetic blessing and a financial curse. Evening Grosbeaks will eat great quantities of expensive birdseed and then suddenly disappear in late winter. • In some areas of Montana, several years may pass with no Evening Grosbeaks sighted, then suddenly they are reported en masse. • The massive bill of this seed-eater is difficult to ignore. In French, *gros bec* means "large beak," and any seasoned bird bander will tell you that the grosbeak's bill can exert an incredible force per unit area—it may be the most powerful bill of any North American bird. • It was once thought that the Evening Grosbeak sang only in the evening, a mistaken belief reflected in both its common and scientific names (*vespertinus* is Latin for "of the evening").

ID: massive, pale, conical bill; black wings and tail; broad, white wing patches. *Male:* black crown; bright yellow "eyebrow" and forehead band; dark brown head gradually fades into golden yellow belly and lower back. *Female:* gray head and upper back; yellow-tinged underparts; dark lateral throat stripe; white undertail coverts.
Size: *L* 7–8½ in; *W* 14 in.
Status: generally uncommon year-round, but sometimes occurs in large flocks, especially in winter.
Habitat: *Breeding:* coniferous and mixed forests and woodlands; occasionally deciduous woodlands, suburban parks and orchards. *Winter:* all forest types; parks and gardens with feeders.
Nesting: on outer conifer limb; female builds flimsy cup nest of twigs and lines it with rootlets, fine grass, plant fibers, moss and pine needles; female incubates 3–4 pale blue to blue green eggs, blotched with purple, gray and brown, for 11–14 days.
Feeding: gleans ground and vegetation for seeds, buds and berries; also eats insects and licks soil; often visits feeders for sunflower seeds.
Voice: song is wandering, halting warble; call is loud, sharp *clee-ip* or a ringing *peeer.*
Similar Species: *American Goldfinch* (p. 162): much smaller; small bill; smaller wing bars; male has black "cap."
Best Sites: Bigfork; Missoula.

HOUSE SPARROW

Passer domesticus

For most of us, the House Sparrow is the first bird we meet and recognize in our youth. Although it is one of our most abundant and conspicuous birds, many generations of House Sparrows live out their lives in our backyards with few of us ever knowing much about them. • House Sparrows were introduced to North America in the 1850s around Brooklyn, New York, as part of a plan to control the insects that were damaging grain and cereal crops. Contrary to popular opinion at the time, this sparrow's diet is largely vegetarian, so its effect on crop pests proved to be minimal. Since then, this Eurasian sparrow has managed to colonize most human-altered environments on the continent, and has benefited greatly from close association with us. Unfortunately, its aggressive behavior has helped it usurp territory from many native bird species, especially in rural habitats. • House Sparrows are not closely related to North American sparrows, but rather belong to the family of Old World Sparrows, or "Weaver Finches."

breeding

ID: *Breeding male:* gray crown; black "bib" and bill; chestnut nape; light gray "cheek"; white wing bar; dark, mottled upperparts; gray underparts. *Nonbreeding male:* smaller black "bib"; pale bill. *Female:* plain gray brown overall; buffy "eyebrow"; streaked upperparts; indistinct facial pattern; grayish, unstreaked underparts.
Size: *L* 5½–6½ in; *W* 9½ in.
Status: abundant year-round.
Habitat: townsites, urban and suburban areas, agricultural areas, railroad yards, other developed areas; absent from undeveloped and heavily wooded areas.
Nesting: often communal; in human-made structure, ornamental shrub or natural cavity; pair builds large, dome-shaped nest of grass, twigs, plant fibers and litter and often lines it with feathers; pair incubates 4–6 whitish to greenish white eggs, dotted with gray and brown, for 10–13 days.
Feeding: gleans ground and vegetation for seeds, insects and fruit; frequently visits feeders for seeds.
Voice: song is plain, familiar *cheep-cheep-cheep-cheep;* call is short *chill-up.*
Similar Species: urban habits fairly unique; female is distinctively drab.
Best Sites: any city or farmyard.

GLOSSARY

accipiter: a forest hawk (genus *Accipiter*) with short, rounded wings and a long tail; feeds mostly on birds.

brood: *n.* a family of young from one hatching; *v.* to incubate the eggs.

brood parasite: a bird that lays its eggs in other birds' nests.

buteo: a high-soaring hawk (genus *Buteo*) with broad wings and a short, wide tail; feeds mostly on small mammals and other land animals.

clutch: the eggs laid by a female at one time.

dabbling: a foraging technique used by some ducks, in which the head and neck are submerged but the body and tail remain on the surface ("tipping up"); dabbling ducks can usually walk easily on land, can take off without running and have brightly colored speculums.

eclipse plumage: cryptic plumage, similar to that of females, worn by some male ducks in fall when they molt their flight feathers and are unable to fly.

extirpated: no longer existing in the wild in a region but occurring elsewhere.

fledge: to leave the nest for the first time.

flycatching: a feeding behavior in which the bird leaves a perch, snatches an insect in midair and returns to the same perch; also known as "hawking" or "sallying."

hawking: see *flycatching.*

immature: a bird that has not developed adult plumage but may be able to breed; compare *juvenile, nonbreeding.*

juvenile: a young bird wearing its first set of nondowny feathers; compare *immature, nonbreeding.*

mantle: the area that includes the upper back and, in gulls, the upper sides of the wings.

molt: the periodic loss and regrowth of worn feathers (one to three times a year, depending on the species).

nonbreeding: an adult bird plumage that is often distinctly duller than that of breeding birds; compare *immature, juvenile.*

precocial: a bird that is relatively well developed and mobile at hatching, usually with open eyes and extensive down.

primaries: the largest and outermost flight feathers of a bird's wing.

raptor: a bird of prey; includes eagles, hawks, falcons, owls and some other species.

riparian: habitat along rivers or streams.

rufous: rusty red color.

secondaries: flight feathers on the trailing edge of the wing, closer to the body than the primaries.

speculum: a brightly colored patch on the secondaries of many dabbling ducks.

stoop: a steep dive through the air, usually performed by birds of prey while foraging or during courtship displays.

subterminal: next to last; usually in reference to tail bands.

terminal: at the end.

tip up: see *dabbling.*

understory: the shrub or thicket layer beneath a canopy of trees.

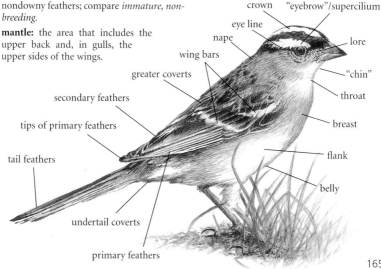

crown "eyebrow"/supercilium
eye line
nape
lore
wing bars
greater coverts
"chin"
throat
secondary feathers
breast
tips of primary feathers
flank
tail feathers
belly
undertail coverts
primary feathers

SELECT REFERENCES

American Ornithologists' Union. 1998. *Check-list of North American Birds.* 7th ed. (and its supplements). American Ornithologists' Union, Washington, DC.

Bellrose, F. 1972. *Ducks, Geese and Swans of North America.* Stackpole, Harrisburg, PA.

Casey, D. 2000. *Partners in Flight Bird Conservation Plan, Montana.* Version 1.0. Montana Partners in Flight and Montana Department of Fish, Wildlife and Parks, Kalispell, MT.

Choate, E.A. 1985. *The Dictionary of American Bird Names.* Rev. ed. Harvard Common Press, Cambridge, MA.

Cox, R.T. 1996. *Birder's Dictionary.* Falcon Publishing, Helena, MT.

DeLorme. 2001. *Montana Atlas and Gazetteer.* 4th ed. DeLorme Mapping Company, Yarmouth, ME.

Ehrlich, P.R., D.S. Dobkin and D. Wheye. 1988. *The Birder's Handbook: A Field Guide to the Natural History of North American Birds.* Simon and Schuster, New York.

Jobling, J.A. 1991. *A Dictionary of Scientific Bird Names.* Oxford University Press, New York.

Kaufman, K. 2000. *Birds of North America.* Houghton Mifflin, New York.

Kaufman, K. 1996. *Lives of North American Birds.* Houghton Mifflin, Boston.

Lenard, S.J., J. Carlson, J. Ellis, C. Jones and C. Tilly. 2003. *P.D. Skarr's Montana Bird Distribution.* 6th ed. Montana Audubon, Helena, MT.

McEneaney, T. 1993. *Birding Montana.* Falcon Publishing, Helena, MT.

Montana Natural Heritage Program, Montana Audubon and Montana Department of Fish, Wildlife and Parks. *Montana Bird Distribution.* http://nhp.nris.state.mt.us/mbd/ Accessed 12 March 2005.

National Geographic Society. 2002. *Field Guide to the Birds of North America.* 4th ed. National Geographic Society, Washington, DC.

Sibley, D.A. 2003. *The Sibley Field Guide to Birds of Western North America.* Alfred A. Knopf, New York.

Sibley, D.A. 2002. *Sibley's Birding Basics.* Alfred A. Knopf, New York.

Sibley, D.A. 2001. *The Sibley Guide to Bird Life and Behavior.* Alfred A. Knopf, New York.

Sibley, D.A. 2000. *The Sibley Guide to Birds.* Alfred A. Knopf, New York.

Cinnamon Teal

CHECKLIST

The following checklist contains 416 species of birds that have been officially recorded in Montana. The list is maintained by the Montana Bird Records Committee and can be accessed on Montana Audubon's website: http://mtaudubon.org/. We wish to thank Montana Audubon, the Montana Department of Fish, Wildlife and Parks, and the Montana Natural Heritage Program for their kind assistance in providing this checklist. Development of this bird list was supported by the Montana Nongame Tax Checkoff.

Species are grouped by family and listed in taxonomic order in accordance with the A.O.U. *Check-list of North American Birds*. Species with fewer than 20 accepted records are listed in *italics*. An asterisk (*) identifies species for which there is current or historical evidence of breeding in Montana (Lenard et al. 2003). The letter "I" in parentheses (I) indicates species that are introduced (i.e., nonnative) to Montana; (ex) indicates species that are extirpated from the state. In addition, the following risk categories are noted: federally endangered (en), federally threatened (th) and species of concern (sc).

Waterfowl (Anatidae)
- ❏ Greater White-fronted Goose
- ❏ Snow Goose
- ❏ Ross's Goose
- ❏ *Brant*
- ❏ *Cackling Goose*
- ❏ Canada Goose*
- ❏ Mute Swan* (I)
- ❏ Trumpeter Swan* (sc)
- ❏ Tundra Swan
- ❏ Wood Duck*
- ❏ Gadwall*
- ❏ Eurasian Wigeon
- ❏ American Wigeon*
- ❏ American Black Duck
- ❏ Mallard*
- ❏ Blue-winged Teal*
- ❏ Cinnamon Teal*
- ❏ Northern Shoveler*
- ❏ Northern Pintail*
- ❏ *Garganey*
- ❏ Green-winged Teal*
- ❏ Canvasback*
- ❏ Redhead*
- ❏ Ring-necked Duck*
- ❏ Greater Scaup
- ❏ Lesser Scaup*
- ❏ Harlequin Duck* (sc)
- ❏ Surf Scoter
- ❏ White-winged Scoter
- ❏ *Black Scoter*
- ❏ Long-tailed Duck
- ❏ Bufflehead*
- ❏ Common Goldeneye*
- ❏ Barrow's Goldeneye*
- ❏ Hooded Merganser*
- ❏ Common Merganser*
- ❏ Red-breasted Merganser
- ❏ Ruddy Duck*

Grouse & Allies (Phasianidae)
- ❏ Chukar* (I)
- ❏ Gray Partridge* (I)
- ❏ Ring-necked Pheasant* (I)
- ❏ Ruffed Grouse*
- ❏ Greater Sage-Grouse* (sc)
- ❏ Spruce Grouse*
- ❏ *Willow Ptarmigan*
- ❏ White-tailed Ptarmigan* (sc)
- ❏ Blue Grouse*
- ❏ Sharp-tailed Grouse* (Columbian subspecies: sc)
- ❏ *Greater Prairie-Chicken* (ex)
- ❏ Wild Turkey* (I)

Loons (Gaviidae)
- ❏ *Red-throated Loon*
- ❏ Pacific Loon
- ❏ Common Loon* (sc)
- ❏ *Yellow-billed Loon*

Grebes (Podicipedidae)
- ❏ Pied-billed Grebe*
- ❏ Horned Grebe*
- ❏ Red-necked Grebe*
- ❏ Eared Grebe*
- ❏ Western Grebe*
- ❏ Clark's Grebe*

Petrels & Shearwaters (Procellariidae)
- ❏ *Manx Shearwater*

Pelicans (Pelecanidae)
- ❏ American White Pelican* (sc)

Cormorants (Phalacrocoracidae)
- ❏ Double-crested Cormorant*

Herons (Ardeidae)
- ❏ American Bittern*
- ❏ *Least Bittern*
- ❏ Great Blue Heron*
- ❏ Great Egret
- ❏ Snowy Egret*
- ❏ *Little Blue Heron*
- ❏ Cattle Egret
- ❏ *Green Heron*
- ❏ Black-crowned Night-Heron* (sc)
- ❏ *Yellow-crowned Night-Heron*

Ibises (Threskiornithidae)
- ❏ *Glossy Ibis*

CHECKLIST

❏ White-faced Ibis* (sc)

Storks (Ciconiidae)
❏ *Wood Stork*

Vultures (Cathartidae)
❏ Turkey Vulture*

Kites, Hawks & Eagles (Accipitridae)
❏ Osprey*
❏ *White-tailed Kite*
❏ *Mississippi Kite*
❏ Bald Eagle* (th)
❏ Northern Harrier*
❏ Sharp-shinned Hawk*
❏ Cooper's Hawk*
❏ Northern Goshawk* (sc)
❏ *Red-shouldered Hawk*
❏ Broad-winged Hawk
❏ Swainson's Hawk* (sc)
❏ Red-tailed Hawk*
❏ Ferruginous Hawk* (sc)
❏ Rough-legged Hawk
❏ Golden Eagle*

Falcons (Falconidae)
❏ American Kestrel*
❏ Merlin*
❏ Gyrfalcon
❏ Peregrine Falcon* (sc)
❏ Prairie Falcon*

Rails (Rallidae)
❏ *Yellow Rail* (sc)
❏ Virginia Rail*
❏ Sora*
❏ *Common Moorhen*
❏ American Coot*

Cranes (Gruidae)
❏ Sandhill Crane*
❏ Whooping Crane (en)

Plovers (Charadriidae)
❏ Black-bellied Plover
❏ American Golden-Plover
❏ *Snowy Plover*
❏ Semipalmated Plover
❏ Piping Plover* (th)
❏ Killdeer*
❏ Mountain Plover* (sc, possibly th)

Stilts & Avocets (Recurvirostridae)
❏ Black-necked Stilt*
❏ American Avocet*

Sandpipers & Allies (Scolopacidae)
❏ Greater Yellowlegs
❏ Lesser Yellowlegs
❏ Solitary Sandpiper
❏ Willet*
❏ Spotted Sandpiper*
❏ Upland Sandpiper*
❏ Whimbrel
❏ Long-billed Curlew* (sc)
❏ Hudsonian Godwit
❏ Marbled Godwit*
❏ Ruddy Turnstone
❏ *Black Turnstone*
❏ Red Knot
❏ Sanderling
❏ Semipalmated Sandpiper
❏ Western Sandpiper
❏ Least Sandpiper
❏ White-rumped Sandpiper
❏ Baird's Sandpiper
❏ Pectoral Sandpiper
❏ *Sharp-tailed Sandpiper*
❏ Dunlin
❏ *Curlew Sandpiper*
❏ Stilt Sandpiper
❏ *Buff-breasted Sandpiper*
❏ Short-billed Dowitcher
❏ Long-billed Dowitcher
❏ Wilson's Snipe*
❏ *American Woodcock*
❏ Wilson's Phalarope*
❏ Red-necked Phalarope
❏ *Red Phalarope*

Gulls & Allies (Laridae)
❏ *Pomarine Jaeger*
❏ *Parasitic Jaeger*
❏ *Long-tailed Jaeger*
❏ *Laughing Gull*
❏ Franklin's Gull* (sc)
❏ *Little Gull*
❏ Bonaparte's Gull
❏ *Mew Gull*
❏ Ring-billed Gull*
❏ California Gull*
❏ Herring Gull*

❏ *Thayer's Gull*
❏ Glaucous-winged Gull
❏ Glaucous Gull
❏ Great Black-backed Gull
❏ Sabine's Gull
❏ *Black-legged Kittiwake*
❏ *Ivory Gull*
❏ Caspian Tern* (sc)
❏ Common Tern* (sc)
❏ *Arctic Tern*
❏ Forster's Tern* (sc)
❏ Least Tern* (en)
❏ Black Tern* (sc)

Alcids (Alcidae)
❏ *Long-billed Murrelet*
❏ *Ancient Murrelet*

Pigeons & Doves (Columbidae)
❏ Rock Pigeon* (I)
❏ *Band-tailed Pigeon*
❏ *Eurasian Collared-Dove* (I)
❏ *White-winged Dove*
❏ Mourning Dove*

Cuckoos (Cuculidae)
❏ Black-billed Cuckoo*
❏ *Yellow-billed Cuckoo* (sc, possibly th)

Barn Owls (Tytonidae)
❏ Barn Owl* (sc)

Owls (Strigidae)
❏ Flammulated Owl* (sc)
❏ Western Screech-Owl*
❏ Eastern Screech-Owl*
❏ Great Horned Owl*
❏ Snowy Owl
❏ Northern Hawk Owl* (sc)
❏ Northern Pygmy-Owl*
❏ Burrowing Owl* (sc)
❏ Barred Owl*
❏ Great Gray Owl* (sc)
❏ Long-eared Owl*
❏ Short-eared Owl*
❏ Boreal Owl*
❏ Northern Saw-whet Owl*

Nightjars (Caprimulgidae)
❏ Common Nighthawk*
❏ Common Poorwill*

❏ *Whip-poor-will*

Swifts (Apodidae)
❏ Black Swift* (sc)
❏ Chimney Swift*
❏ Vaux's Swift*
❏ White-throated Swift*

Hummingbirds (Trochilidae)
❏ *Ruby-throated Hummingbird**
❏ Black-chinned Hummingbird*
❏ *Anna's Hummingbird*
❏ *Costa's Hummingbird*
❏ Calliope Hummingbird*
❏ Broad-tailed Hummingbird* (sc)
❏ Rufous Hummingbird*

Kingfishers (Alcedinidae)
❏ Belted Kingfisher*

Woodpeckers (Picidae)
❏ Lewis's Woodpecker* (sc)
❏ Red-headed Woodpecker* (sc)
❏ *Red-bellied Woodpecker*
❏ Williamson's Sapsucker*
❏ *Yellow-bellied Sapsucker*
❏ Red-naped Sapsucker*
❏ Downy Woodpecker*
❏ Hairy Woodpecker*
❏ *White-headed Woodpecker*
❏ American Three-toed Woodpecker*
❏ Black-backed Woodpecker* (sc)
❏ Northern Flicker*
❏ Pileated Woodpecker*

Flycatchers (Tyrannidae)
❏ Olive-sided Flycatcher* (sc)
❏ Western Wood-Pewee*
❏ *Eastern Wood-Pewee*
❏ *Yellow-bellied Flycatcher*
❏ Alder Flycatcher* (sc)
❏ Willow Flycatcher*
❏ Least Flycatcher*

❏ Hammond's Flycatcher*
❏ *Gray Flycatcher*
❏ Dusky Flycatcher*
❏ Cordilleran Flycatcher*
❏ *Eastern Phoebe*
❏ Say's Phoebe*
❏ *Vermilion Flycatcher*
❏ *Ash-throated Flycatcher*
❏ *Great Crested Flycatcher*
❏ Cassin's Kingbird* (sc)
❏ Western Kingbird*
❏ Eastern Kingbird*
❏ *Scissor-tailed Flycatcher*

Shrikes (Laniidae)
❏ Loggerhead Shrike* (sc)
❏ Northern Shrike*

Vireos (Vireonidae)
❏ *White-eyed Vireo**
❏ *Yellow-throated Vireo*
❏ *Plumbeous Vireo**
❏ Cassin's Vireo*
❏ *Blue-headed Vireo*
❏ Warbling Vireo*
❏ *Philadelphia Vireo*
❏ Red-eyed Vireo*

Jays & Crows (Corvidae)
❏ Gray Jay*
❏ Steller's Jay*
❏ Blue Jay*
❏ *Western Scrub-Jay*
❏ Pinyon Jay*
❏ Clark's Nutcracker*
❏ Black-billed Magpie*
❏ American Crow*
❏ Common Raven*

Larks (Alaudidae)
❏ Horned Lark*

Swallows (Hirundinidae)
❏ Purple Martin*
❏ Tree Swallow*
❏ Violet-green Swallow*
❏ Northern Rough-winged Swallow*
❏ Bank Swallow*
❏ Cliff Swallow*
❏ Barn Swallow*

Chickadees (Paridae)
❏ Black-capped Chickadee*
❏ Mountain Chickadee*
❏ Chestnut-backed Chickadee*
❏ Boreal Chickadee* (sc)

Nuthatches (Sittidae)
❏ Red-breasted Nuthatch*
❏ White-breasted Nuthatch*
❏ Pygmy Nuthatch*

Creepers (Certhiidae)
❏ Brown Creeper*

Wrens (Troglodytidae)
❏ Rock Wren*
❏ Canyon Wren*
❏ *Bewick's Wren*
❏ House Wren*
❏ Winter Wren*
❏ *Sedge Wren** (sc)
❏ Marsh Wren*

Dippers (Cinclidae)
❏ American Dipper*

Kinglets (Regulidae)
❏ Golden-crowned Kinglet*
❏ Ruby-crowned Kinglet*

Gnatcatchers (Sylviidae)
❏ *Blue-gray Gnatcatcher** (sc)

Thrushes (Turdidae)
❏ Eastern Bluebird* (sc)
❏ Western Bluebird*
❏ Mountain Bluebird*
❏ Townsend's Solitaire*
❏ Veery*
❏ *Gray-cheeked Thrush*
❏ Swainson's Thrush*
❏ Hermit Thrush*
❏ *Wood Thrush*
❏ American Robin*
❏ Varied Thrush*

Mockingbirds & Thrashers (Mimidae)
❏ Gray Catbird*
❏ Northern Mockingbird*
❏ Sage Thrasher* (sc)
❏ Brown Thrasher*

Starlings (Sturnidae)
❑ European Starling* (I)

Accentors (Prunellidae)
❑ *Siberian Accentor*

Pipits (Motacillidae)
❑ American Pipit*
❑ Sprague's Pipit* (sc)

Waxwings (Bombycillidae)
❑ Bohemian Waxwing*
❑ Cedar Waxwing*

Wood-Warblers (Parulidae)
❑ *Golden-winged Warbler*
❑ Tennessee Warbler*
❑ Orange-crowned Warbler*
❑ Nashville Warbler*
❑ *Northern Parula*
❑ Yellow Warbler*
❑ Chestnut-sided Warbler
❑ Magnolia Warbler
❑ *Cape May Warbler*
❑ *Black-throated Blue Warbler*
❑ Yellow-rumped Warbler*
❑ *Black-throated Gray Warbler*
❑ *Black-throated Green Warbler*
❑ Townsend's Warbler*
❑ *Blackburnian Warbler*
❑ *Yellow-throated Warbler*
❑ *Pine Warbler*
❑ *Prairie Warbler*
❑ Palm Warbler
❑ *Bay-breasted Warbler*
❑ Blackpoll Warbler
❑ Black-and-white Warbler* (sc)
❑ American Redstart*
❑ *Prothonotary Warbler*
❑ Ovenbird*
❑ Northern Waterthrush*
❑ *Kentucky Warbler*
❑ *Connecticut Warbler*

❑ Mourning Warbler*
❑ MacGillivray's Warbler*
❑ Common Yellowthroat*
❑ *Hooded Warbler*
❑ Wilson's Warbler*
❑ *Canada Warbler*
❑ *Painted Redstart*
❑ Yellow-breasted Chat*

Tanagers (Thraupidae)
❑ *Summer Tanager*
❑ *Scarlet Tanager*
❑ Western Tanager*

Sparrows & Allies (Emberizidae)
❑ Green-tailed Towhee*
❑ Spotted Towhee*
❑ *Eastern Towhee*
❑ American Tree Sparrow
❑ Chipping Sparrow*
❑ Clay-colored Sparrow*
❑ Brewer's Sparrow* (sc)
❑ Field Sparrow*
❑ Vesper Sparrow*
❑ Lark Sparrow*
❑ *Black-throated Sparrow*
❑ *Sage Sparrow* (sc)
❑ Lark Bunting* (sc)
❑ Savannah Sparrow*
❑ Grasshopper Sparrow* (sc)
❑ Baird's Sparrow* (sc)
❑ Le Conte's Sparrow* (sc)
❑ Nelson's Sharp-tailed Sparrow* (sc)
❑ Fox Sparrow*
❑ Song Sparrow*
❑ Lincoln's Sparrow*
❑ *Swamp Sparrow*
❑ White-throated Sparrow
❑ Harris's Sparrow
❑ White-crowned Sparrow*
❑ *Golden-crowned Sparrow*
❑ Dark-eyed Junco*
❑ McCown's Longspur* (sc)
❑ Lapland Longspur
❑ *Smith's Longspur*
❑ Chestnut-collared Longspur* (sc)

❑ Snow Bunting

Grosbeaks & Buntings (Cardinalidae)
❑ *Northern Cardinal*
❑ *Pyrrhuloxia*
❑ Rose-breasted Grosbeak*
❑ Black-headed Grosbeak*
❑ *Blue Grosbeak*
❑ Lazuli Bunting*
❑ Indigo Bunting*
❑ *Painted Bunting*
❑ *Dickcissel* (sc)

Blackbirds & Allies (Icteridae)
❑ Bobolink* (sc)
❑ Red-winged Blackbird*
❑ Western Meadowlark*
❑ Yellow-headed Blackbird*
❑ Rusty Blackbird
❑ Brewer's Blackbird*
❑ Common Grackle*
❑ *Great-tailed Grackle*
❑ Brown-headed Cowbird*
❑ Orchard Oriole*
❑ *Hooded Oriole*
❑ Bullock's Oriole*
❑ Baltimore Oriole*

Finches (Fringillidae)
❑ *Brambling*
❑ Gray-crowned Rosy-Finch* (sc)
❑ Black Rosy-Finch* (sc)
❑ Pine Grosbeak*
❑ Purple Finch*
❑ Cassin's Finch*
❑ House Finch*
❑ Red Crossbill*
❑ White-winged Crossbill*
❑ Common Redpoll
❑ Hoary Redpoll
❑ Pine Siskin*
❑ *Lesser Goldfinch*
❑ American Goldfinch*
❑ Evening Grosbeak*

Old World Sparrows (Passeridae)
❑ House Sparrow* (I)

INDEX OF SCIENTIFIC NAMES

This index references only the primary species accounts.

INDEX

INDEX OF COMMON NAMES

Page numbers in **boldface** refer to the primary, illustrated accounts.

ABOUT THE AUTHORS

PHOTOGRAPH BY BRETT WALKER

CALEB PUTNAM

A birder since childhood, Caleb Putnam has a Masters of Science degree specializing in bird conservation from the Environmental Studies Department at the University of Montana. While living in the beautiful Bitterroot Valley, he has traveled the state in search of birds, racking up 333 species for Montana. He has taught in the University of Montana's ornithology laboratory and has inventoried birds of the Madison Valley for Montana Audubon. Although he recently moved to Michigan, he continues to return to Big Sky Country as often as possible to lead birding tours across the state.

GREGORY KENNEDY

Gregory Kennedy has been an active naturalist since he was very young. He is the author of many books on natural history and has produced film and television shows on environmental and indigenous concerns in Southeast Asia, New Guinea, South and Central America, the High Arctic and elsewhere. He has also been involved in countless research projects around the world ranging from studies in the upper canopy of tropical and temperate rainforests to deepwater marine investigations.